The Young Professional Woman

Breaking Into the Business World & Succeeding

Edited by

Linda Ellis Eastman

⚜ **Professional Woman Publishing**
Prospect, Kentucky

The Young Professional Woman
Copyright © 2013 by Linda Ellis Eastman

Published by:
Professional Woman Publishing
Post Office Box 333
Prospect, KY 40059
(502) 228-0906
www.pwnbooks.com

Please contact the publisher for quantity discounts.

ISBN 13: 978-0-9894428-5-5

Library of Congress Cataloging-In-Publication Data

Cover photo credit: Diego Vito Cervo/ Dreamstime.com

Printed in the United States of America

TABLE OF CONTENTS

TABLE OF CONTENTS
—CONTINUED—

TABLE OF CONTENTS
—CONTINUED—

ABOUT THE AUTHOR

LINDA ELLIS EASTMAN

Linda Ellis Eastman is President and CEO of The Professional Woman Network (PWN), an International Training and Consulting Organization on Women's Issues. She has designed seminars which have been presented in China, the former Soviet Union, South Africa, the Phillipines, and attended by individuals in the United States from such firms as McDonalds, USA Today, Siemens-Westinghouse, the Pentagon, the Department of Defense, and the United States Department of Education.

An expert on women's issues, Ms. Eastman has certified and trained over two thousand women to start consulting/seminar businesses originating from such countries as Pakistan, the Ukraine, Antigua, Canada, Mexico, Zimbabwe, Nigeria, Bermuda, Jamaica, Costa Rica, England, South Africa, Malaysia, and Kenya. Founded in 1982 by Linda Ellis Eastman, The Professional Woman Network is committed to educating women on a global basis regarding, self-esteem, confidence building, stress management, and emotional, mental, spiritual and physical wellness.

Ms. Eastman has been featured in USA Today and listed in Who's Who of American Women, as well as Who's Who of International Leaders. In addition to women's issues, Ms. Eastman speaks internationally regarding the importance of human respect as it relates to race, color, culture, age, and gender. She will be facilitating an international conference where speakers and participants from many nations will be able to discuss issues that are unique to women on a global basis.

Linda Ellis Eastman is also founder of The Professional Woman Speakers Bureau and The Professional Woman Coaching Institute. Ms. Eastman has dedicated her businesses to increasing the self-esteem and personal dignity of women and youth around the world.

Contact:
The Professional Woman Network
P.O. Box 333
Prospect, KY 40059
(502) 566-9900
lindaeastman@prodigy.net
www.pwnbooks.com
www.protrain.net

INTRODUCTION

Linda Ellis Eastman

Many young women are flooding the workplace arena after college and finding challenges every step of the way. Whether the obstacles are gender, racial, or age bias, there are ways to overcome these barriers and thrive in today's work environment!

One of the most key issues for young professional woman is the ability to balance one's personal and professional lives. It is truly critical that you, the reader, learn to place your health, emotional wellness, and happiness on the top priorities. Learn to interview a company and YOU decide if their corporate culture matches your dreams. You be in charge of your life, and don't settle for less.

This book has been designed for you, the young professional woman or the young woman who is stepping into the workforce. Written by international coaches, consultants, and business experts, strategies are shared chapter-by-chapter, providing you with the tools to succeed.

Wishing you terrific success in both your personal and professional lives!

Linda Ellis Eastman

The Young Professional Woman

Breaking Into the Business World & Succeeding

ABOUT THE AUTHOR

JANET CHRISTENSEN

Janet Christensen is President & CIO - Chief Inspiration Officer - of Dynamic Awareness Inc. As a facilitator, speaker, coach and author, she focuses on giving people practical and easy-to-implement tools and strategies to create shifts in perception to transform lives. Janet is an expert in connecting people with their authentic wisdom, intelligence and energy through her unique blend of expertise as a Master Passion Map™ Practitioner, Power Coach®, Performance Management Coach and pre-retirement coach. Her own book will be published in the Fall of 2013. Janet has also authored several published articles and co-authored the books Leaders In Pearls and Expert Women Who Speak, Speak Out, Volumes 2 and 5.

Prior to starting her own business, Janet had over 25 years of success in the corporate world in senior management, sales and personnel. In her role as sales manager for a national real estate company, she twice received the Manager of the Year award for Ontario. In her last corporate position, Janet lead two business operations from impending closure to viability and high profitability in a matter of months through employee engagement and strategic initiatives. Janet has received official recognition for her performance and contribution from The Canadian Diabetes Association, REALTY WORLD-Canada, and Kelly Services. In 2011 she was a co-recipient of the Canadian Association of Professional Speakers President's Award.

Janet now works with clients from around the world, sharing her expertise through leadership training, customized programs, keynote presentations and coaching. She is passionate about helping individuals and organizations create permanent positive change and achieve the results they desire.

Contact:
Janet Christensen
E-mail: janet@dynamicawareness.com
Web site: www.dynamicawareness.com
Dynamic Awareness Inc.
97 Devonshire Ave., London, Ontario N6C 2H6 Canada
Phone: 519-434-5397 Fax: 519-434-8344

ONE

BEING REAL – REMARKABLE, EMPOWERED, AUTHENTIC, LIMITLESS

Janet Christensen

The world of the young professional woman can be simultaneously exciting and daunting. There is a lot of pressure to succeed both personally driven and from external sources, whether it be your boss, family, friends or colleagues. All of this can influence you to take on the persona of a successful professional, however that is defined by people's expectations and evaluations, with the result that someone other than the 'real' you, or only part of you, shows up for work. This pressure to perform and conform can cause you to doubt yourself, lack the confidence to speak your truth and feel like you are doing a dance to meet differing expectations. This becomes exhausting and demotivating.

You are hereby invited and encouraged to take the REAL you to work.

The REAL you is Remarkable, Empowered, Authentic and Limitless.

Being Remarkable

The dictionary defines 'remarkable' as noteworthy and extraordinary. As a professional woman, being noteworthy and extraordinary is a positive thing. Being remarkable is not a result of attempting to be a clone of someone else, or being a second-rate version of you to conform to some ever-changing ideal. You are a unique woman with innate gifts and talents and the only genuine version of you. When you proudly own your uniqueness by being empowered, authentic and limitless you are remarkable.

Being Empowered

The foundation for being empowered is taking responsibility for everything in your life. Understand and accept that the choices that you have made until now have created the results you see today. This can be a challenging concept to accept, let alone to embrace. For one thing, taking personal responsibility removes the option of blaming others for your current circumstances. Yes, there are life events that occur, such as economic downturns, job losses, the loss of a loved one, a natural disaster or a serious illness. While you are not in control of other people, circumstances and events, you completely control how you choose to respond and your attitude about them. You can choose to react as a victim, or choose to respond with empowerment. When you can let go of resistance to and denial of the situations and circumstances you are faced with, you are able to work with the reality of what is. When you are able to evaluate your current situation from a neutral, objective viewpoint without judgement, you empower yourself. Instead of reacting to circumstances, you consciously choose how to respond, making powerful decisions with integrity. This allows you to grow and develop through the challenges and experiences that life presents. It allows you to draw on your strengths and to trust that you will find the people, resources and solutions to move forward. It harnesses your mental, physical and spiritual energies in a positive, pro-active way.

Taking personal responsibility also means being clear about whose version of your life you are living. Everyone is in many relationships of various kinds – family, romantic, friendships, professional, educational, social, to name a few. In most relationships, people have expectations of each other, and in some cases, they may have specific agendas for you. The first step to avoid or change the practice of unconsciously defaulting to others' expectations and agendas for you is being aware of what you are doing. Take a look at all of your choices. Where you are making choices and decisions based on other people's expectations of you, instead of on your truth? Realize that you are choosing to do this, either consciously or unconsciously. It is no one's fault and no one is to be blamed. Our relationships are important - choose to have ones that are mutually respectful and win/win. There will be times when you compromise, or do things that may not be your optimal choice. Realize that these too are your choices and own them. Then choose your attitude to follow. Will you do it grudgingly with resistance, or proactively and joyfully? Where would you like to put your energy?

Ask yourself: "When I am in my power and truth, would this be my choice?" Taking personal responsibility allows you to stand in your personal power. It gives you choice and free will as you create your life by design - choice by choice, moment by moment, and day by day.

Personal Power Vocabulary

The words that you use have a significant impact on the quality of your life. Be aware of the words you are using and shift from destructive and disempowering words to powerful words.

Disempowering words	_Powerful words_
I can't (weak/no control)	I won't (choice)
I should (implies no choice/guilt)	I could (more powerful)
It's not my fault (helpless/victim)	I am totally responsible (ownership)
It's a problem (negativity)	It's an opportunity (open to growth)
Life's a struggle	Life's an adventure
I hope (victim/worry)	I know (confidence/power)
If only (whining)	Next time (learn from situation/choice)
What will I do? (whining/helpless)	I know I will handle it

Responding with Empowerment

People commonly react to situations and issues in 4 ways by choosing to:

- Fight – the best defence is offence

- Flight – removing themselves from the situation instead of facing it

- Freeze – shutting down and not communicating

- Facade – pretending everything is okay. "I'm fine. Nothing is the matter."

- Instead of reacting, you can choose to respond with empowerment and create win/win situations.

- Instead of fighting, choose to respond with **courtesy**.

- Instead of taking flight, have **integrity** and face the issue.

- Instead of freezing, choose to be **open** and communicate.

- Instead of putting on a facade, be **honest** about your thoughts and feelings.

All four aspects – courtesy, integrity, openness and honesty – <u>must</u> be present. When you choose to respond this way, you are empowered and able to overcome your fears and insecurity. If the person does not like what you have to say, the world will not end. It is better to speak your truth than sell yourself out. Commit to speak your truth on your terms, with courtesy, integrity, openness and honesty. This will make you stand out and be remarkable.

Being Authentic

Being authentic means being genuine - the true you with your gifts, talents, strengths and uniqueness shining brightly. However, if you are like many people, you may feel disconnected from your authentic self. Who is she really? How can you reconnect with her?

It is important to be aware of the filters through which you see people, events and circumstances. You, like everyone, have stories that you tell yourself and these form your beliefs and frame your perspective, including about yourself. Your stories and filters begin to form at an early age. As a young child you may have been told not to talk to strangers, do as you are told, not to take reckless chances. These are all messages intended to help you stay safe when you are young. However, if these remain your stories and the filters as an adult, they can sabotage your ability to be empowered, authentic and create the success you desire. If you learned as a child that pleasing others meant being accepted and loved, or in extreme cases staying safe, this may cause you to place everyone else's needs ahead of your own and try to please everybody, which is a disempowering impossibility.

The following are some helpful questions to explore to become aware of when you are expressing your authenticity and when you are not. Resist the temptation to judge and consciously choose to be an objective neutral observer when answering the questions.

Discovering when you feel authentic:

- ○ What am I doing when I feel empowered and joyful?

- ○ What are my strengths, gifts and talents?

- What are 25 (or more) professional and personal accomplishments that I have achieved?

- What am I grateful for in my life?

- What are five key things that I have learned along the way?

- Who are five people that I have positively impacted and how?

- What is my big airy audacious goal (BHAG)?

Discovering how you self-sabotage and what gets in the way of your authenticity:

- What are my stories/filters that negatively influence my perception of people and things?

- Do I have competing commitments? (eg. balancing career and family; financial obligations keeping me in a job I dislike; my wants vs expectations of others)

- Do I put others ahead of myself? (pleasing others to be liked; expectations of others; 'shoulds'/obligations in life, etc.)

- Do I have limiting beliefs and, if so, what are they?

- What are my fears?

- Am I a perfectionist? If so, how does this sabotage me?

- If I procrastinate, how is this self-sabotage?

Use the insights and awareness you gain by answering these questions to consciously make different choices and express your authenticity.

It is vital that you know who and how you want to be in your life. Only then will you be intentional about the life that you create for yourself. You are free to be uniquely you by defining who you are, how you want to be, and how you are going to live your life. Only you can do this. You may have some help, input and support from a coach, mentor or friends, however, ultimately, <u>you</u> choose to live your life by design, rather than by default. It is also important to accept that life is an unfolding journey where ideas and ideals may morph and change as you grow along the way. Ongoing self-awareness is key.

The following are some suggestions and exercises to help you live authentically.

1) Identify your top 5 values. This short list of some commonly held values will help you get started: family, health, honesty, spirituality, compassion, peace, courage, humour, joy, growth, self-reliance, truth, independence, education, respect, adventure, responsibility, creativity, balance. Add values that are important to you, then pick your top 5 and clarify what each one means to you in one sentence. For example, you could clarify 'integrity' as 'doing what I say I will do', or 'health' as 'I lovingly nurture and care for my body, mind and spirit'.

2) Identify your strengths, gifts and talents. You may want to ask trusted friends, family and co-workers to give you feedback on what they see as your strengths, gifts and talents.

A good resource is the book <u>Now, Discover Your Strengths</u> by Marcus Buckingham and Donald O. Clifton. By purchasing this book you get a link to an online assessment to determine your key strengths. Another resource is the *Inventory of Strengths Survey* on the VIA Institute of Character web site: http://www.viacharacter.org/SURVEYS.aspx.

3) Knowing your values, strengths, gifts and talents gives you valuable information to help you with the next step, which is determining your *Why, Be, Do.*

Why are you here? What is your purpose or mission for your life?

Who do you want to **Be**? What is your vision; what impact do you want to have?

How are you going to **Do** this? How will you bring your Why and Be to life?

It is optimal to express each of these in a concise, easy-to-remember declaration:

Why: To help create a peaceful and compassionate planet

Be: To inspire others to love themselves and live to their potential

Do: To lead and inspire through my writing, speaking and coaching

Your *Why, Be, Do* declarations provide clarity, acting as a guidepost for your life and your choices.

4) Define what success means to you. The dictionary definition of success is: 'Favourable end or result; attainment of wealth or fame; accomplishment.' These definitions are all external measures of success, dependent on something outside of you happening. While material success is wonderful, the more a person becomes conditioned by outside factors, the more cut off from their own spirit they become. Many people get caught up chasing success rather than paying attention to what really matters to them most, such as family, health, spirit. You likely know some people who have achieved a great deal of material success, but at the expense of people, the environment, or other things that got in their way. When you measure your self-worth and success by external measures, you hand over your power and self-esteem.

The key to inner success is to know what fulfills you and brings you joy and to bring this into your daily life. This is authentic success that is not dependent on what other people do or do not do. It is measurable on a personal level – you are either doing it or you are not. You find your truth, what resonates for you as an individual.

To create this definition of success, you work with a specific phrase using this formula:

I know I am successful by how (quality/quantity) I am (verb) (object of verb).

For example:

I know I am successful by how much inner peace I am feeling in the moment.

I know I am successful by how much joyful abundance I am experiencing in my business.

I know I am successful by how naturally I am adding value for my clients.

Using this formula forces individuality and makes this about you, not the actions or judgements of others. The statement cannot be dependent on external results. If you find the word 'should' coming up for you, pay close attention as this is an indicator that you are experiencing an expectation that is imposed on you and is not your truth. This success statement only needs to be meaningful to you. It is measurable on a personal level – you are either doing it or you are not.

Once you have your definition(s) of success, there are two aspects to be aware of as you implement this. The first is personal development – relying on yourself to do the work. Only you can make this happen. The second is personal evolution. This involves identifying and making the necessary changes to your surrounding environment to support the changes you want to make. A blend of both personal development and personal evolution are required, and you must be prepared to make personal and environmental adjustments to align with your definition of success. It is also important to connect with the feeling of your success, 'being' this way even before it shows up in your physical reality. Remember, this is a discovery process of connecting with your authenticity. When your choices are based on your definition of success, you can be confident that, no matter what life brings, you will handle it being empowered and authentic.

"If your success is not on your own terms, if it looks good to the world but does not feel good in your heart, then it is not success at all."
—Anna Quindlen

Being Limitless

When you are empowered and authentic, you harness the potential of your body, mind and spirit and tap into what Deepak Chopra calls 'pure potentiality'. Your possibilities become limitless. If you can dream it, you can do it. History is filled with examples of people proving nay sayers wrong by doing what was previously thought impossible.

While the scope of your life may or may not include history making endeavours, you will have personal and professional accomplishments, and you will impact the lives of many people directly and indirectly. When you show up being empowered and authentic, your impact is positive and inspiring. As a professional woman, your opportunities to accomplish great things and to have an influence are many and varied. You influence people and events daily by what you choose, say and do. Often you may be unaware of how your choices, words and deeds impact other people, including strangers who you may never personally meet. The *ripple effect* comes into play as the impact of what you say and do ripples out like ever expanding ripples across water when an object is dropped into it.

"When you live in alignment with your true self, you send out ripples that uplift the entire universe." —Alan Cohen

As Alan Cohen states in this quote, you truly have the opportunity to be limitless.

Embracing the REAL You

When you proudly own your uniqueness by being empowered, authentic and limitless you are remarkable. You stand out as noteworthy and extraordinary.

Let go of trying to be everything to everybody. Embrace your journey of self-discovery and be the unique woman you are meant to be - Remarkable, Empowered, Authentic, Limitless. Discover, define and develop the REAL you and every day ask yourself "What can I put my whole soul into today?"

Be REAL and let your light shine.

Recommended Reading:

The Four Agreements by Don Miguel Ruiz

This Time I Dance! by Tama J. Kieves

Infinite Possibilities by Mike Dooley

ABOUT THE AUTHOR

MICHELE MCLESKEY

Michele McLeskey is CEO and consultant at McLeskey Consulting, Inc., a company she founded in January, 2011 to bring her own brand of common sense and clarity to the food production industry.

Michele founded McLeskey Consulting with the goal of stripping away the layers between leadership and production that exist in many corporations. She imagined new, better ways a company could be run and managed, and saw that she had the leadership skills to build the type of business she envisioned. Her model helps farms and food production facilities improve food safety, quality, and efficiency through increased knowledge, improved procedures, and smoother information flow within their organizations.

When asked about the rewards and challenges of running her own business, she says, "Meeting new people is stressful to me at times," adding, "it's also very invigorating. It's actually a process of teaching a lot of people, which is amazing, and I get to work with different people all the time, meeting them on a level where they're not worried about impressing me, because I'm there to assist them. They're laying all their cards out, being completely open and honest, and I'm able to help them right off the bat."

Passionate about teaching and learning, Michele, an alumnus of Arkansas State University, has spoken repeatedly at the Arkansas State University Agricultural Student Leadership Conference. There, she speaks to students about succeeding in agricultural business.

Michele grew up on a farm in rural Arkansas near the border of Missouri and Tennessee, but McLeskey Consulting works with farms, corporations, and food production facilities throughout North America and Europe, reaching into all areas of agriculture and food production.

Contact:
Michele McLeskey
Office: 731-334-1665
Cell: 731-267-9913
Email: michele@mcleskeyconsulting.com
Address: McLeskey Consulting, Inc.
Office: 13628 Loren Ln.
Fayetteville, AR 72704
Mailing: P.O. Box 473
Tontitown, AR 72770
Website: www.mcleskeyconsulting.com

TWO

AWARENESS: WHAT EVERY WOMAN NEEDS TO KNOW

Michele McLeskey

Welcome to Michele's intro to Business101 lessons that were hard learned for me over the last two years while starting my company, McLeskey Consulting, Inc. I'll share interesting lessons I discovered and the fascinating ways in which I learned these not- so-fun lessons.

I love to refer to the last two years of starting my company as my spiritual journey of a common woman with zero skills in starting a business to becoming the CEO and "Face" of McLeskey Consulting, Inc. and making it work for me! Since 2011, I have been in a constant state of fright about starting a business and I thank God every day for this opportunity. My learning curve was Mount Everest as I had no clue how to start a business! So I basically had EVERYTHING to learn about starting a business in 30 days, filing incorporation paperwork which took several months, tracking finances was a slam dunk after 2 weeks on the internet researching the best of the best, where do I go for advice when everyone I know works for someone else and learning to be the "CEO" as I laugh. So sit back and listen to my somewhat entertaining but mostly educational path. Please laugh, have fun with my mistakes and successes because this will continue to be my "paying it forward" moment for all women who think they can't.

Just a quick recap about me to get you in the mood, I was raised in a small farming community in the Northeast Arkansas countryside. We are "honest and genuine", to a fault, means bold/brutal speak from a southern girl who is about five foot two inches in height. Did I mention I am an extreme introvert? I was born to two very independent- thinking parents that influenced all six of us kids. I am the 4th girl and 5th child, respectively. Therefore I have wildly fantastic dreams of grandeur in thinking I could start a company at the ripe old age of 43. Stop laughing, take a drink of your Dr. Pepper and calm down. I know, perish the thought that we raise our little females in the south to be independent thinkers. My parents raised our family as southern democrats so I protect what is mine. Speaking skills are getting better each day, good Lord willing and the creek don't rise, and I'll be a much better speaker / orator / teacher tomorrow. Although I was known as "Chatty Kathy" with family & friends in my younger years, I am not so much nowadays with the general public or acquaintances. I tend to be pretty shy as a norm but if you approach me I'll greet you like an old friend and hold a steady conversation until you'd like to move on to greener pastures. Oh don't get me wrong I have just as much to say as anyone else, I figure if you want to know you'll ask like I do otherwise you don't really want to listen to me chew your ear off.

I'd say with this chapter I am building on the basic lessons I've learned over the last 2 years and partially explained in two previous chapters *"50,000 Foot View Versus Ground Level"* in the book *"A View From The Top Exceptional Leadership Strategies for Women"*, and "Succeeding in Communications Means Reading Between The Lines" in the book Breaking the Barriers A *Woman's Toolkit For Success"*.

I decided to look at the individual elements that are very critical for us, as women, to thrive in our work environments. So the basics are as follows and I call them directives:

Directive #1: Do not compromise your principles, period.

Directive #2: Trust is earned, period.

Directive #3: BE AWARE - Know the Big Picture & Day-to-Day Operations.

Directive #4: Recognize positive & negative behaviors within your business interactions.

Directive #5: Work hard, but Play harder!

Let's tackle Principles, Directive #1: Do not compromise your principles, period. Be who you are, don't change for anyone. Well this implies you actually know who you are. We are fluid human beings so take a temp check to understand the basics of who you are as a person.

I did this with my all-time favorite training course, a 360° Leadership Training/Evaluation Class from **_The Leadership Trust_** with Dr. Holly Latty-Mann called **"Personalized Leadership Development Program"**. Doc Holly as we like to call her is a licensed clinical psychologist with many years under her belt. Excellent teacher and a damn fine person to boot, who taught me quite a bit about myself because I was willing to learn. And yes it was just that simple!

I have taken three Meyers-Briggs personality tests over ten years, one commonality is **my basic personality stays the same within reason,** I am naturally or normally an INTJ.

My 2002 test Scores: **I**-8   **N**-13   **T**-6   **J**-16

My 2007 test Scores: **I**-2   **N**-2   **T**-4   **J**-20

My 2012 test Scores: **I**-22 **N**-23 **F**-3 **J**-25

The number scale with the opposing traits on each end. As you answer the survey questions, you fall to one side or the other.

Where you focus your attention: "Extraversion" 30, 20, 10, 0, 10, 20, 30   **"Introversion"**

The way you take in Information: "Sensing" 30, 20, 10, 0, 10, 20, 30   **"Intuition"**

The way you make decisions: "Thinking" 30, 20, 10, 0, 10, 20, 30 **"Feeling"**

How you deal with the outer world: "Judging" 30, 20, 10, 0, 10, 20, 30 **"Perceiving"**

For the Extraversion versus Introversion classification of my personality, this highlights where I focus my attention. My tests scores ranged from 8-2-22 over the 10 years. A few factors affecting these changes were moving to a new position/company/area but with a pretty good selection of friends in 2000, promoting to a mid-level manager & performed lots of public speaking/training in 2005 and starting a consulting company in 2011.

For Sensing versus Intuition classification of my personality this highlights how I take in information. My tests scores ranged from 13-2-23. A few factors affecting these changes were moving to a new position/company/area as a way to further my career in 2000, promoting to the head of a quality department of fifty versus seven employees in 2005 and starting a consulting company and utilizing information for charting of my company, goals, and plans of action in 2011.

For Thinking versus Feeling classification of my personality this highlights the way I make decisions. My tests scores ranged from 6-4-3. A few factors affecting the changes were moving to a new position/company/area all while learning a new culture like who are the sharks/guppies and how to swim with them so I could be successful in 2000, promoting to the head of a quality department while learning to balance day-to-day logic decisions versus department head in 2005 and being the CEO of a company in 2011.

For Judging versus Perceiving classification of my personality this highlights how I deal with the outer world. My tests scores ranged from 16-20-25. A few factors affecting the changes were moving to a new position/company/area required heavy daily planning for even small tasks in 2000, department head promotion & being molded to match others who were very successful within the company in 2005 and being sole proprietor of a new company in 2011.

I don't fight the sway from my normal / comfort zone of personality. Adjusting to the business/social setting just allows me to stretch who I am. Being a big picture person is tempered with the information I utilize in my day to day operations for me and my company's success. Now that I have moved to the Feeling intersection side it isn't such a strain that I moved to a deeper judging stance. I work to balance making decisions based on who I am with respect to my values and moral compass all the while tempering the Judging side of my personality. Luckily for me I crossed over to the feeling side of the above trait which compensates with my social skills. While heavy Judging aids me greatly in starting my company by being able to judge people/their intentions from one preliminary visit; I do watch my words now, more than ever as I realize I have the ability to do harm my business without this trait in check.

So as you can see, you can alter your basic personality somewhat by being flexible but you will revert back to your most basic of personality traits to feel normal when you are alone. Learn what environment you thrive in, these are your "strengths" and swim successfully in that pool. Stop concentrating all your efforts on the areas where you are floundering, these are your "weaknesses" and should be noted and enhanced but NOT focusing all your energy on this area. WARNING: "It is not fun to try and be someone you are not. This only makes your life hard. So **know** you, **like** you, **feel at peace** with you and your choices made every day. Principles are what make you who you are when no one is watching or listening. I had more than one occasion when my principles were challenged over the last 45 years. So protect who you are and stand up & be counted as this action feels right for you. However, "it ain't for the faint of heart". To **paraphrase** a movie quote from "*A League of Their Own* - "There is no crying in business, suck it up and deal" thank you Tom Hanks! And now for the fun fact, I opened my eyes reluctantly in 2007 but have been keeping them open and learning each day. Be open to learn...........

Next we move on to Trust, Directive #2: Make everyone earn it, every day. Our trust is a sacred gift and ONLY the most loyal of family, friends and business partners should have it. Unfortunately this is not always the case so I fall back on my directive – Make everyone earn it, every day. I talk in greater detail about communications in the book **"Breaking the Barriers a Woman's Toolkit for Success".** My chapter, **"Succeeding in Communications Means Reading between the Lines",** tries to help everyone understand the aspects or foundation of successful communications. I explain about a length of time but really this depends on the two individuals and their experiences, depth of trust needed, day to day working environment and so much more. But I will say this one comment; it has been hard for me to have trust for someone that does not have the same principles as you do. This does not mean that someone has to be exactly like you, no what I am suggesting is the foundation that we use to establish trust is built over time, related to our principles and we use these to measure everyone, not just the people who are different from us. I have friends who run the spectrum of the rainbow! Men, Women, mild mannered (i.e. wallflowers) to flamboyant behaviors, stylish dressers to completely not caring what they look like to anyone, book smart nerdy college graduates to street smart/savvy dropouts, Artists to Brick layers and the one thing that holds true for all is "they earn my trust, every day" as I do theirs. The minute I fail, they let me know and vice versa.

This brings us to AWARENESS – Directive #3: BE AWARE: Know the big picture focus of your company & most especially the Day-to-Day operations. These are two very different and distinctive focal points.

Get smart about how to build a Company correctly from the ground up, the first time! I hired a lawyer for starters because He is smart about law and I am not. Most of you need assistance filling out incorporation paperwork, putting together consulting contracts, understanding others contracts, impacts to your business with changes, expansion, moves to your business.

Then I consulted with my new lawyer to find & hire a solid CPA that could/would grow with my business. As I expand my services and grow, I wanted day to day information on every conceivable subject. Also, my lawyer suggested an Insurance Agent that could cover all insurance needs - Professional Liability, E&O, Travel, Automobile and Medical. Did a little research & found I have a pretty amazing Financial Consulting company. Met my Website Designer through a family friend, this turned out smashingly! My website is incredible and I take no credit! And quite by accident, I stumbled upon an old friend who is now my IT Support and who I will make it my life's work to have him join my team permanently as soon as I can fiscally manage. After I had what I considered to be the basics of a solid support team, I started looking at experts in other areas. Still searching for some of these but my company is young and growing.

Next, be honest about your current professional Skills, if you can get more or better skills/training to expand your business then do as fiscally possible. I did in 2007, went for three classes with certifications in my first year that expanded my business more than three fold. I am now a qualified trainer in a section of my field and auditor for two separate divisions. Tackle this like all your other company goals, by listing what is lacking in your company and searching the most fiscally sound avenue to achieve!

Be smart about success planning! Plan to succeed or you are most definitely planning to fail! I think I am paraphrasing a quote. *"If you do not plan for success, you can count on failure. If you are not thinking forward, you are moving backward." Confucius.* I sit down with my plan at least once a week to keep it fresh in my visual mind. If I keep my goal/plan in front of me then I don't lose focus. I also can work out the daily changes. Change is inevitable. So let's end with BE AWARE or FOCUS on the here and now while keeping your eyes on the future prize. Use whatever tools help you stay focused on the here and now, while keeping an eye on the future mapping of your company!

Then we have Behavior Recognition – Directive #4: Recognize positive and negative behaviors in your Day-to-Day business interactions. Take the positives and leave the negatives, I say! I guess this is old fashioned people watching at its very basic nature for some of it, so this comes naturally for me as an introvert. This requires you to understand a little about human behavior and you can learn this by researching a little, either online or in a class room setting. Watching the Movies/Films or TV Shows will show you exaggerated expressions or behaviors. When we are happy, we smile. When we are sad, we are quiet or cry. We are basically the same but the idea is we know these basics of everyday behaviors, so what am I asking you to learn?

I am asking you to monitor empowering skills, positive words used to show praise and thoughtful actions by others. Watch for people who set up others for success rather than failure.

Watch for anyone that is positive with/about you rather than negative when you make a mistake.

Watch for manipulative behaviors in others, like I'll only help you if you help me first. Or Diva/Queen behavior by men and women who think they don't have to work or try to get you to do all the work and then they take the credit. Also watch for the ones that are intimidated by your personality so they try to undercut you at every turn either in meetings by negatively opposing your EVERY idea. Watch out for people that always want to work their connections and not introduce you to theirs so you can make your own.

Take the good and leave the bad by emulating the good and not letting the bad in you before it becomes a behavior of yours. Acting in particularly bad way one time can be counted as a mistake but twice, it is now a negative habit that will require great effort to stop.

And Last but not least the FUN – Directive #5: Work hard, Play harder! Have fun in this life time, make room & plans for the really important parts of your life - family and friends, charities & causes that are near and dear to your heart.

As we get older these actions are more critical to our everyday lives. Do not get so invested in making a career that you forget to make a life. I did everything wrong in the first part of my life by putting my time and energies in the wrong things. Just listen to the word I used, things. Wow, I am so saddened by not getting it earlier in life and concentrating on the people in my life that made me rich beyond any money that I could have earned. Money is cold and does not love you. It is an inanimate object that is to be used for your benefit, not cherished. Family is warm and loves you even when you are the biggest dork this side of the Mississippi River! Family is to be cherished and NOT USED. Good luck with that one and learning your bad behaviors early on in life so you can stop them before they become a pattern of behavior that is almost unbreakable and always detrimental to your happiness.

Now I am concentrating on cherishing the friends I have made/ will make throughout my life. Friends, who are really your friends won't use you and will be there when the chips are down. Our really good friends will be there in the jail cell with us, saying "Wow, let's do this again sometime" or I have heard they will help you bury the bodies... I, thankfully, haven't tested either of those theories but will let you know if I do.

Let's just say I am not perfect & won't claim to be. I am just a regular person who has learned some hard lessons along the way. Good Lord willing and the creek don't rise; I'll keep learning new lessons each day. The minute you stop learning, you stop living and are stagnant like bad water in a scummy pond. Learn these lessons and please don't make the same mistakes I made. Good luck with your business and living the good life. And thank you for letting me tell you my upside down story.

ABOUT THE AUTHOR

Barbara J Cormack MNMC, AFC(IIC), CIAC

Barbara is a Spiritual Life Coach, Mentor, Facilitator, Trainer, and Speaker. Born in Southern Rhodesian (now Zimbabwe), Barbara commenced her training as an Accountant in Malaŵi. After moving to the UK, Barbara soon reached her goal to work, as a Financial Analyst, in the City of London. Her third career-choice gave Barbara the opportunity to travel extensively (Africa, UK, Europe, USA and Canada); where she spent many years living and working as an IT financial software specialist and project/programme manager. At the beginning of this century, another career change saw Barbara qualifying as a Master Coach, becoming an Accredited Fellow Coach (IIC), and starting her own business. This now allows her to combine her extensive background and experience with a keen insight into the demands of balancing the personal with the professional.

Coaching is a wonderful journey of self-discovery and achievement.

From an early age, Barbara was very intuitive; selecting only to demonstrate the use of her intuition after training as a coach. Although her career choices were always based on her intuition or 'gut feel'; she now uses her intuition actively in her everyday life, with her clients, colleagues, and friends.

After many years of transition, Barbara now has the ultimate 'virtual working life'. This allowed her to move to her dream destination (her little piece of Africa in Europe; Madeira, Portugal). After her divorce she found herself on the move, and now lives in rural France.

Stop Dreaming, Start Achieving.

Author of Creating Sustainable Change, and a columnist for Magna Intuitum (Cormack's Capers); Barbara is available to coach, train students, carry out IT projects, facilitate or mentor from anywhere in the world; and travel to attend speaking opportunities.

Contact:
P.O. Box 582
Chatham
Kent
ME4 9BY
www.nyasa.biz
barbara@nyasa.biz
+44 (0)20 8144 2067

THREE

CALM CONFIDENCE

Barbara Cormack

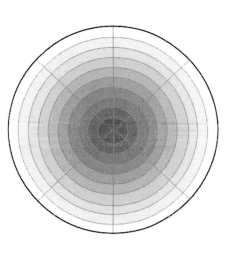

L ife is a combination of phases and segments. Often the phases happen without you being aware of them – being born, learning to walk, school, college/ university, work/career, marriage, family, grand-parents, and retirement to name the 'standard' range; whereas other phases will be planned – changing job, changing career. Throughout each phase of your life, you have a range of segments that cross each phase – friends, significant other (partner/husband/wife), finance, work/ career, personal growth, energy, self-esteem, physical fitness, fun and recreation, optimum health, fitness, holidays, hobbies, and money and/ or finances. This can be represented by an adapted Wheel of Life. As a Spiritual Life Coach the Wheel of Life is used to represent a helicopter view of your life as it is today; but for the purposes of Calm Confidence the phases can be represented by the circles starting from the centre of the circle – your birth. The segments are represented by the spokes of the wheel. As you move through each phase of your life, you have more options in each segment and through the decisions you take (consciously or unconsciously) the segments become more defined.

Moving from one phase of your life into another doesn't always bring with it the feelings of confidence; and taking the step from school to college or university and then onto join the world of work is something that has changed over the years. Often in today's world it is more difficult to get your first job or even a new job.

Remember, moving into the phase of work gives you the opportunity to *create your own success*. High school subjects were designed around providing an education for what was and still is known as the 'main-stream' careers – accountant, engineer, doctor, dentist, solicitor, secretary, teacher, and even the armed forces. Whereas today's careers include options like IT consultant, alternative health therapist, astrologer, as well as the more 'main-stream' careers. With the development of technology the career opportunities, although grown in variety, have decreased in number.

Everyone is entitled to happiness ♥ health ♥ wealth ♥ love ♥ friendship ♥ true expression ♥ peace of mind; and breaking into the business world is a wonderful step into your own future, which when taken with Calm Confidence will give you the opportunity to achieve your wildest dreams.

Life is not easy for any of us.
But what of that?
We must have perseverance and above all confidence in ourselves.
We must believe that we are gifted for something
and that this thing must be attained.
—Marie Curie

Confidence is generally recognised as a state of being certain that a chosen course of action is the best or most effective way; or that a suggestion, proposition or prediction is correct. Self-confidence is being confidence in your own state of being, of your own decisions, and is recognised as having confidence in yourself.

The decisions you take now will have an impact on your whole life. Whether these decisions are taken consciously or unconsciously, you will start a chain of events that will take you one step closer to the future you chose; or will it?

The first step is to truly understand what you want from your life is to start to capture your inner most thoughts. Your **journal** is one way in which you can capture your dreams; your aspirations; your inner most thoughts, concerns, and fears. Although there are many definitions of your journal it is really *your personal and private document*, which allows you to capture your own thoughts, fears, concerns, barriers, dreams, aspirations, and unspoken goals. Finding somewhere quiet; where there are no disruptions, no interruptions, no phones, no-one wanting to talk to you; gives you the opportunity to capture exactly what is 'on your mind'. Often these are thoughts that you may not want to share with others or maybe even voice. They are often known as your inner most dream – that dream you don't believe that you can achieve. Capturing your thoughts exactly as you hear them, whether they make sense or not; releases them from your unconscious mind. It is important that you capture them just as you hear them; don't try to analyse them, or to rationalise them, or to think about them – just write them down. Your journal will allow you to capture your inner most dream or dreams – that/those dream(s) you've never told anyone about.

Capturing your inner most dream(s) through your journal allows you to start to truly understand what you want from your own life. Each thought you capture will consolidate and clarify your dream(s). As you capture your thoughts you'll find that they may create or define a single or a number of dreams. Each of these dreams may be in a segment of your life or may cross the boundaries of the segments of your life. Achieving just one of these dreams will take you into a new phase in your life.

After a period of time, as your dream clarifies through your thoughts; the next step will be to create your dream as a goal. Although there are many techniques that allow you to do this and the simplest technique is to use the SMART(ER) acronym. Select one dream at a time and take it through the following process:

- o   S stands for SPECIFIC!

- o   M stands for MEASURABLE!

- o   A stands for either ATTAINABLE, ACHIEVABLE and AGREED!

- o   R stands for RELEVANT and REALISTIC!

- o   T stands for TIME-BOUND and TIME-FRAMED!

○   E stands for EVALUATED and EXCITING!

○   R stands for RECORDED!

Coaching is a wonderful journey of self-discovery.

It's at this point that you will truly start to discover your own internal hidden dreams. You are about to start your own journey of self-discovery. Using the information that you've captured in your journal; you'll be able to create your own goal. Each element of your goal must be clear and well-defined. Without absolutely clarity you will not be able to achieve your goal. As you define the *specifics* of your dream you will go through periods of internal self-discovery. It's important that as you discover new elements of the internal you, or you gain new learnings and experiences, that you capture these in your journal. Acknowledge them! Without knowing the specifics of your goal, how would you be able to *measure* that you have achieved it? An example of a specific and measurable goal is one where you want to 'lose weight!' If you didn't know how much weight you wanted to lose, how would you know that you've achieved your goal? So rather than defining a goal to lose weight, you would define a goal to lose a specific amount of weight. Although your goal may feel that it is not *attainable* or *achievable*, each goal is attainable or achievable; if you *agree* that you really want to achieve it. Frequently your inner most dreams are the only ones that you really want to achieve, but until you agree that you want to achieve it, you won't! It may sound harsh, but without your own agreement, your goal will probably remain your dream. It maybe that although you've agreed that you want to achieve your goal that you feel it is not attainable or achievable. One of the things to remember, is that in goal achievement you will take one step at a time to achieve your goal – you will not be trying to achieve the whole goal in one step. The larger the goal, the more steps you may have to take. However, it is important that you create a goal that is *realistic*.

There is nothing stopping you creating a goal from your dream. For example your dream maybe to run your own company which employs 500 people and earns several billion dollars a year. You can do this as long as you are realistic about the time that it might take you to achieve it. *Relevant* goals are your own goals. You may often feel that the goals you should be achieving are those that will make other people happy; but really, you should only be achieving dreams that are yours. Setting goals that are relevant to the direction you want each segment of your life to take is important. It's undemanding to take the easy way out, where you find yourself achieving someone else's dream and achieving their goal. The goals you chose to spend your time and energy achieving should be those that are relevant to your life.

> *You are never too old to set another goal or to dream a new dream.*
> —C. S. Lewis

Time Bound or *Time Framed* goals are interesting. As a Spiritual Life Coach I am aware that the spiritual world works on a different time to that us humans work on. Phrases like 'go with the flow' and 'it will happen at the right time' come to mind; but what research shows is that without a time frame you will not work towards living the life of your dream and achieving your goals. When setting a time frame it is important that you are specific and measureable – in this you must have the date, month and year included (some say the time as well).

Although E stands for *evaluated* as well as *exciting*, I know that unless you are truly excited about the goal you have defined, you won't achieve it. A goal you are excited about should be one that you live, breathe, touch and feel at every moment of every day. It's the goal that makes you tingle when you think about it.

Recording your goal in short sentences that are written in the present tense, positively, and personal are your opportunity to be absolutely clear about what you want to achieve. All those thoughts that you've had, all those ideas that you've had are now brought together into a single focus. If you take the goal to lose weight, and today is 4th January, 2013; writing something like 'Today is the 31st December, 2013 and I have lost 2 stone' gives you a very clear goal that by the end of this calendar year you will have lost 2 stone in weight.

> *'People too weak to follow their own goals,*
> *will always try to find a way to discourage yours.'*
> —J. Johnson

As you go through this process of understanding and capturing your dreams; and then defining your own goals; it is important to understand who you can share this with. Some people close to you may not want you to achieve your goals. This is not based on whether you can or whether you can't, but on their fears of change. It is normal for them to wonder that by achieving your dream, what changes are you making to their lives?

Having understood and clarified your dream, and then defined your goal; now is the time to start looking at achieving it.

'If you think you can do a thing
or think you can't do a thing,
you're right'.
—Henry Ford (1863 – 1947)

Henry Ford's statement is an accurate one; but you sometimes feel that you can do something until one very small fear raises itself and everything comes to a halt. Yes, you can select to work with a coach who will support you in every element of the achievement of your goal in a non-judgemental, non-directional manner while maintaining your confidence in every element of your conversation; but you can do this too.

Your journal is the one tool that you have to capture your inner most secrets – that fear that stopping you achieving your dream. By using your journal as your confidant you will allow the **Universal Thought Process** to provide you with a level of unconscious support. A major component of your Universal Thought Process is your unconscious mind (also known as your power centre); and it functions at every level of your being and within every cell of your body. The Universal Thought Process is a major component of the Law of Attraction; and although there are many definitions of the Law of Attraction, it really means that you get what you focus your thoughts onto and into.

We gain strength, and courage, and confidence
by each experience in which we really stop
to look fear in the face …
we must do that which we think we cannot.
—Eleanor Roosevelt

Putting all your thoughts, concerns, fears, goals, achievements, successes, and questions into your journal; gives your unconscious mind the opportunity to let them go. Just the act of writing them down gives you the feeling of having support. By writing in your journal you are letting them go and now allowing your power centre work with the Universal Thought Process. Without realising it your unconscious mind will work through your questions, your concerns, your fears; and as you capture your next and future thoughts in your journal, you'll find the answers presenting themselves. Those *eureka* moments!

Visualisations are important to achieving the life you wish to live. Being able to clearly visualise your own future as you would like it in a positive, present tense and personal way helps to keep you focused on your own goals. Visualisation maybe simply seeing you living your dream, or creating a picture board of you living your dream. Taking one step at a time allows you to move closer towards your goal. Sometimes the steps are small ones and at other times they may feel huge. Whatever size the step is, taking one step after another towards the future you visualise keeps you moving towards achieving your goal and your dream.

> *Believe in yourself!*
> *Have faith in your abilities!*
> *Without a humble but reasonable confidence in your own powers*
> *you cannot be successful or happy.*
> —Norman Vincent Peale

Building your own *calm confidence* is not something that will happen overnight. It will start with a sudden realisation that you have started to believe in your own self-confidence. Self-confidence is being confidence in your own state of being, of taking your own decisions. Gradually you will begin to realise that the journey you are on has become a journey of self-discovery, a journey of achievement, a journey of successes, and a journey that has started to build your own self-confidence.

Another tool that will help you continue to develop your own self-confidence is **meditation**. It's a skill that allows you to get beyond the 'thinking' mind and move into a deeper state of relaxation and awareness. One purpose of meditation is to relax your body, calm your mind (conscious and unconscious) and quieten those many thoughts, fears, concerns, and questions. Quietening your thoughts gives you the space (and time) to honestly focus on creating and maintaining your ability to continue your journey of self-discovery and achievement. There are many ways and techniques which you can select to meditate and these encompass a wide range of spiritual or psychophysical practices. Whichever way you select to meditate, the way or technique more often involves turning your attention inwards to a single point of reference – focusing on your breathing, or waves breaking on the beach, or a candle flame, or a meditation CD/DVD, or a piece of music, or something similar. Whether you practice meditation now or wish to learn how to meditate, the outcome of meditation is to move your mind, body, and spirit from the busy place it is in now, to the achievement of a higher state of consciousness, a place of quiet and a deeper state of relaxation; creating and maintaining your own Calm Confidence.

Kindness in words creates confidence.
Kindness in thinking creates profoundness.

Kindness in giving creates love.
—Lao Tzu

An exercise that will help you develop your Calm Confidence is a simple combination of the tools that you've explored in this chapter. Using your journal provides an opportunity of openness and honesty with yourself. Your journal allows you to capture not only your inner-most thoughts, fears, concerns, goals, achievements and successes; it also allows you to become very specific, measurable, agreeing, realistic, time-bound, excited; whilst recording every goal that you dream you could achieve. Meditating provides an opportunity to clearing your mind.

Select a time every day in which you can spend at least an hour with yourself, where you have no appointments afterwards. Take your journal and your favourite pen or pens and find that quiet space where you will have no disturbances and settle comfortably. It is advisable to have a glass or bottle of water with you. Quietly go into your own selected meditation. Let your mind become empty of all thoughts. Let your body relax. Let your spirit wander. Feel yourself floating in a sea of calmness. As you begin to come to the end of your meditation, bring yourself back into your own surroundings and ask yourself the one question that you need an answer for today! It's the one question that will help you move into the next step of your goal.  It's the one question you know you need to ask yourself to conquer a fear or face a concern. Whatever it is, ask yourself that question. As you feel your mind start to give you the answer or answers, capture them in your journal – no interpretation of what you are capturing, no analysing what you are hearing or feeling – just write it all down. Your thoughts and your feelings!

As you begin to realise through the detail that you are capturing in your journal, that you are taking each step towards your own selected goal(s), that you are succeeding at each task you undertake, that you are achieving each milestone you set, that you are being successful, that you are moving ever closer to your dream; you'll begin to understand that internally you now have your own Calm Confidence.

Breaking into the Business World and Succeeding
is a journey of self-discovery and achievement!
—Barbara J. Cormack

ABOUT THE AUTHOR

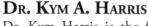

DR. KYM A. HARRIS

Dr. Kym Harris is the founder and CEO of Your SweetSpot™ Coaching and Consulting, LLC. The mission of Your SweetSpot™ is to ensure that diverse talent reach their professional and personal potential; and to guide organizations in maximizing the potential of their human capital through individual coaching, team coaching, and facilitated development programs.

Dr. Harris is a board certified Executive coach with an Ed.D. in Organizational Leadership. She is committed to helping women and diverse executives establish strategies for achieving increased professional and personal effectiveness. Dr. Harris is known for her action oriented coaching model, which is grounded in value-based decision-making, the pursuit of authentic relationships, and personal accountability. Described as a "velvet hammer," she utilizes a strategic and intuitive approach to guide clients out of their comfort zones in a way that minimizes discomfort and amplifies desired results.

Dr. Harris' 27-year career in Human Resources and Talent Development represents leadership and executive roles in higher education (University of Miami and Emory University), and corporate America (The Home Depot and Cox Enterprises). She holds a Bachelor's degree in Psychology from Rutgers University, a Master's degree in Business Administration with a concentration in Human Resource Management from Nova Southeastern University, and a Doctorate degree in Organizational Leadership from Argosy University.

Dr. Harris is a dynamic keynote speaker who shares her personal and professional life lessons through colorful, humorous, and moving stories that entertain and impart powerful lessons about work and life. She is available to deliver keynotes and facilitate conference workshops.

Contact:
Dr. Kym A. Harris
Founder and CEO
Your SweetSpot Coaching & Consulting
drkym@liveinyoursweetspot.com
(678) 524-9492

FOUR

LESSONS FROM THE FUTURE

A LETTER TO MY 25 YEAR–OLD SELF

Dr. Kym Harris

Dearest Kim,
I have learned that reflection is a powerful thing. I do not take enough time for it because life is so busy. I had an inkling of what the future had in store, but could never have imagined all the twists and turns life would take. I would like to share some insights with you.

I know that twenty-five was the magic number for you. Your expectations about what you would have accomplished were high and now that you are at that milestone, you are disappointed in yourself. All you have to show for your efforts at this point is a nice car, a great wardrobe, and a lot of debt. This is not how you envisioned the big two-five. Please know that this is actually a time to celebrate because what you are feeling in *this moment* will influence your decisions and actions for the next twenty-five years. *Now* seems like an apropos time to offer a bit of encouragement as you begin to recalibrate and set a course for the future. What you are feeling will fuel behavior that is *goal driven* and you, my dear, will achieve every goal that you set. My advice, aim high! You will experience challenges and learn lessons along the way that will inform your thinking and your choices. You will also experience much success. I am *here* to tell you that everything will be fine, so exhale and relax.

Having the hindsight that you could not possibly have, I want to share a few lessons that you will learn along the way. I know you well enough to know that initially you will not consider this advice seriously. I also know that at some point this letter will become a frequent reference point. Therefore, I will begin with this, "be kind to yourself." Know that you are intelligent and capable. Some things will require a bit more effort on your part, but your natural ability to excel will always win out. Replace the negative self-talk with words that encourage and fortify you. Life is a dance Kim; choose the moves that work for you.

People will come into your life and influence your view of the world, some for a season and others for a lifetime. There will be a man with whom you will fall deeply in love. This man will teach you what it means to be strong, a quality you will demonstrate throughout your life. Although his presence will be for a season, his impact will last a lifetime. His death will motivate you to move outside of your comfort zone, try new things, and take some risks because life is short.

You are resilient Kim. You will fall down, but rise with speed and grace. Others will admire this about you. Keep in mind that as important as it is to rebound, it is crucial that you address the issues that led to the fall. Do not allow your desire to "keep it moving" prevent you from addressing unresolved issues and conflict. It will be uncomfortable and awkward to deal with issues that make you feel vulnerable, but do not let those feelings stop you from facing the hard stuff head on. In the absence of resolve, issues will resurface. Resolving issues when they emerge will build skills you will need later when there is much more at stake.

Kim, right now, you do not understand the strength of your presence. Over the next few years, you will get glimpses of it and not recognize it for what it is. Make no mistake; your presence is an asset. However, it will intimidate some people. When you hear that for the first time, you will be stunned. The strength of your presence will flavor your interactions with others all of your life. Knowing this now will help you manage it later. Dial back on your intensity and allow others to see your lighter side. Be intentional about letting people get to know you. Share more of yourself. You will learn along the way, that life just "ain't that serious." With that said, do not shrink so that those around you will be secure. Do not pick-up the baggage of others and make it yours. I want you to emerge as a woman who is comfortable with herself and unapologetic for who she is.

I know that you have visions of being a successful executive and it will happen for you. Be warned though, women do not easily achieve the heights you want to reach in your career. It is even harder for

Black women. Patience, tolerance, and diplomacy are tools you must master to reach the level of success to which you aspire.

People will see the leader in you and ask for more. When they ask, give it consistently. Realize that your standards are high and not everyone will be able to meet them. Meet people where they are and value the contributions and perspectives they bring to the table. You will find that your perspective is often different from most. You have a unique way of seeing things; this is a strength and the source of your creativity. Enter every situation prepared to share your views, and then share in a way that is confident and open to the opinions of others.

Kim, do not run from feedback. While initially, you will believe that the perceptions of others are erroneous, some observations will become consistent. You will gain a friend along the way that will share this advice, "you follow yourself wherever you go." Everyone is a work in progress, even you. Feedback is information that feeds growth; develop an appetite for it. Not everyone is comfortable with his or her flaws, but you will learn to manage your imperfections perfectly.

You need to know that not everyone will provide the direct communication you prefer, so you will have to look beyond the surface to hear the real message. You will learn that it is not always about people understanding you; you will have to make an effort to understand others as well. Look past titles and see the person, recognize their vulnerabilities, and meet them there. Your professional relationships will be richer because of your efforts.

Courage will become a core value, especially in your career. You will recognize it in others, be proud of yourself when you display it for all the right reasons, and justify times when you should have been more courageous. Do not allow fear or ego to prevent you from dealing with issues head on. Also, try not to judge others who do not demonstrate the courage you think they should. Courage is your value. The risks you are willing to take do not make sense for everyone.

You will make career decisions based on money; and walk away from an accomplished career in higher education, to pursue opportunities in corporate America because of the financial rewards they provide. You will learn that Corporate America is not an environment in which you thrive. In this world, people that do not understand you will label you. Know that those labels do not represent the woman you are. Do not allow those experiences to create self-doubt and diminish your confidence. You will learn quickly that while the money is great, not all the handbags and shoes in the world even when you can afford them will bring you happiness and fulfillment.

The lessons from this experience will teach you that your needs are basic and provide clarity about two more values, independence and flexibility. Because of your experiences in corporate America, you will question your career moves and kick yourself for not investing more time in the environment that suited you better. You will wonder if a bit more patience would have allowed you to achieve the same level of success with less battle scars. Could you have made different choices? The answer to that question is 'yes.' Would they have been better choices, there is no way to know that. Just know that when the dust settles, you will land well.

You are not going to believe this, but that doctorate degree that you ran from in college will eventually catch up with you. Once again, you will wonder, "what if?" and then realize that the perspective that you brought to your doctoral study was the result of years of experience. The timing will be perfect.

Your education, successes, failures, lessons, and stories become the framework for your future. Each will leave you with a wealth of knowledge, experience, and skill. The experiences that cause you the most joy and pain will be the fuel that accelerates you into the field of Coaching. As you read this letter, you will have no idea what that involves. Just know that it is your calling. You will stand on your stories and achieve an unfamiliar level of success as a result. Your past will qualify you for your future.

Over the course of your career, a core value, financial security will be threatened when you are downsized, not once but twice. The first time will be early in your career. You will emerge from that experience as a successful leader in higher education. This is an opportunity that you would not have pursued had you not been laid off. The second time, you will be more seasoned and professionally accomplished. From this, you will emerge an entrepreneur. As you learn to lean into your strengths, you will gain confidence in your abilities to build a business that fulfills your vision of a gratifying career. Once you make the decision to move in the direction of a career that best serves you, the universe will conspire to help you. As an entrepreneur, you will find your sweet spot and thrive.

Young women that aspire to do more will watch you and you will serve as their role model, even when you do not realize it. In fact, you will mentor and learn from many young women. A woman several years your junior will teach you a powerful lesson. From her you will learn that because others look up to you, the weight of your behavior is considerable. Be mindful of your words and your actions, this responsibility is part of your purpose.

Guess what Kim? You will fall in love again. This man will support and nurture you and your dreams. He is the faceless man in that reoccurring dream. You will know that it is he because his stature, form, and presence will match the dream. He will teach you the importance of transparency. Through him, you will learn how to communicate in a way that enhances understanding. He gets you and appreciates your quirkiness. His presence in your life will bring you joy. He will become your best friend.

As I close this letter Kim, I want to remind you to enjoy every aspect of your life. Spend quality time with your family, take vacations, and enjoy your friends. Life is about more than work. Take in all that life has to offer. Know that who you are is more than enough. Believe in yourself. Life is going to be sweet. Enjoy the journey.

With Much love and admiration,

Kym - "I have indeed emerged comfortable with myself and unapologetic for the woman I am."

To those who read this letter

This letter was thirty years in the making and there is a lot more I could have shared. It was hard to write and stirred up many emotions. As I read it, I am reminded of my strengths and my areas of imperfection - some of which I have simply accepted and some I continue to work on.

Let me encourage you not to wait thirty years. Each day, month, year provides insights from which we can learn and grow. Be intentional about *your* learning. Make letter writing an annual ritual. Do it at the end of every year and reflect on your lessons. Conscious introspection reminds us of our accomplishments, which are a source of self-confidence. It is also an opportunity to forgive ourselves for things we could have done different.

Take the time to reflect on your accomplishments, failures, lessons, and relationships. What have you learned? What will you do different as a result? How have you grown? What opportunities did you miss? What did you absolutely love about the past year? How can you get more of *that* in the coming year?

Reflect, plan and move forward with intention.

ABOUT THE AUTHOR

BOBBIE CRUDUP QUALLS

Specializing in professional coaching and empowering young women to develop themselves into exemplary leaders to serve humanity is Bobbie's deepest passion .

Ms. Qualls is an advocate teaching and leadership educator. She received a Rank 1 certification in Administration Leadership and Masters Degree in Counseling and Bachelors Degree in English Literature .

Ms. Q (as she is affectionately known) served as a Distinguished Educator from Kentucky Department of Education (1998-2000) and retired as a Distinguished Leader (Consultant) from Jefferson County Public School (2001). Having served as a Vice Principal, Distinguished Educator and Distinguished Leader, her greatest career joy was serving as an English Literature **teacher**. Currently she serves as a teacher educator on Kentucky Teacher Internship Program Committees for University of Louisville.

She also holds certification in Zeta Organizational Leadership (ZOL) from Zeta Phi Beta Sorority, and certifications in Women's Issues and Diversity and Professional Coaching from Professional Woman Network. Ms. Qualls has received several recognitions because of her service to humanity. NAACP High School Teacher of the Year; Great Lakes Region: State Director of the Year, Woman of the Year, Kentucky Service Award, and Finer Womanhood Award (Zeta Phi Beta Sorority), March of Dimes Service Award, Distinguished Educator Cadre Award, and Outstanding Woman of America Award.

Ms. Qualls is a **member** of Community Baptist Church, Educational Advisor of Newburg Youth Council, Professional Woman Network , International Advisor board (PWN), Acorn State University Alumni Association, Life Member of Zeta Phi Beta Sorority, and a partner of Crudup -Ward Day Care and Activity Center.

She is co- author of Bruised **But Not Broken, Transformation: Reinventing the Woman Within, How to Break the Glass Ceiling Without a Hammer: Career Strategies for Women, and Sister to Sister: A Guide for African American Girls** in the PWN Library.

Contact:
Bobbie Qualls
8212 Thornwood Road Louisville, KY
quallsbf@aol.com

FIVE

CHILDHOOD VALUES PERMEATE... WORKPLACE

Bobbie Crudup-Qualls

Wow! Mom, have you heard about the exuberant young professional...
impressive credentials, graduate degrees, sparkling image, profound
*earning power, **walking tall** and speaking assertively! My mom,*
exemplifying humility and compassion, smiled and exclaimed, 'did she
***walk** in with her 'childhood home training' (we call them **VALUES**)*

Absolutely! Your childhood values permeate and transcend into the workplace daily. As a child you are taught many values (i.e. honesty, hard work, integrity, trust, teamwork, persistence, service, confidentiality...) that help shape and mold you into the person you blossom into. Your parents, educators, mentor, and community that you belong to become an instrumental part of the professional you transcend into today (no matter where you live.)

As I was traveling from the Caribbean Islands, to U.S.A and to Hawaii (the mainland) 2012, I diligently reflected on my contributing chapter for an upcoming book ' Childhood Values Permeate into the Workplace'. After engaging in conversation with several leaders, I decided to use this grand opportunity to **interview** some highly skilled and influential professionals. These leaders assessed the workplace / company's values with their own childhood values. They have found their core values; those values are guiding and directing them through their professional journey.

So embark on this Value Journey with me. Study the leader's values, and observe how they aligned their childhood values with their workplace values. I will respectfully share some 'golden value nuggets' with you.

All Aboard! Meet the **interviewees...**

Please try to keep 'this complete chart on 1 (same) page if possible (add/delete as needed)

Childhood Value Interview Model Format

Book Title: *The Professional Young Woman: How to Break Into The Business World ...*

Chapter Author & Title: *Childhood Values Permeate into WORKPLACE*

Chapter Author: Bobbie Qualls

Chapter Goal:

1. Interview 10 Professionals

2. Essential Question: What major VALUE did you learn as a child and practice throughout your career that you would recommend to a young professional woman in the workforce today?

Contributor's/ Interviewee's Name:	Professional Position/Title:
Sherri L. Wallace, Ph.D.	Associate Professor, University of Louisville

PART I: Identify 1-2 VALUE(S). Using a scenario, an incident, event or a favorite quote etc., describe /explain the childhood value taught /reinforced by a parent, relative, or personal role model, etc.

1. **Honesty (be truthful)** – <u>Be true to yourself and others</u>. This way you never have to remember what you have said and done. Your reputation and work will speak for itself.

2. **Authenticity (be genuine)** – <u>Be who you are</u>. You will earn the respect and trust of others around you. People who are pretentious will eventually be discovered and viewed as "users" and "self-centered." Your reputation for authenticity can transcend into leadership positions because people will trust your judgment and insight. Intimidation comes from

being uncomfortable with self. Authentic people are self-aware, and not afraid of exploring themselves for growth and/or recognizing and engaging others.

PART II: State briefly how you model, practice or incorporate your childhood value(s) in the workplace.

I bring honesty and authenticity into the classroom through the course I teach, my research and public service. As a teacher, scholar and social change agent, I am a manifestation of my values.

PART III: (Optional) **Please share a "value-learning activity or exercise" that is or can be used in the workforce.** If the activity or exercise is published or has copyright, please include the full author attribution or citation.

There are many cultural competence "self-assessments" available **to examine and interrogate our assumptions, beliefs and value**s that we take with us into society and the workplace. **Please visit: http:// www.hillcrest.logan.k12.ut.us/web/html/International_week. html/Cultural_Competency_Interactive_Activities.pdf;**

Also, a lot of job training activities can be found at "Teaching Tolerance" http://www.tolerance.org. I recommend **"Hidden Bias" assessment**, http://www.tolerance.org/hidden_bias/

Childhood Values: Commitment & Focus
(Antoinette Crawford-Willis, Ed.D)

"The older I get the more wisdom I find in the ancient rule of taking first things first... " —Dwight D. Eisenhower

Antoinette, you can't be in every pot that boils but when you pick your pot...try to stay until what you are cooking is done." My mother needed me to learn that if you make a commitment always stay focused and try to follow through ...completion.

Cooking, not me! I always told my family that I would never cook; I would have someone to prepare my meals for me. Daddy would shake his head and mom would smile and say well come to the kitchen and keep me company. She never made me boil water...

...I was in the kitchen (again) watching my mom cook dinner.... she informed me that I would need to consider an alternative career if something happened "God Forgive" with my dancing (degree in theatre and dance) . I ran off a list of careers that I could pursue if ... or when I stopped dancing. How...? I gave her a wide-eyed stare and said "I don't know but I will... She said you need to pick one thing and focus in on that one item.

Do you see me stirring in every pot on the stove or one pot at a time? I began internalizing that question. I got focused and committed; I returned to school and received Masters of Arts degree; I received my doctorate in Higher Education and Adult Learning, in 2012.

Value Tip: Commitment is extremely important in the workplace because it reflects your sense of duty and determines focus. Your commitment enables you to incorporate a sense of accountability, integrity and builds a positive attitude. Commitment is key because it's one of the steps towards your ladder of success. What are you totally committed to and focused on today?

Childhood Value: Respect
(Shamika Stewart-Qualls: Special Education Instructor)

"Treat people as if they were what they ought to be and help them become what they are capable of becoming." —Goethe

When asked to think of a **childhood value** that I also carry into the work place, there wasn't one that quickly came to the forefront. But in quiet moments I could hear the voice of my grandmother saying "the only thing in life people want is to be treated with respect". Then she would say "treat people the way you want to be treated. If it is honesty you want, give them honesty. If you want them to care, care for them, if it's love, love them." The most important value however is respect.

As an Educator, respect is an important treasure to have. The foundation of respect is what most relationships connecting home and school are built upon. A respectful relationship between parents, students, and colleagues is essential. As a Special Education Teacher Chairperson, it is my job to lead my team using respectful tactics. I show genuine concern and compassion for their creativity and ideas. I respect and value their opinions and celebrate their contributions to the team. In effort to bridge the gap between parents and school that currently exist within our learning communities, I act as a liaison. I honor the beliefs, values, and personal choices of the parents.

Instructing my students through multiple measures and varied modifications takes effort, balance, and patience. While some days are daunting and some are more strenuous than others, respect is the glue that bonds instruction and comprehension. I respect my students' independence and individuality...yes, I embrace their disability with respect...

Value Tip: Demonstrate Respect Daily in Workplace/ Organization

Google http://www.buzzle.com/articles/respect-in-the-workplace. html: Respect in Workplace

Value: Excellence - Always do your best.

(Edwin Fox: Financial Advisor)

"We are what we repeatedly do. Therefore, excellence is not an act. It is a habit." —Aristotle

I was about six years old and my chore was to take the garbage out and empty it into the trash can. I was being lazy and instead of pouring the trash in the can, I missed the can and the trash ended up on the ground. I left it! My father saw it and made me clean it up with a lecture about doing your job well, regardless of what the job is or your perceived importance of the job. After the lecture and teaching, he checked out my attitude and walked toward the car.

I am diligent as I provide sound professional advice of excellence regarding the investment of my client's dollars. I continually read and digest data regarding the stock market. I keep abreast of what the best analyst say and combine that information to make sound reliable decisions. Providing support and advice during time of market volatility is a necessity. When I make a decision on behalf of my clients, I have done everything I can to make an informed and intelligent decision. Yes, confidentiality is a virtue: I take my client's confidence in me very seriously.

Value Tip: Stay informed and keep abreast. Keep your mind transformed? Annually read Stephen Covey's book: The 7 Habits of Highly Effective People.

Value: Honesty & Character Development

(Debra Lowery: Educator)

One of my sisters was going on her first babysitting job, so Dad called all of us in the family room and taught us a crucial lesson. If you see money anywhere whether it's on the drawer, on the counter, or even on the floor, leave it there; it doesn't belong to YOU. He proceeded to share one of his childhood incidents …

"I knew those pears didn't belong to me, but I grabbed some off Mr. _____ tree anyway; after receiving my major consequence from Mama, I had to walk MILES back to return them." I learned as a young boy, honesty is the best policy and your word is your bond.

Everybody can act like they are somebody are famous words spoken by Mama. We received a lesson in Character Development daily. Our school report card was the 'measuring instrument'. Dad was proactive and assured us, you may can't get all A's and B's in your books but you can always get an A in conduct.

Honesty is an essential foundation for your success. Being honest will earn respect and trust which will reward you success in your career. Developing character starts with doing what's right. Value of honesty (and other values) were first taught to us by our parents and grandparents; they taught basically through 'value sayings' by emulating and disciplining.

Value Tip: Implement these 6 ways to create a climate of honesty in the workplace: model it, embrace honesty with assertive communication; if an error occurs, solve unethical behaviors and actions; celebrate and rewards ethical behaviors; follow company policies/guidelines and do what you say you are going to do. Reflect: How will you create a climate of honesty…

Air Force Values: Integrity, Service, and Excellence
(Lisa Moore: Lieutenant Colonel)

"Always give your best in everything you do", echoed my parents. They taught and trained me how to excel in all that we do. More importantly, they modeled the best! I watched them work untiring giving 100 percent as they established a Dry Cleaning business from the ground up and supported the community by helping those in need.

'Stay in the Word, Praise God, and give Him the glory for every, 'little bity' blessing, said Mom. So, on Sundays you know where I was… I then had to go into the community and serve. These teachings and service helped me overcome the trails of military life.

The Air Force recognizes integrity first, service before self and excellence in all we do as its core values. These are values every member must believe in and more importantly, must live by. I entered the US Air Force as an enlisted member and was commissioned after 11 years of service. I am now a Lieutenant Colonel and have won many awards for excellent performance. As a member of the United States Air Force for 23 + years, I live by these core values daily and they have been extremely worthy and beneficial for my country and for me.

I challenge you to implement my values in workplace: Stay grounded, keep the faith, serve others, show generosity, and be honest even when no one is looking…

Value Question: How will you integrate the US Air Force values (Integrity, Service before Self, and Excellence in all we do) into your workplace / organizational culture? Explain

_____

_____

_____

_____

_____

_____

_____

_____

Childhood Value: Empathy

(Amber Moss-Qualls: Professional Development Trainer)

As a child, I recall watching that famous last scene in "The Color Purple" in which Nettie and Celia are reunited after decades of separation. Beautiful purple flowers sway in the wind in front of the southern porch. A car can be seen traveling up the driveway and a league of beautifully dressed Africans stand outside to greet the mother and sister having been torn apart from long ago. As the characters cried in response to the overwhelming joy of being reunited, so did my mother and sister. Oh, did my sister really cry... At the age of six, I couldn't understand why my family was crying. I asked my mother, who replied these are "happy tears." What they were doing was **empathizing** with the characters. That day I began to learn and appreciate the value that comes with truly understanding all facets of the human experience. The ability to empathize is what has allowed me to touch a cord with those I encounter in my personal / life.

Empathy may seem like an unorthodox value in the workplace. Values that are more "top of mind"... tenacity, honesty, and punctuality.... Empathy, you see, waits quietly in the background, for the moments in which a person's real life issues, forces their way through the guise of professionalism and intrude on the workplace. A managers divorce, the loss of a child, a marriage proposal. Those are the times that the ability to empathize will set you apart from your colleagues.

An instance in time: Colleague was going through the devastating loss of her son-in-law. Our office supported her step by step through her grieving process. Empathetic listening strategy was used; we acknowledged and validated the colleague's emotions / needs. ..I purchased a book for her.... became a resource for healing and relationship building. That humanistic experience brought our office closer together than any team building activity.

Value Question for the Professional: What's the value of empathy in the workplace? Explain the phrase "put yourself in someone else's shoes". Remember, empathy comes from the heart.

_____

_____

_____

_____

Childhood Values: Integrity & Commitment
(Kesha Hodge Washington: Lawyer)

'I have nothing to offer but blood, toil, tears, and sweat", proclaimed
Winston Churchill.

One of my earliest lessons in integrity came from my paternal
grandfather (Caribbean: St. Thomas). As a child, I remember when
someone was telling him about a "quick money" scheme that involved
"taking advantage of the system." My grandfather abruptly told the
person that he was not interested and that the person "should look an
honest day's work, if he needed money." I later asked my grandfather
why he wouldn't even listen to what this person was saying. My
grandfather said, "When you get money dishonestly, it only passes
through your hands and when the dishonest dollars leave, it takes your
honest dollars too." In other words, there are no shortcuts! If you
want to get something, you have to work for it! If it comes through
dishonest or questionable means, it will be short lived, transitory, and
take more from you when it leaves than what you got from it. It is a
rather simple concept, but one that I try earnestly to follow daily.

Commitment was a value that was instilled in me from my parents
throughout my life, but driven home in my first semester of law school.

My parents are avid believers that each generation should be
better off and given more opportunities that preceded them, so they
sacrificed everything for children. When I overheard parents talking
about ways to 'cut back on money' I suggested attending public school:
no monetary cost. My father made a point to sit me down and school
me: "you are a child. Enjoy childhood; you have rest of life...adult
responsibilities...As long as I have life and strength I will provide...

just promise...you'll reach your goals...Never give up!" 3500 miles away from home, I journeyed to fulfill my dream...attend law school and become a successful lawyer. Few days before my first set of final exams...my father suffered a heart attack (his directives from hospital bed---stay in school...)

I celebrated my ten year anniversary as a licensed lawyer. As my father congratulated me and celebrated with me on that milestone, we talked about that hospital bed conversation (Daughter, we love you, be blessed, do the best that you can do: reach for your passion: goals) He went on to say that, sometimes that means that we (your mother and father) had to sacrifice so that you all can move forward." I sincerely learned that commitment to a principle or person is easy when the road is smooth, but **commitment is tested when there is adversity.**

Integrity and commitment are two of the most important values that I learned from my parents/ grandparents. Those two values are very indicative of a person's character. These precepts still hold true for me today (whether I am in the office, courtroom, at home, etc...) My personal and professional experiences have solidified the wisdoms of these teachings. I am forever grateful for these lessons.

Value: Integrity
(Jazmine Rubin: Love Truth -Executive Director)

My mom (native of Caribbean Island) reared me to adhere **consistently** to very strict moral / ethic code of conduct. In the midst of these high expectations life was filled with delicious Caribbean cuisine and celebrations. Yes, even in the kitchen she was consistently teaching and modeling integrity. Thus, integrity has always been a strong value that I hold near and dear from childhood into my professional life.   It has taken many forms and was taught in many different ways.

- Through family stories I was taught how important one's character is; these lessons helped shape my value system as they impact my life

I actually can hear my mother's words ringing out as I was leaving for school with a slice of buttered toast in my mouth as I rushed out the door, *"He that keeps his tongue keeps his life!!!"* I think back and smile to myself because I remember rolling my eyes from hearing this statement –what I didn't realize was a lesson that was pounded in my brain to help shape the professional woman I am today. I found myself making sure that I thought about the words that flew out of my mouth before I simply reacted to situations that come up regularly...   We must engage people with small steps and small victories which will leads to great success!!!

- Lessons were reinforced by teaching using quotations: "No one can make you feel inferior without your permission"- Eleanor Roosevelt... "Know Thyself" Plato

As I was packing my clothes in preparation for college, Mom's words start ringing out again--- Jaz, while you are in college --- know yourself and be the best you can be. Mom's message was truly reaffirmed in my life when I stumbled upon E.E. Cummings message: "To be nobody but yourself — in a world which is doing its best, night and day, to make you everybody else — means to fight the hardest battle which any human can fight--- and never stop fighting."

- Modeling through Presentations: Serving as Mentor "Love Truth Organization"

...as I stepped into the delicious aroma smelling kitchen, my parents smiled and applauded me for the exceptional 'Love Truth Retreat' I implemented that week.. We began celebrating. I realize the power of proactivity: Proactive professionals value planning,   rejoice over accomplishments and transmit positive energy.

Value Quotation: Explain Author S. Covey's Habit #1: Be Proactive

_____

_____

_____

_____

_____

Value: Wisdom Modeled
(My Daddy: Mr. Andrew Bennett Crudup)

As I journeyed home (Mississippi: January 2012) to visit my 89 year old Dad, I asked him for some 'home training' VALUES to share with Young Professionals...With a twinkle in his eyes and an authoritative but humble stance, he said tell them:

"The righteous leader walks in his **integrity**...Psalm 20:7

A Charge to keep I Have... (Favorite Song) ...They have a charge and a duty to **serve**

Work: work together: Disagree but don't "fall out" / be a **team** and help carry the load

Don't take anything that doesn't belong to you (Be **honest** and upright)

What you say you are going to do, do it! Your word is your bond

Bridle THAT tongue: Listen to understand

God has a plan for their life; plans to prosper them… give them HOPE…Jeremiah 29:11"

With a sprint in his walk, Dad hurried outside and fed his dogs; with words of wisdom and a song always in his heart, I could hear him singing, *This Little Light of Mine, I'm Going to Let it Shine…*

Bravo, Young professional (my grandchildren and all future leaders)! I am confident, as you emerge into the workplace you will embrace your core values and be an asset to humanity. Surely, your values will determine your destiny!

Notes:

_____

_____

_____

_____

_____

_____

_____

_____

_____

_____

_____

_____

_____

_____

_____

_____

_____

_____

_____

_____

_____

ABOUT THE AUTHOR

AMICITIA (CITA) MALOON-GIBSON

Dr. Amicitia (Cita) Maloon-Gibson established MGAA-Professional Development Institute (PDI) to help others to succeed and develop strategies for mastering business, careers, life and relationships. A professional and expert at "Growing and Empowering Future Leaders now!" A Career, Business, and Empowerment strategist who inspire others to succeed without limitations. Through her keynotes, seminars and retreats, Amicitia shares effective strategies for leadership, career and entrepreneur strategies. Her audiences learn how to achieve, believe and live the dreams of their life and the stepping stones to success strategies. The author and co-authored several books. She is featured in local, national, global professional magazines and federal magazines. Her voice is recorded in interviews sharing her effective leadership, career and entrepreneurial strategies. She is a retired Lieutenant Colonel, who served during Desert Storm, Desert Shield and Iraqi Enduring Freedom. She is renowned and her travels are global and international. She serves on several corporate and Non-profit boards: Christian Services Charities, Neighbor to Nation, Tuskegee Airmen-GDCJ Chapter, Women's Army Corps Veterans Association and Professional Woman Network Advisory Board.

Contact:
MGAA Professional Development Institute
Attn: Empowerment Doc
P.O. Box 411482
Melbourne, Florida 32941-1482
Office Number: (321)-537-5002
Web Sites: www.empowermentdoc.com
www.maloongbsoninstitute.com
www.citagibson.com
Non-Profit: www.mgc4e.org

SIX

FINDING A MENTOR

Dr. Amicitia (Cita) Maloon-Gibson

Several months ago in during myself empowerment session, I came across an article by authors Beverly Kaye and Devon Scheef who describe short-term mentoring relationships that comprise "mentworking," a process combining mentoring and networking and enabling participants to give and receive in relationships in which everyone is both learner and teacher. "You'll be sharing your knowledge and abilities with others," the authors write, "serving as a mentor to many. In other words, each 'mentworker' receives and gives brain power to others, creating multiple short-term learning teams."

During the course of my careers many opportunities of "mentworking" were part of my professional growth and development. A mentor or mentors are critical to success in any occupation and academia. The focus is to find a mentor that you admire for their achievements and success in a career that parallel where you want to go. Important in this process is find someone that you can trust, that will commit and will give you honest feedback that will facilitate development and growth in your career of field of study. Ensure that your mentor is the right "fit" for you; meaning personality and values should be similar to yours. Also, there are times when you may get a mentor whose main purpose is to derail and distract you from your goals. Identify this early and avoid the pitfalls of wasting time and energy being steered down the wrong path. Good mentors are great listeners and will support your goals and objectives.

The term, **Mentor** derives from the Greek word for "*steadfast*" or "*enduring.*" In Greek mythology Ulysses asked his friend Mentor to be a friend, guide, and teacher of Ulysses' son Telemachus.

The term Mentor has numerous definitions depending on the specific functional field and role of the individual. There are several key definitions that will apply in this chapter relevant to Mentor and mentoring between the mentor and mentee (protégé) and they will be included throughout the chapter.

Who is a Mentor?

There is no single definition to define a mentor; however this definition encompasses most of the characteristic of a Mentor.

Definition:

Mentor: A trusted friend, advocate and role model for a younger (sometimes older) and less experienced person. A mentor possesses a set of skills, experiences, or qualifications which enables him or her to foster the development of a youth (or adult). However, mentoring is not age specific and is applicable to adults in any career field or occupation. Having a mentor can be a significant, empowerment influence in a person's life, especially youth in the 21st Century.

Mentoring like learning can be a lifetime process of empowerment and exchange of intellectual knowledge.

Who is the Mentee or Protégé? In the mentoring relationship this is the individual that is considered "junior" or "a newbie", in most, but not all cases. The Mentee is the beneficiary of the mentoring partnership or relationship.

America's Mentoring Umbrella:

The Corporate Mentoring Challenge (CMC) addresses America's dropout crisis by encouraging and promoting corporate support of mentoring both locally and nationally. The CMC recognizes outstanding corporations from all over the country that have created, expanded or partnered on mentoring initiatives this year.

The Corporate Mentoring Challenge is sponsored by the White House Office of Faith-Based and Neighborhood Partnerships and the Corporation for National and Community Service in collaboration with MENTOR. The National Mentoring Partnership. This recognition challenges private corporations to create or expand and existing initiative within their companies to encourage employee participation in mentoring programs for youth in communities across the country.

MENTOR is the lead champion for youth mentoring in the United States.

They serve young people between the ages of 6 and 18, and MENTOR's work over the last two decades has helped millions of young people find the support and guidance they need to build productive and meaningful lives.

Statistics on Mentors and the shortage:

Currently, 18 million children in the United States want and need a mentor, and three million have one. MENTOR's mission is to close that "mentoring gap" so that every one of those 15 million children has a caring adult in their life.

The Goal of MENTOR:

MENTOR helps children by providing a public voice, developing and delivering resources to mentoring programs nationwide and promoting quality for mentoring through standards, cutting-edge research and state of the art tools.

The National Mentoring Partnership is guided by leaders representing the business, government, education and religious sectors. These dedicated individuals are actively engaged in the strategic planning and implementation of MENTOR programs and policies and serve as the organization's chief ambassadors for youth mentoring.

The Findings:

MENTOR determined that youth in the very high-risk category need multiple interventions and that mentoring would not be nearly as effective for them as it would be for youth in the other risk categories. Therefore, MENTOR focuses its efforts on recruiting mentors for those who could most benefit: young people in the high and moderate risk categories, as well as 10 percent of youth considered low risk – a total of 18 million youth, or 50 percent of all young people in the U.S.

Finding a Mentor

Mentoring can be described as action where one individual helps another individual to grow, develop and be self-empowered. A connecting of a mentor and mentee is a serious life changing decision for both individuals; and the fact is that everyone mentors, some mentor better than others. Finding a mentor is not as challenging as you would think. However, prior to finding a mentor you should research and prepare yourself to ensure that you get a "good" fit as a mentee.

The functions below are identified as important roles that are performed by mentors. First you should perform a self-assessment of your personal history and identify a person who has contributed to your developmental needs in one of the several roles. Below list several behaviors or skill sets for each role that is important to your growth and development.

Active Listener

_____

_____

_____

_____

_____

Encourager – Motivator

_____

_____

_____

_____

_____

Coach – Guide

_____

_____

_____

_____

_____

Advisor – Counselor

_____

_____

_____

_____

_____

Role Model

_____

_____

_____

_____

_____

Expert - Problem Solver

_____

_____

_____

_____

Teacher – Challenger

_____

_____

_____

_____

Sponsor – Advocate

_____

_____

_____

_____

_____

Spiritual – Values

_____

_____

_____

_____

Document your expectations. What knowledge are you seeking? How frequent would you like to meet with your mentor? How much time do you want mentor to commit? Duration you anticipate this mentorship relationship to last? Documenting these expectations from the beginning will ensure that the mentor and mentee relationship is understood.

_____

_____

_____

_____

Find someone who you can gain knowledge and experience from. The model mentor is respect professionally and has a career that you seek to emulate. Seek an individual who is competent and successful in your career field. Additionally, an important characteristic to consider is the individual's personality. Having the ability to communicate with your mentor, is key to having an experience that will be fulfilling.

After you've made the decision of what you are seeking out of your mentor relationship, there are a variety of resources you can consult.

In a recent article and interview conduct between Lily Whiteman and myself, for the *Federal Times Newspaper* these are following recommendations suggest by me: " recommends you begin a mentoring relationship with two documents: a worksheet/questionnaire for your mentee and a set of binding agreements between you (mentor) and your mentee.

The worksheet/questionnaire is intended to help your mentee conduct a rigorous self-assessment of his strengths, weaknesses, short-term goals and long-term goals. The resulting information should help you both identify the focuses of your future coaching sessions, which skills you should help the mentee develop and which obstacles you should help him conquer.

For example, suppose the mentee's worksheet reveals that he is doggedly aiming for a leadership position but has a fear of public speaking — a skill that is obviously required of effective leaders. Your mentee's worksheet responses would suggest that you should encourage your mentee to improve his public speaking skills, no matter how intense his fear may be. So after explaining to your mentee the importance of developing his public speaking skills, you might, for example, suggest that he join Toastmasters International, take a class or receive individual coaching on public speaking. After the training, you might want to help identify or arrange opportunities for your mentee to use his improved public speaking skills.

In addition, the worksheet responses may reveal the types of expertise you should offer and the types of support the mentee needs. For example, suppose you are a woman and your mentee is a young woman who is striving to break certain types of glass ceilings. These results suggest that you should share any relevant experiences or observations you may have about breaking similar glass ceilings, and that you should regularly initiate discussions about your mentee's progress in this area.

The worksheet should also ask mentees to describe their expectations for the mentoring relationship so that you can gauge whether their expectations should be negotiated further.

The binding agreements — or contract — between you and your mentee will help protect your investment of time and energy in your mentee. This document should establish what types of communication you both will use and how often you will communicate. Will you, for example, plan regularly scheduled face-to-face meetings or e-mail conversations, or will the mentee contact you as needed? Whatever mode of communication you choose, both of you should double-check that neither of you is pledging more time than you can realistically spare.

Also, the contract should establish rules of accountability for your mentee. For example, this document should commit the mentee to being coached and showing up on time to your planned meetings or phone calls; cite how much notice the mentee should give if he must cancel a meeting or phone call; and warn the mentee of consequences he can expect for failing to give notice (unless he is involved in an emergency). For example, the contract may state, "If the mentee fails to show up at more than X number of meetings without giving notice, the mentor-mentee relationship will be dissolved."

In addition, the contract should prepare the mentee for the full range of feedback you will provide. "I use the contract to ensure that each mentee will be open to feedback — good or bad, positive or negative. Some people just want to be pumped up. But my contracts tell mentees that they can expect to hear the truth from me (in a tactful way)."

"If I see a problem, I will discuss alternative courses of action with them but I won't tell them what course of action to take. This is all part of teaching mentees to take ownership of their goals, and empowering mentees to make decisions for themselves."

SAMPLE MENTORING AGREEMENT

This agreement documents our mutual interest for entering into a mentoring relationship for personal/organizational purposes and period of time specified below. We agree to meet regularly according to a prearranged scheduled, discuss personal/organizational issues freely and openly, respect differences of opinion and point of view, protect confidences and identify specific developmental tasks to be accomplished.

This agreement will end on

_____

The personal/organization's goals are

_____

_____

_____

_____

_____

_____

_____

_____

_____

Our regular meetings will occur on

_____

_____

_____

_____

Periodic reviews will occur on

_____

_____

_____

_____

_____

Developmental assistance and assignments are requested for the following areas:

_____

_____

_____

_____

_____

Mentor's Signature & Date   Mentee's Signature & Date

_____   _____

Closing thoughts, visualize success, seek good mentors, and learn from mistakes. Persistence, this is the key to success, but you must keep the faith and stay in the race, because the end is better than the beginning. You must know yourself, know your job, and your field of expertise.... Your attitude, character, and integrity determine your altitude. Develop goals that are specific and attainable, and remain balanced.

"Watch your thoughts, for they become words. Choose your words, for they become actions. Understand your actions, for they become habits. Study your habits, for they will become your character. Develop your character, for it becomes your destiny."

References and other resources:

Mentoring.org (http://www.mentoring.org), published by the National Mentoring Partnership, covers issues on youth mentoring.

One to One: A guide for Establishing Mentor Programs. Washington, DC: U.S. Department of Education.

Growing and Empowering Future Leaders Now, Amicitia Maloon-Gibson, ISBN9780972796453, 2012.

Notes:

_____

_____

_____

_____

_____

_____

_____

_____

_____

_____

_____

_____

_____

_____

_____

_____

_____

_____

_____

_____

_____

ABOUT THE AUTHOR

MICHELLE RICHARDSON, MCC (IAC)

Since founding Momentum Works Inc. in 2001, Michelle has coached thousands of people including entrepreneurs, corporate managers, individuals, groups and teams. She specializes in the areas of leadership, meaningful success, passion, and personal evolution. One of a limited number of IAC Master Certified Coaches in the world and a former Instructor for CoachVille, Michelle has excelled as a leader in the professional realm, in the community, and among her peers. A firm believer in continuous growth and skills development, she is passionate about working with people to support their success both professionally and personally. Her highly successful business background includes Microsoft and SuperPages; add this to her unique blend of training and life experiences and it's a winning combination.

Michelle is a champion for the greatness that exists within all of us. Her Vision is to have a profoundly positive impact in the world and, as evidenced by a nomination for the YWCA of Vancouver Women of Distinction Award, she is doing just that. Called to Evoke Greatness on a Global Scale, she makes progress toward this through her relationships, coaching practice, programs, seminars, workshops, TeleClasses, webinars, Inspirational Tips, and her book "From Surviving to Thriving: 7 Simple Steps to Help You Live a Life You LOVE!".

Michelle loves to spend time with her family & friends, travel, and go play outside. Also an accomplished athlete, whatever she does, she plays to win.

Visit Michelle's websites to learn more about her and the business & life-changing products, programs and services she has created since 2001.

Contact:
Company Name: Momentum Works Inc.
Address: 300 - 3665 Kingsway
Vancouver, BC V5R 5W2 CANADA
Telephone: 604.630.3073
Email: michelle@momentumworks.com
Websites: http://momentumworks.com and http://michellerichardson.ca
Facebook: http://on.fb.me/marFBpage
Twitter: @mrichardsonca
LinkedIn: http://bit.ly/MRLinkedIn
Pinterest: http://bit.ly/PinMR

SEVEN

BE TRUE TO YOU

Michelle Richardson

'Be True to You' Defined

To 'Be True to You' means to do what you know is best for you, and not do what you know is out of alignment with who you are and what is important to you. It is accomplished by maintaining your integrity, orienting around your Values, and establishing boundaries that ensure you remain true to yourself. Seneca is quoted as saying "What you think of yourself is much more important than what others think of you." I agree wholeheartedly. Being true to you is the best way I know to honour yourself, have a positive opinion of yourself, and be at your best in your career and life.

In the early stages of your career, you may find it challenging to be true to you. When you are new and lack experience, it might seem natural, even necessary, to defer to others. There is a lot on the line and it's easy to allow your desire to excel to eclipse your commitment to be true to yourself. It's important to remember that you were chosen for good reason; you have a valuable skill set and the potential to make a positive impact in the company. Having said that, there will be times when listening, learning, and following are your best course of action. Provided that what is being asked of you aligns with your Values, allows you to maintain your integrity, and respects your boundaries, this is a perfectly natural and acceptable dynamic in the workplace as you embark on your career.

1. Maintain Your Integrity

Integrity is not one thing; it is a combination of things. It is this combination and your dedication to upholding it that results you being in integrity. When you identify and observe these elements in your life, you will enjoy enhanced results at work, in relationships, and in your overall sense of success.

One of my favourite definitions of integrity is this one from Barbara De Angelis: "Living with integrity means: Not settling for less than what you know you deserve in your relationships. Asking for what you want and need from others. Speaking your truth, even though it might create conflict or tension. Behaving in ways that are in harmony with your personal values. Making choices based on what you believe, and not what others believe."

First and foremost, being in Integrity starts with you; this means making sure your needs are met, living in alignment with your Values, and making choices that support you to live life in integrity with yourself. Some of the ways you can accomplish this are:

- putting yourself first

- following through on commitments you make to yourself

- expressing yourself honestly (i.e. thoughts, feelings, fears, reservations, etc.)

- making choices that are consistent with your beliefs, Values, etc.

- telling yourself the truth

When you honour yourself in these ways, you reinforce your self-worth and enjoy many benefits. Once you have your own requirements met, you will experience less stress and more success.

Keeping commitments is an important aspect of integrity. Ensure that you choose your commitments carefully and limit your commitments to those that you truly want to make. Some of the strategies that can be of value in this process are:

- consider the payoffs of keeping commitments vs. the prices of not keeping them

- identify the short-term gains of saying 'yes' and replace them with long term rewards of saying 'no' when appropriate

- become very clear about your priorities; this makes it easier to choose commitments that are aligned with your priorities and decline those that aren't

- keep in mind that upholding commitments to yourself is equally as, if not more important than keeping those you make to others

- pay attention to the dynamics that occur if you do break a commitment (i.e. patterns, influences, etc.). Ask yourself:

- What do I really want?

- Do I want to rethink this?

- Am I changing my mind about this commitment?

- What can I do to repair the damage?

- What short-term payoffs was I pursuing?

- What long-term benefits does this commitment represent?

By following through on commitments, you will gain respect, stand out, feel better about yourself, and enjoy higher quality relationships with yourself and others.

Speaking your truth is another important aspect of integrity. There are many areas in which the opportunity exists to speak your truth. By speaking your truth, you maintain integrity and demonstrate a willingness to hear the truth from others. This bodes well for you in a business environment and in your personal life.

Some common areas of truth are:

- how you feel

- what you know

- what you observe

- facts/information

- what you want

- what you do

- your results

- your reservations

- your level of trust

- your goals

- your thoughts

- your expectations

Some ways of being untruthful are:

- avoiding issues

- cultivating ambiguity

- implying

- generalizing

- allowing someone else to take the blame

- withholding

- distorting

- distracting attention

- hiding feelings

- denying thoughts, feelings, intuition (to yourself or others)

Speaking your truth is an effective way to demonstrate leadership, strength, and honesty in the workplace and your whole life. It is also a powerful way to enhance self-esteem, improve relationships, and reduce stress.

As much as you might understand that maintaining integrity is critical to success, you might, at times, compromise your integrity in some way. When this occurs, it is helpful to understand what you have allowed to influence you to do so. Some common influences are:

- your ambition

- the influence of others

- what people may think of you

- what you think of yourself

- your fears

- unmet needs

- taking the 'easy' route

- habits

- people/relationships

- the situation itself

Once you understand why you chose to compromise your integrity, you will be in a position to reflect on how to adjust in an effort to avoid doing so in the future. It might be of value to enlist the support of others to help you with this by sharing your tendencies with them and asking for specific support to ensure you maintain your integrity moving forward.

There are many potential benefits to maintaining integrity. By choosing those that hold the most meaning to you, your commitment to maintaining integrity will be strengthened, as will your relationships and your results. Understanding the various elements of integrity can help you identify your strengths and the areas you want to improve. Once you gain this awareness, you will be well equipped to develop strategies that will help you to maintain your integrity.

We tend to hold people who maintain their integrity in high esteem; by placing a high degree of importance on it from the beginning of your career, you will be true to yourself, set yourself apart, and support your success.

2. Honour Your Values

Your attitude and approach to life are informed by your Values; they are the things that are most important to you. Your Values are based on choice, faith, and who you are as a person. They encompass what you stand for and what you stand up for in life. Your Values gratify and attract you; you are naturally drawn to them.

When you live in alignment with your Values you will enjoy a sense of meaning and fulfillment. Fulfillment is an outcome that most everyone desires and it is achieved by being true to you. By identifying your Values and living in alignment with them, you will have taken important steps toward having a highly successful and deeply rewarding career and life.

Your Values are what you naturally lean toward or are drawn to do; there is little, if any, effort involved. For example, some people are natural leaders; they were leaders as children, and they continue to lead the way throughout their life. Someone with the Value of leading doesn't have to force themselves to lead – they do it naturally.

The Values to which I am referring are the broader, deeper Values that are unique to you; they are not based on external rules or expectations. Your Values are tailored to you, by you, and may be experience based, culturally based, genetically based, or a combination of these things.

Some indicators that can help you determine your Values are:

- if it comes naturally to you, it's probably a Value

- if it resonates deeply, it's likely a Value

- if it triggers a strong emotional response, it's probably a Value

- if it's been important to you for a long time, it's likely a Value

- if you light up at the thought of it, it could be a Value

- if you're doing it to get something else, it is not a Value

It is important to identify your Values for many reasons; among them are:

- they can be used to guide you when needs, problems and other issues arise

- they play an important role in times of conflict

- goals are easier to attain when they are Values-based

- by elevating to live by your Values, you become more purpose-driven

- they are a source of fulfillment

- they act as a 'compass' that can help you in many areas, including:

  o decision making

  o goal setting

  o direction

  o relationships

If something goes against what you stand for or believe in, it represents a Values issue. When you are engaged in something that goes against your Values, you will strongly resist it and probably refuse to continue with it.

Values are optional and, as such, are often set aside in favour of more 'pressing' matters. There are many things that have the potential to stand in the way of operating in alignment with your Values. Some of them are:

- needs

- 'shoulds'

- incompletes

- procrastination

- expectations

- stress

- habits

- over committing

- roles

- conflicting priorities

- upbringing

- money

- obligation/duty

- adrenaline

- pipe dreams

These things (and others) tend to dominate most people's lives. As long as this is the case, Values won't have much of an opportunity to be expressed or guide someone's life.

Once you identify what gets in your way and address those things, you create the space for your Values to be fully expressed and, in time, you will live your life in alignment with your Values. Until your blocks are overcome, it is not possible to be truly Values-oriented; Values simply cannot be expressed fully in the face of constant struggle against what is in your way.

Determining your Values, connecting with why they are important, and identifying the 'blocks' that are stopping you from living a Values-based life will put you in a strong position to make the required adjustments. Once you start to remove these blocks, you will clear a path to orienting your life around your Values. Values afford a greater sense of fulfillment, authenticity, ease, and more. Even if you don't quite reach your goals, the experience you have in the attempt will create fulfillment because they are Values-based.

Go to http://momentumworks.com/resources.html; download the 'Clarifying Your Values' document and use it to determine your Values. Identifying your Values will take time and learning to live in alignment with them is longer process still, but the benefits are well worth the effort. When you live your life in alignment with your Values, you will make great strides toward being true to you and achieving meaningful success in all that you do.

3. Establish Your Boundaries

In the early stages of your career as you attempt to make a name for yourself, it's easy to fall into the trap of working long hours, putting your personal life on the back burner, and not taking time for yourself. In the long run, this will work against you. Not only will you set expectations that are impossible to meet long term, you will burn yourself out and negatively impact your effectiveness. It is important to establish healthy boundaries from the outset in order to be at your best and do your best work. There will most certainly be circumstances that require extra time and energy, but make that the exception and not the rule.

The Merriam-Webster Dictionary defines a boundary as: Something (as a line, point, or plane) that indicates or fixes a limit or extent.

In the Oxford English Dictionary a boundary is defined as: A thing which serves to mark the limits of something; the limit itself, a dividing line.

The purpose of establishing boundaries is to protect and take care of yourself. Learning how to set boundaries is central to being true to yourself, respecting yourself, and honouring what's most important to you. Everyone has a right to establish boundaries to protect themselves from others. We not only have the right, but must also make the commitment to take a proactive approach to managing expectations, as well as how we allow others to treat us.

Boundary setting is a way to remind yourself of your worth, the importance of your feelings, and your right to choose what you are and are not willing to accept from the people and situations you encounter. The process of defining, establishing and maintaining boundaries is an empowering and self-honouring one.

Personal Boundaries:

- provide a basis from which to let people know when their actions, behaviours, and expectations are not acceptable to you

- are imperative for healthy professional and personal relationships

- signify your right to say 'no' to what isn't right for you

- are a way for you to take care of yourself, no matter what happens, where you go, or who you're with

- when defined, help you know and understand yourself better

- indicate that you know, value, trust, and listen to yourself

- demonstrate your belief that what you want, need, like, and dislike is important

Your boundaries protect you from taking on the feelings, expectations, and agendas of others. If you are not aware of and/or enforcing your boundaries, you'll be so preoccupied with trying to make everyone else happy, that you'll be exhausted and have little hope of giving your best.

Determining Your Boundaries

As with many things in life, awareness is the first step in learning to set boundaries. Perhaps you want more space, respect (from yourself and/or others), time, energy, or personal power. Maybe it's less pressure, fewer demands, more assistance, or something else that you want. Boundaries tend to announce themselves in several ways; some of which are anger, complaining, feeling threatened, overwhelmed, or victimized. Physical indicators may include a tight chest or throat, a knot in your stomach, a well of emotion, a lack of energy, or something else. All of these are clues to boundaries that require your attention. If you find yourself doing or feeling any of these things, identify the personal boundary and establish it using the process outlined in the Boundary Setting document located at: http://www.momentumworks.com/resources.html.

External boundaries allow us to tell other people when they are behaving in a manner that's not acceptable to us, for instance when someone adds to your workload unexpectedly, or is critical of you. Internal boundaries allow us to set personal limits for ourselves, such as protecting our personal time, limiting working hours, or ensuring that we get enough sleep to function effectively.

Here are some examples of Personal Boundaries to get you started:
External Boundaries: *I do not allow people to...*

- criticize me

- take their anger out on me

- invade my personal space

- insult or belittle me

- tell me what to think

- insist that I do things that compromise my integrity, cross my boundaries, or conflict with my Values

Internal Boundaries: *To protect my personal limits I will...*

- ignore the phone or turn the ringer off if I don't want to be disturbed

- stop working at a time that leaves adequate room for my personal life

- return calls or e-mails in a timeframe that works for me

- change my mind

- reserve a place in my home that is off-limits to others

- say 'no' to anything that doesn't work for me

It is important to understand that you cannot set a limit with someone and also take care of their feelings. While some people may be happy to respect your boundaries, others may be hurt, angry, or disappointed in you. These are not your feelings to take on, it is up to the people in your life to adapt to your boundaries, or not. A strong support system can be helpful as you establish and enforce boundaries. Your first responsibility is to honour yourself. Your beliefs, strength, and resolve will be tested when you set boundaries, but you will feel much better about yourself as a result of doing so.

There are times when we allow people to infringe on our personal boundaries. This is particularly likely at the beginning of something important, such as a job, a relationship, or in other situations that there is a lot on the line. Some of the reasons we allow our boundaries to be crossed are that we want to avoid conflict, we lack clarity about them, it seems like too much effort, or we downplay their importance.

If you have a hard time standing up for yourself, agree to things you really don't want to do, have difficulty saying 'no', or take things personally, it could be that you:

- want to be liked or accepted

- dislike conflict

- feel like a good person when you do things for others

- don't want to hurt anyone's feelings

- worry about what other people might think

It can be easier to say 'no' to something/someone when:

- you are very clear about your priorities

- you are living in alignment with your Values

- the request is inconsiderate to you or others

- it could hurt you or someone else

- you would feel bad doing it

- the demand is inappropriate

- you don't want to do it

Once you have figured out the people with whom, and situations in which you tend to have the biggest challenge setting boundaries and why, you can begin the process of clearly establishing and enforcing those boundaries moving forward.

Learning how to set boundaries is vital and necessary in order to be true to you. It requires that you embrace the responsibility to take care of and protect yourself when necessary. By learning to communicate your boundaries directly and honestly, and enforcing them, you will enjoy healthy relationships with yourself and others.

Choose to Be True to You

Being true to you in your career and life is paramount to meaningful success, confidence, self-esteem, and fulfillment. When faced with decisions or tasks that do not align with who you are, what you value, and what you know to be in integrity, always choose what you know is best for you. At the end of the day, you go home with yourself and there is nothing more important than having the highest regard for the person you see in the mirror.

Notes:

_____

_____

_____

_____

_____

_____

_____

_____

_____

_____

_____

_____

_____

_____

_____

_____

_____

_____

_____

_____

ABOUT THE AUTHOR

ANDREA FOY

Andrea Foy is an award-winning international author, speaker, consultant and coach. ***Andrea Foy Consulting (AFC, LLC)*** is a personal and professional development company design to provide a unique program of professional development seminars and workshops for individuals, businesses, and corporations. Andrea conducts workshops and seminars on topics such as: Women's Issues, Business Skills, Diversity, Image Consulting, Personal Success Strategic Plan and the Hire Power Series. Andrea is a Certified Professional Coach, a Certified Diversity Training Consultant and a Certified Facilitator with Moovin4ward Presentations. She is also an Independent John Maxwell Leadership Coach. She has been personally trained by her mentors John C. Maxwell and Les Brown.

Ms. Foy's knowledge of business and professionalism comes from over 25 years of customer service experience working for the public and private sector for companies such as Sharkey Modeling and Talent Agency, McDonald's, Sears, Delta and USAir Airlines, American Express Financial Advisors and the Federal Government.

Andrea is an Advisory Board member for The Professional Woman Network and has served as a keynote speaker for the PWN International Conference.

Education:
> BA in Liberal Arts specializing in Communications
> MS in Business and Technology specializing in Management and Leadership

Books:
> Hire Power: How to Find, Get, and Keep a Job. (2010)
> Co-author - Single and Loving it: a Handbook for the Single African American Women (2012)
> In The Still of the Night: Personal Safety for Women (2012)
> Co-author - My Vision, My Plan, My Now (2013)
> About AFC:

Certifications:

Women's Issues and Diversity	Professional Presentation Skills
Women in Management	Leadership Skills for Women
Coaching	Personal Success Strategic Plan
Leadership	John Maxwell Leadership Coach

Professional Organizations:
> Professional Woman Network (PWN)
> Toastmasters International (TMI)
> Moovin4ward Presentations (M4P)
> Women in Business Networking (WiBN)
> National Association of Professional Women (NAPW)

Contact:
Andrea Foy
info@andreafoy.com
www.andreafoy.com

EIGHT

PERSONAL SAFETY FOR THE YOUNG PROFESSIONAL WOMAN

Andrea Foy

How to Break into the Business World & Succeed is for the young woman entering the workforce ready to take to world by storm; this chapter is about keeping yourself safe while doing it. As you learn the strategies to break into the business world, you should also know how to be safe in the brave new world you are about to enter.

Some women, by the time they make it to the corporate world, have already traveled extensively, others have not. Even if you think you are a seasoned traveler, you still probably have not traveled to the extent that you may find yourself doing now that you are a career woman. This chapter is a reminder to some and will be enlightening to others as to the best way to make sure you come back from every trip, business or pleasure that you embark on.

All By Myself

Recently I met a young lady at a conference. As we got to know each other over lunch, she revealed to me that, at 30 years old, this was her first trip ever by herself. She had travelled with family, girlfriends, her kids and her husband, but never all alone until then. She flew by herself, rented a car, stayed alone at a hotel and even went shopping and sight-seeing. The look of accomplishment on her face was revealing. I shared with her that as a young flight attendant in my early twenties, while it wasn't my first time traveling alone, I still was very nervous about travelling alone on a regular basis. In fact, on my very first layover, fresh out of flight attendant training, I was sent to the middle of New York City by myself to stay overnight. No pressure!

As I remember, the hotel shuttle came and got me at dinner-time but I went to the hotel, checked in and ate peanut butter crackers and water that I had in my luggage. I didn't even venture out to see if there were vending machines nor even check out the restaurant. Safe in my room, I pushed a chair in front of the door of my hotel room, turned on all of the lights, and sat in the middle of the bed, listening for any noise possible. Might I add this was a top hotel and most likely very safe, but it was New York City. By the time I was supposed to report for duty again the next morning, I was exhausted from not getting any sleep. As I sat there, sleep-deprived, I realized then and there, that I had to make a decision either to quit my career after my first trip or learn how to relax and be safe and see the world.

Lest you think travelling alone is not a big deal, I would remind you of the recent headlines of a young mother going to Turkey alone, to take photographs: She never returned. Also, we all know the Natalie Holloway story of her going to Aruba with a group of friends and chaperones; she never came back. In fact, on one of my international trips, a group of flight attendants went shopping. One woman wanted to buy something in a store but there was a long line so she told the rest of us she would catch up with us. As she crossed an alley next to the store she was grabbed and drugged down the alley, in broad daylight, at a tourist area and while we were a few hundred yards away! They grabbed her by the throat so she couldn't scream, but thanks to a scream from another tourist, the muggers ran away before she was really hurt or killed. They took money and her purse but she, because of training, had left her Passport and ID in her room. If she would have lost those documents, it would have been difficult of not impossible for her to come back to the States. (Tip for international travel) She was shaken and bruised, but alive. I say all of this to remind you: Women are always targets, alone, with friends etc. There are too many stories in the news for us to not pay attention to.

I have actually had women say to me when I was travelling, "Aren't you afraid to go all of those places?" Or "How did you do all of that stuff alone?" Being a flight attendant was a gift because before I did that I might not have travelled much alone but because I had to, I realized that even if you are alone, there's no reason you cannot enjoy yourself to the fullest on business trips and on vacation.

As a new corporate employee or business owner, you will no doubt travel by yourself at some point in your career. Whether it is for business or pleasure, here are some reminder tips on how to be safe while travelling. So let's go over some things to remember. These tips are taken from my book; In The Still Of The Night: Personal Safety For Women, published by Professional Woman Publishing. (probooks. net) I have taken some of the more applicable tips for young women new to the corporate or business world, other tips for cruises, campus, home safety, etc. can be found in the book.

Travel

- DON'T – Talk to strangers. I know it is polite or even romantic to meet someone on an airplane or on a trip, but try to resist doing it too much. There was a story in the news several years ago of a woman who claimed she met a man on a flight, had a few drinks with him and then when they landed, she for some reason went with him into a terminal in the airport that was marked 'under construction' where he allegedly assaulted her.

- DON'T accept dates with people you meet while travelling. If he is really interested, he should allow you to take his business card and you call him, when you are ready. Men that are in a hurry to get to know you may be married or worse, psychotic!

- DON'T - Try and look cute while traveling. This is the time to wear sweats and tennis shoes. Even if you are going straight to a meeting, you can change in an airport restroom rather than attracting attention by wearing sky high heels and expensive clothing.

- When someone else book's a hotel for you, do your own due diligence ahead of time. Use Google street maps to take a look around the hotel you are staying at. Check out reviews and ratings as if you booked the hotel yourself.

- If you get a bad feeling, try and get your hotel changed before you leave. Good companies should accommodate you on that request. Beware those who don't.

- Be reasonable, asking for a hotel with inside doors is reasonable. Don't be a diva, just be safe.

Hotels

When you arrive at your destination, make sure you are comfortable with the location, floor, etc. Remember these tips to ensure your safety and comfort:

- Let the valet help you with suitcases.

- Look around, notice how close the elevator is to your room, look for alcoves, and notice how close you are to the stairwells. Count the number of turns to your room, hallways look the same in hotels.

- Go into your room, open the doors, and brace them wide open with your luggage.

- Go into the bathroom and make sure the shower curtain is pulled back and check behind the door.

- Open all closet doors, and look inside.

- Check behind long curtains

- Check under the bed.

- Limit trips in an out of your hotel room once you check in; you may draw attention.

- Stop and ask the valet or concierge for advice on where to go shopping, sightseeing or to eat.

- Get the hotel's business card with the address and put on your person, not in your purse.

- Keep your cell on your person, either with a holder on your clothes, in your pocket or in a wristlet.

- Do not to carry a big purse.

- Only carry a small amount of money and an ID it. Better yet, wear something that has pockets and leave your hands free.

- If your purse gets stolen; call your hotel first so they can lock your hotel room or go straight to the front desk.

- Leave a trail of bread crumbs. Let people know where you are going. Try not to get too distracted texting or talking that you do not pay attention to who is around you.

- Leave a copy of your itinerary friends also. If it is a business trip, make sure someone in the office has your itinerary and emergency contact info.

Dating and Dining

Again while traveling, you need to eat and eating room service is boring, lonely and expensive. That doesn't mean you should accept a man offering to buy you dinner. But if you do:

- Trust your gut feelings. If a place or the way the man acts makes you nervous or uneasy, leave. Always have a cell phone and make sure it is fully charged. Have money for a cab.

- Be careful how much you drink, if anything, in restaurants or bars as well.

- Don't accept beverages from someone you don't know and trust unless it is brought to you by a waitress.

- Do not let anyone you meet 'see' you to your hotel room. He may pretend he wants to protect you, but may want to harm.

- Do not get up and leave your food or drink unattended and then come back to it, you never know…

Taxi

- Do not get caught up texting, reading emails, etc. unless it is to tell someone where you are.

- Don't use Gypsy cabs, also known as hacks. These are usually unlicensed cabs, most importantly most are uninsured.

- Know where you are going before you get in a taxi. Google it or they may just drive you around to run up the fare or worse take you someplace you don't want to be.

Car

If you decide to drive or have a job that requires you to drive a lot, keep these tips in mind:

- Use only the well-known restaurants, gas stations, and travel areas when you need to take a break.

- Stay on your guard. Bad guys have been known to pick out women who are alone and follow them as they leave the area or station.

- As always if you are followed at night by a car with a flashing light, stay in the car, doors locked, and keep the cell phone ready to use.

- If you are traveling alone and a car "bumps" into you, don't stop to exchange accident information. Drive to the nearest place with people and then get out.

- If you don't have a cell phone: keep a blanket, warm clothes, a pair of boots, snacks, water and a flashlight in your car always, for emergencies.

- Do not stop to help people; if you want to assist someone whose car has broken down, go to the nearest phone or use your cell phone and call the Police.

- Plan your driving for day trips, if possible.

- If you get carjacked, give it up. No car is worth being injured or losing your life over.

ATM

Believe it or not, ATMs are a source of muggings and robbery's, keep these tips in mind at home or traveling.

- Try to use machines you are familiar with, and try to use terminals located in banks rather than independent terminals.

- Use ATM inside shopping malls that are well lit with much foot traffic.

- Be aware of your surroundings. Look around before conducting a transaction. If you see anyone or anything suspicious, cancel your transaction and go to another ATM.

- If you must use an ATM after hours, make sure it's well lit.

- Never walk away from an ATM with cash still in hand. If you are going to count your money, do so at the ATM.

- When making an ATM transaction from your car, be aware of your surroundings. Keep your eyes and ears open, and keep car doors locked.

Conclusion

These tips I have talked about in this book are not only for travelling, a lot of the do's and don'ts substitute for dating advice as well, especially on the first few dates. Keep aware of your surroundings, do not drink excessively, and know where you are going and let your family and friends know, finally do not leave your food or drink unattended. Definitely check out your room thoroughly before you relax and unwind, but most important don't let these tips scare you into not travelling around the world! Bon voyage! There is no reason to live in fear of crime and violence. This means we can go where we want, do what we want and not be afraid of the bogeyman that can hurt us. There is however reason to take reasonable precautions. And in doing so, you will have deterred most criminals from choosing you as their victim. Knowing how to protect yourself from danger can and will liberate you from not living your life to the fullest.

The harder you make it for the criminal to victimize you, the more likely he is to go ply his trade elsewhere. You won't have stopped the criminal from being a criminal, but you will have stopped him from choosing *you* as a victim.

This chapter was not intended to scare you into being paranoid, but to liberate you into living life to the fullest, by being safe and smart.

As I said in the beginning, I was surprised at the number of women who admit being afraid to travel unless someone was with them. There is no reason to have that fear when you know what to do and are careful. Whether you are at home, traveling by air or ground, dating or on a cruise you can have the time of your life.

Notes:

_____

_____

_____

_____

_____

_____

_____

_____

_____

_____

_____

_____

_____

_____

_____

_____

_____

_____

_____

_____

ABOUT THE AUTHOR

REV. DR. LILLIE MADISON JONES, M.S., M.DIV, ED. D.

Lillie Jones is a nationally distinguished educator, whose mission for many years was "that no child be left behind." Her degrees include a BA, M.S., Ed. S and Ed. D. She received a Master's of Divinity in 2003. Additionally, she is a Board Certified Coach and received CPLC Certification from the Professional Christian Coaches Institute. She is also a trained Appreciative Inquiry Coach. Her passion is leadership development and matriculated in a series of leadership programs including "Leadership at the Peak" through the Center for Creative Leadership in Colorado Springs. She was one of the first group of women inducted into the Society of Our Wise Women at Bennett College. Dr. Jones is a graduate of the Shalem Institute of Spiritual Formation with a certificate in Leading Contemplative Prayer Groups & Retreats. She is currently founder of Full Measure Living Coaching and Consulting, LLC.

When she retired as Interim Superintendent of the Guilford County School System, her dedication and effort had positively impacted many children. Dr. Jones has been a teacher, principal and Deputy Superintendent. As a United Methodist Pastor, her commitment to personal empowerment and spiritual development are at the center of her willingness to contribute her talent and her wisdom. She served as pastor of a two- point charge from 2001 –2006. During her tenure as a pastor, she initiated a summer camp (AACCC=Academic, Artist, Creative Christian Camp) to prepare K -12 students for school.

Dr. Jones was a community activist in Mooresville. She organized the Annual Community MLK Service, as well as a catalyst in organizing the first MLK Community Breakfast. In 2008, she was the keynote speaker and spoke on the topic: "We are the ones we have been waiting for." Having served on numerous community boards, she is currently the Program Development Chair of the Gulfside Association in Waveland, Mississippi.

She is a sought after speaker and retreat leader. Some of her topics are "The Power of a Praying Woman," "Just a Sister Away" "Listening to God" and "Sisters, I Got Your Back." Other speaking engagements have been keynote presentations at Annual Conferences of the United Methodist Church and contemplative prayer retreats for the community. Most recently she was the 2011 Baccalaureate Speaker at Bennett. A scholarship was established in her honor at the closing event. Her publications include "Revitalizing Middle Schools," The Guilford County Process", contributor to *Child by Child* by Dr. James Comer and "Help Students Soar to Success" in *Bizlife*.

Dr. Jones was both a Coordinator of Ethnic and Justice Ministries and District Superintendent in the Western North Carolina Conference of the United Methodist Church.

She has been married 46 years to retired educator and artist, Fred Jones. She has two children, Giselle & Rick with six grandchildren.

Contact
Dr. Lillie Madison Jones
P.O. Box 2372
High Point, North Carolina 27261
(336) 688 9512
lillielmadisonj@aol.com
www.fullmeasureliving.com

NINE

QUIET TIME

Lillie Madison Jones

...the floods came,
and the winds blew,
and burst against the house;
and yet it did not fall,
for it had been founded upon the rock."
—Matthew 7:25

Sarah Sue Ingram, staff writer of the *High Point Enterprise*, wrote this about me back in 1985: "Her day begins before sunrise. The still stillness of the hour holds special meaning, and she uses it to record reflections." I was 42 at the time in my educational administrative career and realized the absolute necessity of quiet time, which had actually begun ten years prior. Intuitively, I knew that if I was to going to be a leader of influence, I had to be spiritually grounded. Hence, I will share a few personal experiences in this chapter that I pray will demonstrate the importance of setting aside time to continuously examine your life. I endeavor to also propose a rationale for quiet time as well as suggest resources for you as you begin to aspire toward making *quietude* a part of your lifelong necessities.

"An unexamined life is not worth living"-Socrates.

Ultimately, you have to acquire various disciplines as a way to become grounded. This grounding can lead to authentic leadership in all your endeavors such as career and community. Being well grounded, as part of the young professional *character* file, is a key not only for success but also for effectiveness. What does one gain in being successful without being effective? In the end, "being" is more desirable than "doing." To "be" is grounding so as to become truly human. Being human acknowledges that you are made in God's image.

The attainment of this acknowledgement is developing a process through which one spends time reflecting on daily experiences. Daily experiences encompass spiritual disciplines that are compatible with your particular learning or personality style. Whatever you decide, the disciplines should be ones to help you to develop spiritually, emotionally and intellectually. I would argue that the young professional needs to carve in her schedule a structured time to be quiet, to be still so as to consistently sustain renewal. This stillness, this quietness, assists in maintaining a friendship with the SPIRIT which will lead into all truth. Through such an endeavor, the establishment of a lasting balanced vision will be fostered. "Without a vision, the [person] perishes" (Proverbs 29:18).

As a way of suggesting ways to cultivate a "quiet time" – a time to be holistic and fruitful, choose a quiet place (a place without distractions), and comment or answer the questions below:

1. What does it mean to be quiet?

2. What is my definition of "quiet"?

3. What is preventing me from taking the time to be still in order to know?

4. When will I determine the importance of quiet time?

5. What is Sabbath time?

6. Am I willing to incorporate Sabbath time away from my job, ministry or any other vocation?

7. As I determine my destiny for accepting the need for quiet, what approach would be most comfortable: auditory, visual or kinesthetic?

8. In light of question #7, do I know who I am?

9. What do I think will be the reward for spending time in "quietness"?

10. When is the best time for me to set aside time for quiet?

11. On a scale of 1 -10, with 10 being the highest, how deep is my desire to have time for quiet? Check (one)

    1__2.__3.__4.__5.__6.__7.__8.__9.__10__

12. What do I have to lose by not spending quiet time every day?

13. How important to do I think intentional breathing is essential as opposed to shallow breathing during quiet periods?

14. What part does SILENCE play in the quiet process?

15. When will I begin structuring or scheduling quiet time?

The purpose of the personal inventory is to provide introspection as to the possibilities of "quiet." Adjective synonyms for "quiet" include still, calm, placid, tranquil, peaceful, silent, Nouns specified are calm, quietness, quietude, calmness, and peace. Some verbs are calm, quieted, soothe, pacify, tranquilize and appease. Results of quiet can mean to be composed, graceful, elegant, gentle, peaceful, and serene. Such characterizations explain explicitly whysuch a person is described as one with "quiet" strength.

> *If you are wise therefore you will show yourself a reservoir and not a canal. For a canal pours out as fast as it takes in; but a reservoir waits till it is full before it overflows, and so communicates its surplus...Be filled yourself; then, but discretely, mind, pour out thy fullness.*
> —Bernard of Clairveaux, Sermons on Song of Songs

For a quiet time to be meaningful, one has to employ spiritual disciplines such as meditation, contemplation, silence, solitude, guided imagery, journaling, Sabbath time, reflective reading or writing. Note: you choose the discipline that is compatible with your vital needs. Vital needs are what you need to have a holistic life.

As principles of living, silence, solitude and Sabbath time have all been part of my journey the majority of my life. As a result, they have been compatible with my ability to lead from the "heart." I also believe that they put me on the contemplative path. This is to say that early on as a beginning career woman, this path began to help prioritize in me a balance between the body, soul and spirit. What is unique, as you will discover, is that once you establish the chosen disciplines, whichever ones they may be, you will begin to schedule the time for them and will feel naked when you try to escape or make some excuse not to follow through.

Notwithstanding the importance of solitude and Sabbath time though, my focus in this chapter will be on **silence.** Whether we realize it or not, there is a need for silence in our lives. Not the kind of silence many had to endure when growing up. Silence then was used as punishment. "Go to your room and be quiet." If you didn't have a room, you were doomed to a corner. Either way you were given a chance to reflect. My first positive experience with silence, however, was through a Quaker Retreat (In the Oaks) when I was a junior in High School. This experience gave me such a peaceful feeling that led me on a journey of wanting more, of yearning to embrace the spirit that made me feel whole. It was only when I began my career of teaching and learned about the Upper Room academies and the Emmaus Walks that promoted the importance of being quiet- of being centered.

During those years and even through two retirements, I would intentionally frequent Retreat Centers. One such retreat experience, occurring only about three years ago, will always stand out in my mind though. It was a four-day respite of quiet that I would spend at an Episcopal Center called Kanuga.

A new beginning of retirement was much on my mind prior to going to Kanuga. As I prepared to leave for what was called an

Autumn Refresher at Kanuga in the fall of 2010, I received this prophetic message:

"Get seriously quiet before Me, says the Lord, for you are approaching a turning point where you will need direction and guidance. This will be a break- away moment, a line of demarcation that will separate the past from where you are now and where you are headed. Your past experiences will have very little relevance to what is upcoming, but do not be afraid. This is not a bad thing; it is only a course correction which will produce kingdom destiny in your life. Look forward to all that I have prepared for you."

The retreat at Kanuga was a perfect setting for me. The conference center was situated on 1,400 mountain acres near Hendersonville, North Carolina, with scenic Kanuga Lake at its center. I love the mountains! Mountains have always made me feel closer to God and have provided a sense of refreshment over the years. Additionally at the time, leaves had begun changing, and to behold the grand foliage and array of awesome incredible colors in a natural environment contributed to my sense of soul being. Reflectively, I believe the purpose of this particular Kanuga retreat assisted in the quieting of my soul.

Upon my arrival, I received a text from my son Rick: "Mary died today." Mary was one of my dearest friends. I plunged into despair wondering what I needed to do. I had always been there for Mary, even when she became terminally ill, and had visited her in a nursing home immediately after another friend's funeral. I had been told that she would not recognize me, but I could tell by the twinkle in her eye that she knew me. Needless to say, but I struggled with whether or not I should leave. One of the retreatants said to me, "Lillie, perhaps you will receive the healing and discernment you desire by remaining at the conference." Knowing Mary so well, she would have wanted me to stay.

I needed silence. I had a private room overlooking the mountains and a partial view of a pond. The room was very comfortable and gave me a chance to practice my meditation twice a day and to walk the labyrinth. My intent for those four days of quiet (even during meals) was spending time away in quiet and in prayer, and questing to hear God's voice to garner some assurance of his Will in my life during this particular season. The theme of the retreat prophetically was "Friendship with God, others and self". What an appropriate theme to focus on friendship when one of my best friends had just died. Yet, on the other hand, it was a time to renew my relationship with God, my friend. The teacher was Dr. Margaret Guenther, currently a full-time spiritual director and retreat/conference leader. All of her books resonated with me: *The Art of Spiritual Direction, Toward Holy Ground: Spiritual Directions* for *The Second Half of Life*, and the *Practice of Prayer*. In addition, her mini lectures on friendship were profound. I used her book: *My Soul in Silence Waits: Meditations on Psalm 62* as my key reading during the week. What ended up being my mantra in the silence was "Wait." "No more pushing." "Eyes have not seen." "Wait, my child." Somewhere I read about the sacrament of waiting: "We get tired, constantly standing at the ready instead of relaxing and waiting for the order of things to work its way through during the time of transition." Being in silence helped me to recognize that my worries cannot do much.

Silence meant leaving to God what was beyond my reach and capacity. Additionally what I learned at that time was that silence was the first language of God. Meister Eckhart, German theologian who wrote many books on spiritual psychology, stated that "*Nothing is so like God as silence."* A moment of silence, even very short, is like a holy stop, a sabbatical rest, a truce of worries.

Ultimately, the silence during this particular retreat at Kanuga reminded me that God and my dear friend were now communing together: "for to be absent from the body is to be present with the Lord." Thus I received my confirmation that my physical presence at the time of her death had no bearing on where her soul was now residing.

So how does one begin the discipline of silence? Professional career women are adept at planning. The time of silence must be part of your calendar and daily routine as everything else. This time can become your lifeline. Here are a few suggestions:

- Choose how you will spend this time. As a career professional, you will be more apt to stick to this process if it is planned.

- Select a reading. As a beginning, I would recommend *The Daily Reader for Contemplative Living: Excerpts from the Works of Father Thomas Keating*.

- After reading, use at least 15 minutes for just listening. Begin practicing listening so as to hear what the Spirit is saying.

- Cease talking. This means eliminating conversation from your thoughts. I found Centering Prayer twice a day for 20 minutes has become a norm.

- Journal thoughts at the end of centering or your reflections after reading.

- Pace yourself. There is no need to be in a hurry.

- Use music or yoga in preparation for quiet time.

What is this mystery called silence? It is a practice of being present in the moment. It is a time of quieting thoughts, letting go, listening, being and becoming. ("Silence is a source of Strength"-Lao Tzu). For me, it helps to do some affirmative exercises to facilitate relaxation such as yoga or focused breathing.

Once silence becomes the norm, you will intentionally seek places where you can have that solace to sustain your professional and private life. When I spent eight days at a retreat center at Snowmass, Colorado, it gave me time to build a stronger relationship with God. This was a place where the spiritual discipline of silence was enhanced through hours of intentional practice. Silence simply means the cessation of speaking with words. But silence can be just sitting still and becoming motionless or experiencing the stillness of a completely dark space. On the other hand, silence may be a conduit for shutting off a flow of thoughts, ideas, or imagery that blocks and interferes with giving God first place. How can this be best realized? Just how effective can this be?

Consider these three possibilities: correct posture, concentration and spiritual focusing (recognizing the Holiness of God, the Holy Spirit). Let's explore each one to assist in answering the previous questions. Correct posture, for an example, has to do with sitting (ideally) erect in an upright chair with feet placed comfortably apart, with arms and hands resting on the legs. Concentration entails choosing a sacred word, sacred gaze or sacred breath as a means of communing with God. Theoretically, this process defines what is known as Centering prayer. In this mode, one shuts off distractions from the subconscious mind that stimulate the flow of images, allowing them to literally fade away-as the sacred choice becomes the catalyst.

Centering prayer is best realized as a time of worship where allowance is made to set aside 20-30 minute segments—twice a day (or more) to hear the Spirit speak. Centering prayer evolves from the words of Jesus who said these encouraging words to His disciples: "When you pray, enter into your secret closet, and God, the Father, who sees in secret, will reward you openly" (Matthew 6:6).

In Snowmass, centering prayer was greatly realized by the aesthetic beauty of mountains, sky, trees, and being in the company of a set of people who enjoyed corporate silence—bringing about synergy through a collective mind.

How does one maintain quietness on a regular basis? Psalm 4: 4 states, "Meditate within your heart on your bed, and be still." Meditation is or should be a purposeful act where one trains the mind through practice to declutter. Decluttering the mind will give you room to be the creative being that God intended you to be. In other words, no matter what happens, you simply dance to the music because the spirit will lead you.

My greatest advice to the young career professional, in conclusion, is to give yourself permission to schedule "quietness" in your daily activities which will ensure that your mind will always be full of clarity in order to deal with the many viccisitudes of life.

Notes:

_____

_____

_____

_____

_____

_____

_____

_____

_____

_____

_____

_____

_____

_____

_____

_____

_____

_____

_____

_____

_____

_____

_____

_____

ABOUT THE AUTHOR

Rev. Dr. Tracie A. Saunders

Rev. Dr. Tracie A. Saunders is an Associate Professor of Anesthesiology and Assistant Professor of Obstetrics, Gynecology, and Reproductive Medicine and has been an Attending Anesthesiologist at SUNY Stony Brook University Medical Center (SBMC) since 1995 after completing her anesthesiology residency at St. Luke's-Roosevelt Medical Center in New York City. She specializes in high risk Obstetric Anesthesiology, is a founding member of the Resource Center for Spirituality and Health Care Education at SBMC, and serves on the SBMC Institutional Ethics Committee. Dr. Saunders earned a Bachelor of Science degree in Mathematics at Spelman College, Atlanta, Georgia in 1985, a medical degree at Boston University School of Medicine in 1990, and a Master of Divinity from Union Theological Seminary of New York City in 2010. She was awarded the Maxwell Fellowship from Auburn Seminary given to those seminary students who show the promise of excellence in future service in parish ministry. The award committee wrote that Dr. Saunders:

"cares deeply about the pain and suffering of people and believes that health is a state of complete physical, mental and social well-being, not merely the absence of an infirmity. She brings this empathetic understanding with compassion to her faith community as a teacher and a preacher. She will be a quiet wind of change in any parish setting."

Dr. Saunders was ordained in the Gospel Ministry at Faith Baptist Church, Coram, New York on December 18, 2010. She has been married to her husband, Eric, Sr. for 27 years and they have been blessed with two children, Amanda and Eric, Jr.

TEN

DON'T GET DERAILED

Rev. Dr. Tracie Saunders

Getting into the business world and succeeding starts with a vision and is sustained with passion. We have to have a strategy to stay focused on the vision because there are a multitude of hurdles that have to be overcome. It takes courage and perseverance to overcome all of the hurdles. Don't be surprised if you are smart, educated, have funding, have a network of friends, and a supportive family, but still have to battle against the glass ceiling of racism and/or testosterone.

We are in the 21st century and there remain people oppressing women, especially women of color. The difference is if they are smart about it or maybe even in denial about it, they are stealth about it. They are sheep in wolves clothing. This is a reality that has to be acknowledged and expected especially for those women who aspire to enter traditional male dominated professions like mine, medicine and ministry.

In medicine and in ministry, beware of people, especially older men in charge, professing equal opportunity and civil rights, while relentlessly oppressing women. They say all the right things, preach about social justice more than Christ crucified. Maybe they ordain a few weak women that won't speak up and speak out but behave more like timid little girls. Be careful when he appoints his wife co-pastor to maintain control, while the deacons are powerless because they don't know God. Watch when he stops having church meetings because they "get out of hand." The truth is that they get out of hand because the pastor doesn't respect other people's opinions. Watch when the male pastor invites himself to the women's ministry meetings and interrupts to give the women a lecture because we "don't understand" what's really happening.

Pastor Smith of 25 years in a Baptist church who appointed his own wife as co-pastor felt the need to be in attendance at a women's ministry meeting. He had the nerve to come late to the meeting and sit separated from the women seated around a long rectangular table. He got a chair and sat six feet away but in the middle as if he was in charge. This pastor who told me, his protégé, about how he behaves at meetings, usually not saying anything and just listening. But those meetings were majority men. What made him think it was okay to interfere in our meeting, especially if we are a congregational church?

But are we a congregational church? I thought we were. We are a Black Baptist church in the northeast. We are not Catholic or Episcopal. He told me years ago during my training that we were congregational. Now when I argue that women should be safe to express themselves at a women's ministry meeting, he says, "No!" He says that there are different types of congregational churches. Oh really! Does he mean dictatorial congregational churches? If a woman at a women's ministry meeting wants to suggest fellowshipping more with other local church women, is that wrong? Is that negative? Why would the co-pastor offend her for saying that? Why would the co-pastor call that negative? The pastor blasts that she has been saying that for 20 years. Then he started lecturing us at our meeting about how this woman is a trouble maker. The pastor who usually only listens at meetings lectures women at the women's ministry meeting about how this woman who said, "I'm going higher in the LORD," is fooling us and that we are too naïve or dumb or spiritual to figure it out. So he has to explain it to us.

Thank you God for showing me, as plain as day, that the only one trying to fool us is this man. Only God knows how this pastor is going to fix this with me. He hurt the women. That is the one thing you don't do in front of me and expect me to be quiet. My Christian therapist and my sister Valerie have been telling me since I first got ordained to go to the pastor and tell him how I feel about our church. Specifically, I asked him about church meetings. I have never been to a church meeting. I was in seminary, learning about church polity and trying to figure out my church. I decided to let it go and wait until I got ordained when I would have leverage. After I got ordained, I asked my pastor when the next church meeting would be and he said in three months. Well it is now two years later and it never happened. The worst part is that I don't think it was ever going to happen. It is a fraud or a lie or an untruth. Our church is a dictatorship. That is why he appointed his own wife co-pastor. There was no vote. God help us.

I told my counselor and my sister that I would say something to the pastor when God said so. God had to tell me when, where, and how. That is what happened on Sunday at the women's ministry meeting. God prepared me before the meeting by having me preach on Revelation two times within two weeks before the meeting. God also told me to listen carefully. I listened not only with my natural ears but with my spiritual, heavenly ears and oh dear. My pastor and co-pastor had Satan's agenda. Christ had nothing to do with their agenda and that has been a problem for a long time.

Even if some women had plans to sabotage the meeting, there is a way to handle it so that the other women don't get hurt. AND, we are not stupid women that cannot figure out the motives of other women! How disrespectful and oppressive for this man to lecture us at our meeting. They made the meeting a hostile environment and an unsafe place for women.

So now what do I do? Do I leave the church? Do I start my own church? Do I find another church with a potentially even more oppressive pastor? NO, NO, NO! I'm staying right where I am! God made it so clear. He said, "Look at the women. They are afraid and intimidated. They need a voice. You are their voice. Speak up for them." I spoke up for the women and I did not back down when the pastor insulted me by saying I don't see that the woman is trying to start trouble. I never did that before. I've challenged my pastor before, but not like that with such passion and authority.

It is very interesting how the women's ministry started a bible study from the book of Esther two years ago but we never finished it. Vashti and Esther are perfect examples of women who had to risk everything and stand up for themselves and their people. More specifically, they had to stand up to men and speak out against their abuse and oppression of women and vulnerable people. We have to finish this bible study. I'm not sure exactly why, but the women in my church don't have a voice. They are intimidated and afraid to speak up for themselves and challenge their pastor and co-pastor.

This is really bizarre since they are supposed to be shepherds that love their sheep. Their behavior at the meeting was anything but loving. It was horrible. It was obvious how hurt the women were. Jesus said that it would be better for one of his disciples to tie a milestone around his neck and be thrown into the sea than to hurt one of his little children. Jesus is not only talking about little children, Jesus is talking about vulnerable people who need care, help and guidance. These women are Christ's daughters, how dare a pastor hurt them.

Do no harm. That is my motto as a physician and as a minister. I told my pastor that not only are we free to speak because we live in the United States, we have freedom of speech, but we are free in Christ Jesus! He said, "No!" Really! A woman is not free to speak her heart and what she wants for the ministry when the floor is opened up for comments and suggestions? Sure Caesar would agree with him, but it is wrong. The only Lord that lords over me is Christ!

Thus I will never give up my passion and authority, both given to me by God. The following Sunday I was assigned to officiate for communion. I prayed, I fasted, and I asked God to help me. I read scripture and I sang my gospel songs. I read my minister's handbook to find a way to make this communion extra special. I added the Lord's Prayer in the beginning of the ceremony for the whole congregation to say it together. But first, when my pastor took the position of the officiate in the middle of the communion table, I had to decide if I would challenge him. Not really. I already decided before I got to church that I was going to do what I was called and assigned to do by God. So I stood beside him, looked him in the eye and said, "You don't want me to do this?" He said, "Oh, you're on the list for today?" I said, yes as he moved from behind the table and walked all the way around to the other side. I took my authority.

Dr. Trombone would be so proud of me. That is what she screamed in my ear five times at the end of women's retreat three months before. "TAKE YOUR AUTHORITY, TAKE YOUR AUTHORITY, TAKE YOUR AUTHORITY, TAKE YOUR AUTHORITY, TAKE YOUR AUTHORITY!" I vowed that I would but I didn't know that this is what it meant. I am at a crossroads. Do I ignore the fact that my mentor insulted me and the women of our church? Do I ignore that he disrespected and violated our space at our meeting? Do I ignore that he did not apologize? Do I ignore the fact that we still don't have church meetings? Do I ignore the fact that he and his wife hurt people? Do I get rid of my "Do No Harm" rule? The most important question is do I get derailed from doing what God called me to do, minister to hurting women? No. I will not get derailed. These are eight steps to prevent getting derailed:

1. Stay on track to reach your goals

2. Take care of yourself, reboot if necessary

3. Don't believe the lies

4. Watch your mouth

5. Take courage

6. Believe in yourself

7. Never give up

8. Have fun and enjoy the journey

Step 1. Stay on track to reach your goals. Continue to perform with excellence. Don't procrastinate, be early, leave late, be consistent, and meet deadlines. In other words whatever the objective requirements are to reach the goal do them. Keep focused. Things like education, certificates, degrees, and other credentials such as ordination cannot be minimized or taken away. They are leverage, so even if you fail a test, don't give up, take it again. If you don't get into medical school the first try, attend a post-baccalaureate program, and try again. The same thing for law school, business school, education, whatever the goal. Each requirement is a hurdle that you have to get over, just keep going forward.

Step 2. Take care of yourself. Protect your body, soul and spirit from the stress associated with achieving your goals. Take time to meditate, pray and be quiet. God is always speaking to us so be quiet long enough to hear what the almighty has to say. Eat well, exercise, get plenty of rest. Revive yourself in God's purpose and calling for your life. Remember the vision, it used to be your first love. Is it still your first love?

Step 3. Don't believe the lies. Ask God for wisdom, knowledge and discernment to distinguish the truth from the lies. This requires divine help because all too often the lies are longstanding and deep seated. Powerful people believe the lie that they know better than the people they lead. I'm sure Caesar believed he knew what was best for the people of the world. Powerful people also love controlling other people and convince themselves that it is for the good of the people. These are all lies.

Step 4. Watch your mouth. Be careful who you speak to about the struggles and the trouble. There are plenty of spies and double agents out there. Even, or especially in the church. Don't gossip.

Only share the story if the person can make a difference and help the situation. Usually this is not the case. Just talk to God.

Step 5. Take courage. Have courage. Be courageous. How many ways can I say this? It takes courage not to get derailed. Courage to speak up and speak out against oppression or injustice. Courage to be alone or lonely. It is rare for the masses to back up the challenger. How many times have I spoken up in a meeting and no one else backed me up? Then immediately after the meeting several people come to me and thank me for speaking up. It is amazing and annoying. I have to forgive these people. God created me to speak up and I don't mind doing it. Apparently, most people just can't do it. God told me, just like he told Moses and Joshua and Jeremiah the people need a voice so take courage and speak out.

Step 6. Believe in yourself. You were chosen by God.

Now the word of the LORD came to me saying,
'Before I formed you in the womb I knew you,
and before you were born I consecrated you;
I appointed you a prophet to the nations.'
Then I said, 'Ah, Lord GOD! Truly I do not know how to speak, for I am
only a boy.' But the LORD said to me,
'Do not say, "I am only a boy";
for you shall go to all to whom I send you,
and you shall speak whatever I command you. —Jeremiah 1:1-1-7

God knew us before we were formed in our mother's womb. God separated us from others before we were born. God ordained us to speak God's words to nations. Therefore, I have to conclude that God believes in God's creation. Yes, God believes in us.

Step 7. Never Give up. Winston Churchill said, "Never, never, never give up." Always persevere and continue doing what you know God called you to do. Do it on whatever scale you can while living peacefully with everybody. For example, I will not give up and leave my church because my pastor did something horrible. I was called to be a voice for God and for women and I will continue to do that no matter what. I will continue to represent God wherever I go. Just because things get ugly doesn't mean that God made a mistake in calling me or I didn't hear God right. No, I heard God perfectly and that is why I am having all of these challenges. The devil is trying to get me to shut up, but I won't.

Step 8. Have fun and enjoy the journey. Every day that there is life in my body is a good day. I am so grateful for every breath I take. Life is so precious and fleeting. Every day we must act as though it is our last and enjoy it. Enjoy the people we are with no matter what the circumstances. Smile, laugh, and look for the good in all things. Be positive and look for the beauty in all of God's creation. Remember what Jesus said, "Come to me, all you that are weary and are carrying heavy burdens, and I will give you rest. Take my yoke upon you, and learn from me; for I am gentle and humble in heart, and you will find rest for your souls. For my yoke is easy, and my burden is light." (Matthew 11:28-30) We must be light and easy like Jesus.

Deaconess Beatrice blessed me at the end of choir rehearsal. She came up to me and said, "thank you for doing the Lord's Prayer for communion." This beautiful saint has been praying that we would say the Lord's Prayer in worship service for years. Our church stopped saying it in worship service once the former pastor retired 25 years ago. She was grieved in her spirit because she noticed that the children in vacation bible school never heard it before, let alone memorized it.

God is so faithful to have blessed my efforts to make this particular communion service special. Communion is supposed to be about Christians coming together, united in Christ to remember the sacrifice that Jesus made for the world.

Jesus' crucifixion is the epitome of courage and perseverance. Jesus is our example of not getting derailed. How many times did the Pharisees and Sadducees try to derail Jesus? They tried everything they could to stop Jesus from completing the mission to save the world. Even Jesus himself tried to get out of completing the mission. It took courage for him to submit to God's plan for him to die a horrible, violent, and very painful death. Jesus' three year ministry gives us a model of not getting derailed in the face of difficult circumstances. He had a circle of friends that he taught and left a legacy. He prayed a lot, especially early in the morning. He gave himself to people. He was a source of healing. He was always focused on doing God's will. He did not focus on his enemies, his immature friends, or the outrageous end of his earthly mission. He focused on God. That's the answer. Don't get derailed, focus on God.

Notes:

ABOUT THE AUTHOR

Marcie Wingfield Shanks

Marcie Wingfield Shanks was born and raised in Central Kentucky where she now resides with her husband, son, and three step-children. She studied and taught dance for over 18 years. After studying chemistry, chemical engineering and math she received her B.A. in Liberal Studies with a focus on environmental science. For fear of giving up an unbelievable opportunity she found herself learning and managing her family's retail automotive dealership for 8 years. In the last year she has been recovering from a complicated autoimmune disease after years of chronic pain. Her struggles to return to vibrant health have led her to develop a love for total wellness and a desire to help others.

Her skills include certification in Women's Empowerment Coaching through Professional Women Network, teacher certification in Yamuna® Body Rolling and Yamuna® Foot Fitness. These modalities helped her manage musculoskeletal pain, as well as strengthen and realign her body during recovery. She will receive her Master's in Integrated Marketing Communications in 2013 from West Virginia University and her Health Coaching Certification from the Institute of Integrated Nutrition in 2013. She desires to use her unique background to coach, inspire, and support those struggling with chronic illnesses restore their health and wellness through a multi-disciplinary approach.

Contact:
Marcie Wingfield Shanks
Dimensions Wellness
P.O. Box 183
Eastwood, KY 40018
www.dimensionswellness.com
marcieshanks@gmail.com

ELEVEN

DEFINING YOURSELF

Marcie Wingfield Shanks

The business world is brutal, unforgiving, and daunting. It is also exciting, challenging, and fulfilling. I was young when I entered the professional workplace. I was fortunate enough to have an entrepreneur for a father that saw the value of me being in his automotive dealership at the age of fourteen. Every summer, and during school breaks I would work in his small business in different departments depending on where they needed the most help. I also started teaching dance during this time, so in essence I had two jobs at a young age. I learned a lot about life and business in those four years before college.

One of the most important things I learned early on was if you don't want to do the grunt work, you'd better work really hard in school, get a stand out education, and get out of the classroom experiences. Those days washing cars and picking up trash on the dealership lot, paid off in motivation for my high school and college years. My time as a teenager at the dealership also allowed me to see that being a successful business professional wasn't just about making money. My dad was doing something he really loved; he was also involved in, and giving back to the community, and led a balanced work and family life. I learned at an early age those were the things that made someone truly successful. It is the kind of success I hope for each of you as you journey into the professional world!

So, you have aspirations to become a successful business professional in a highly competitive world. Where exactly should you start? Start by taking stock of yourself. When we examine ourselves in a meditative way it gives us the opportunity to look at our interests, motives, hopes and dreams in an analytic way: separating out our emotions and fears of not being able to be successful at something and revealing where our hearts truly lie. I learned this lesson the long and hard way. For a long time I had aspirations and goals that I thought would make me happy professionally because it was prestigious work, or I thought it would make my parents proud, but it wasn't really in my heart. I didn't love it. I spent 8 years learning and managing my family's automotive dealership with the intention of buying out my father, essentially acting as the owner, before I decided it wasn't for me. It was a great opportunity, but at the end of the day it just didn't meet my definition of "success". For this reason I urge you to look objectively at your professional aspirations. Do you love the subject matter; does the career have an aspect that involves something you excel in, that brings you joy? Part of finding success is knowing you're starting in the right place for you.

To figure out if you're starting in the right place make a list of your interests, your strengths, and your weaknesses using the table below. Make this table as large as needed to list all the things that bring you joy and happiness, the skills you have, and ones that you are interested in developing. Really dig deep and think of all those "wants" that you've mumbled over time, "I really want to learn photography, "or "I really want to learn how to use Photoshop." Sometimes we are interested in too many things and that can become a weakness or distraction from our success but identify these things and then prioritize them accordingly. When you make your list of interests think about what are the things that you enjoy the most? Once you have completed your list and filled in your strengths and weaknesses, you'll want to label the focus area in order of importance. Decide the relative importance of each of your interests based on marketability for your career, your strength level, ability to monetize, and your enjoyment level.

I've given you my example below. I'm almost finished with my Masters in Integrated Marketing, which I enjoy very much, and that is a very easy skill to monetize since so many people need help with digital marketing these days, and is at the top of my skills professionally. You'll see my other top area includes health and wellness. I'm finishing my education in health coaching and beginning to build a practice. I also intend to add public speaking to my list of skills, but I know that I need to primarily focus on the marketing and health and wellness right now. You'll also see the lower importance of some of the other skills and interests I've listed.

Interests/ Skills	Strengths	Weaknesses	Focus Area
Marketing	Good with people, ideas, masters degree	Very little big corporation experience	1

Dance	Long history of dance from time I was young	Hard on my body but enjoyable	5
Crochet	Interesting skill but not a big money maker, good for gifts	Haven't done in a long time, takes lots of TIME	6
Photography	Enjoyable and useful in many different areas	No fancy equipment, just my personal camera	4
Health &Wellness	Personal experience, always interested in helping people and passing on knowledge, broad range of skills	Education not completed yet	2
Public Speaking	Would be valuable skill for my business	Get nervous in front of lots of people, would need lots of development	3

Another important aspect of your strengths and weaknesses to consider is your personality. One way to evaluate these strengths is through the Myers & Briggs Type Indicator®. I took this test as part of the NADA Dealer Academy preparing to take over our family dealership, and the results were invaluable for understanding interactions between personality types in the workplace, and how to have your best performance based on your strengths. For more information about Myers & Briggs visit www.myersbriggs.org. If you are having trouble identifying your strengths you may want to talk to someone that you respect that knows you well that can provide some insight. You may also want to consider some of these books I've found helpful over the years:

- The Purpose Driven Life by Rick Warren

- Finding Your Direction by Bill Cantrell

- Now, Discover Your Strengths by Marcus Buckingham & Donald O. Clifton Ph.D.

- Discover Your Sales Strengths by Benson Smith & Tony Rutigliano

Now that you've filled out your table, which of your interests coincide with your strengths, and can you see yourself making them into a career? You should focus your interests in the area that satisfies the most aspects of success. Does it spiritually satisfy you, hold your interests, provide financial stability, meet your social needs, is it intellectually stimulating, and do you feel like you are bettering the world by doing it? Your total wellness and overall happiness will determine your personal success in this world, so it is important to consider how all these factors are tied together when you begin a new endeavor.

Once you have given some thought to your talents, their importance to your success, and how you can manifest them in a career; it is important to reflect, pray, or meditate on what you have uncovered. Often when we take stock of ourselves, slowing down from the busy world to dig deep, we find things that surprise us and it takes time to process these things. It is important to let them sink into our psyche to create a new vision of ourselves. When making decisions about the direction of my life or taking on new projects and endeavors I have often prayed, "Lord, if this is the right path for me please calm my fears, give me a spirit of hope, renew my strength to try something new, and give me your peace about the direction of my life." Reading my bible has also brought me great strength and vision for God's plans for my life (I highly recommend The Maxwell Leadership Bible – see resources). Sometimes I find it helpful to bring clarity when I sit and meditate on my path, do yoga, go for a walk, or talk to a trusted friend. You have to find what works for you, what brings you peace about your direction, so that you know moving forward you are setting yourself up for success.

Arming Yourself for the Professional World

Now that you are sure about the direction you are headed, your strengths, and where your heart lies it is time to get prepared for the business world. Of course a traditional education will be important in most careers in the professional world, but there are underlying skills that make candidates stand out and rise to the top quickly. What are they, and how can you get them?

1. **Positivity** – is essential in the business world. I've found this to be true personally and in my employees. When you stay positive about your skills, problem solving, those around you, and your outlook, you draw others to you with positive energy. If you focus your outlook to be positive and try to always find the bright side in things you will begin to exude this energy effortlessly. It can take some training and dedication to stay positive, but it is a skill worth acquiring. In the business world employers are looking for problem solvers that bring synergy by bringing people together, if you have a positive outlook this role will come naturally to you. When tasked with hiring a new employee I would much rather have the positive employee with less experience, but a clear positive outlook on life. As opposed to an employee with experience, but has a definite negative energy, and complains about how bad their last experience was instead of providing solutions. When hiring a positive person you know the likelihood of training, motivating, and creating synergy within your team is much higher than with a person that is very negative. For training in this area I would recommend the books: The Power of Positive Thinking by Norman Vincent Peale, and Something to Smile About: Encouragement and Inspiration for Life's Ups and Downs by Zig

Ziglar. Start building your positive outlook now by listing some of the positives that you can bring to the workplace:

_____

_____

_____

_____

2. **Be authentic** – being authentic is about integrity in the workplace. Integrity is important, valuable and often hard to find in the corporate workplace. So what does being authentic look like in the professional world? It means to know what you stand for, what is important to you, and what you will and won't do for success. It means being honest in billing, not taking credit for others work, giving your true opinion when asked, knowing professional and personal boundaries, and being willing to admit when you are wrong if you make a bad decision or a mistake in your work. Being authentic in the professional world is about not blowing smoke and therefore building trust, because trust builds teamwork and respect. When others respect you because you are authentic you will be sought out for your opinion, because they know that if they ask you, you'll be honest. If you have the best intentions of the company at heart in your opinions, you will quickly find yourself with more and more responsibilities, employee camaraderie, and potential promotions. Being authentic, honest and having integrity in the workplace will give you a feeling of personal satisfaction that will last much longer than any worldly

measurement of success. Some of the best books I've read on this subject matter are in this order: Principle-Centered Leadership by Stephen R. Covey, The SPEED of Trust: The One Thing That Changes Everything by Stephen M.R. Covey, and Developing the Leader Within You by John C. Maxwell.

Being authentic is not always an easy decision to make; you have probably encountered situations that made you uncomfortable either in a classroom setting, previous work experience, or through friends. Perhaps you were asked to do something like cheat on a test or assignment, cover up something that you knew wasn't right, or maybe you were approached in an unprofessional manner by someone in authority. Whatever the situation think about how you handled it. Did the outcome make you feel good or bad about the choices you made? Do you feel like you handled the situation with integrity? Take a few minutes to think about these situations and jot down anything that comes to mind about what you did, or what you might do differently in the future. It is important to have confidence in your ability to maintain integrity, because at some point it will be tested.

_____

_____

_____

_____

3. **Networking** – is an invaluable skill to have when entering the professional workplace. Networking is the cultivation of

productive relationships both personally and professionally. This is something you can start at a very early age, such as in high school and college. By participating in groups, clubs and organizations with people of similar interests you are building a network of people that know you. I have always considered myself a "contact hoarder". I was always the person to volunteer to make contact lists for groups and if anyone ever gave me their number for any reason, I always kept it in my phone. You never know when someone you met might come in handy. I recommend becoming a contact hoarder so that you always have your network contact details at hand. My father always said, "It's not always what you know, as much as whom you know." People have a certain level of comfort with someone they already have a relationship with; referrals from trusted friends are a great benefit of networking. Maintaining a strong network is invaluable to your professional success.

a. **Online networking** – Another important aspect of networking today is digital networking. This includes sites such as Facebook, LinkedIn, MySpace, and Twitter, Bebo, and other smaller niche sites. Do not underestimate the importance of online and social networking! Many employers Google you and look at your Facebook account, or other social media profiles before hiring candidates. So not only is it important to present yourself well online, but showing that you are good at networking never hurts either. It is important to brand yourself well when online and think about how others will view the information and how it will be received. I am particularly fond of LinkedIn for business networking online because it allows you to highlight yourself much like an electronic resume. For more information on branding yourself check out the book: Branding Yourself: How to Use Social Media to Invent or Reinvent Yourself by Erik Deckers and Kyle Lacy.

b. **Professional and Service Organizations** – another important part of networking is being involved in groups where you can relate to others in a meaningful way. Professional and service organizations are a good place to accomplish this task. Much like groups in high school and college, being involved in groups outside of work provides additional value to your experience and opportunity to network. If your area has a professional association such as attorneys, marketers, public speakers, I would strongly recommend getting involved with that group. There are many options when choosing outside networking experiences depending on where you live. Many women find Junior League to be valuable, as well as Habitat for Humanity, Rotary, Kiwanis, Business Networking International, and any other club that you feel personally drawn to based on your values and its' service opportunities. In my opinion one of the most significant factors of truly successful professionals and leaders are their servant's hearts. Learning to serve others through organizations teaches us to serve others in our professional lives as well. When we have servant's hearts by choosing to help those around us, we can't help but find success in our professional life. Brainstorm some organizations that you think would be valuable to you in the future:

_____

_____

_____

_____

The secrets to success as a young professional depend on what lies within you. For this reason it is important to take time to define yourself, your skills, interests, and strengths. Arming yourself with positivity, authenticity, and networking skills will give you a big advantage in whatever field you choose to pursue, as these are the building blocks of a leader. I wish you great success as you enter the professional world!

I have been blessed to learn nearly everything about the business and professional world I know from my two fathers: earthly and heavenly. I dedicate this chapter to them.

Other Great Business and Leadership Resources
Drive: The Surprising Truth about What Motivates Us by Daniel H. Pink.

How to Win Friends & Influence People by Dale Carnegie.

Fish! A Proven Way to Boost Morale and Improve Results by Stephen C. Lundin Ph.D., Harryn Paul, and John Christensen

See You at the Top by Zig Ziglar.

The 21 Irrefutable Laws of Leadership by John C. Maxwell.

The Five Dysfunctions of a Team by Patrick M. Lencioni.

The Maxwell Leadership Bible (2nd edition). New King James Version. John C. Maxwell and Tim Elmore Executive Editors.

The One Minute Manager by Kenneth Blanchard, Ph.D, and Spencer Johnson, M.D.

The Seven Habits of Highly Effective People: Powerful Lessons in Personal Change by Stephen R. Covey.

Who Moved My Cheese?: An Amazing Way to Deal with Change in Your Work and in Your Life by Spencer Johnson M.D. and Kenneth Blanchard Ph.D.

ABOUT THE AUTHOR

PEGGI PEASLEE

Peggi Peaslee has worked in a strategic capacity in the fields of Human Resources, Technology, Internet Strategy and Program Development in various industries. Peggi partners with businesses and departments within organizations using an inclusive, team-building approach to strengthen relationships and achieve responsibility and accountability for success. She is currently the Chief Operating Officer at United Cerebral Palsy of Central Arizona.

In addition to her full-time employment, Peggi works as a strategic partner with individuals, couples and groups to guide the process of achieving desired success that is measurable. She works collaboratively with her clients to ensure understanding, setting goals and action plans that assist each client in attaining their desired goals. Her company, Desert Coaching, donates 10% of proceeds from each package to a charity of their choice.

Life is a journey and Peggi seeks to live a life of continuous learning that leads to new paths, new people and greater fulfillment of her legacy. Her life experiences have taught her that in all situations, we all need to visualize our future and take action if we truly desire change and success. We achieve our goals by opening our mind, heart and eyes to new possibilities. When we stop to listen, watch, feel and learn from others while breaking down our own barriers, we can begin to embrace diversity and learn from each experience to ultimately achieve our own goals. She teaches and speaks on topics that lead to personal responsibility and accountability for every choice.

She enjoys and cherishes spending time with her husband, family and beagles, exploring Arizona, traveling, volunteering in the community, yoga and cultural dance.

Contact:
Desert Coaching website: www.desertcoaching.com
Email: Peggi@desertcoaching.com
Phone: 480-393-6347

TWELVE

BUILD YOUR LADDER, THEN YOUR DREAM

Peggi J. Peaslee

"The message is clear: plan with attitude, prepare with aptitude, participate with servitude, receive with gratitude, and this should be enough to separate you from the multitudes." —Krish Dhanam

What is your dream for your career? This is not your next goal; we are talking BIG, really, really BIG, about the very top step of your personal ladder. Do not settle for second best! Write your ultimate goal in the dream cloud below.

As a young professional just starting in the business world, you should have big dreams and always keep them in your line of sight. So how will you achieve this goal? More important, do you believe in your goal? Breaking into the business world as a woman, regardless of your age comes with a myriad of emotions and logic. This is the wonderful, complete package that we have to offer because we can think and act logically while leading with our heart and instilling collaboration in work teams and organizations. There is a difference between how men and women think but neither need to sacrifice who they truly are to become noticed and succeed. Men are typically hunters, single mission focused like completing the project while women tend to be gatherers, multi-tasking, creating sustainability and helping others along the way. Think of it this way – men want to hunt the animal to provide immediate food while women want to plant and collect seeds that continue to grow. Both roles are needed for success but take different approaches.

Seeing the Top versus Experiencing the Climb

Julie is new to the business world. Fresh out of college, eager and feels worthy of a management position. After all, she did excel in college and feels she has earned her place in the business world.

She is offered a job at a local radio station as an office assistant. Her many attempts in applying for management jobs has failed and she continuously hears that she is not qualified. Frustrated but needing a job, she accepts the role as an office assistant. Her heart is not in it and although she is thankful to have a paying job, she resents having to start at the bottom. After several months of doing her work, she speaks with her manager about opportunities for growth. Her male manager, Mr. Smith, explains that she is just not ready and does not have the life or industry experience to move ahead right now. He encourages her to keep learning. She leaves his office and becomes disengaged with thoughts of seeking new employment somewhere else where her worth will be recognized. Julie has not made many friends at the radio station anyway so changing jobs won't be a big loss, as she sees it. She continues on this path, becoming increasingly frustrated and treats newer employees with less respect since they are below her. She knows she wants to make it to the top and be noticed so trudging along must be the best way to prove she can do it on her own. She is on a personal mission to show her boss that she is smart and worthy of a promotion. In meetings, she corrects his errors and points out her knowledge on the topics.

The newer and lower degreed, Karla, participates but in a different way. Karla is the one who tends to toss out ideas and allows everyone else to jump in and share. Karla was hired three months ago and has already been given more opportunities. Karla comes in each day, greets everyone with a smile and offers to help anyone in need. Julie always has the full plan of every detail so why is Karla moving above her? Why is she being offered special assignments and a promotion?

Julie is angry that her seniority, great ideas and knowledge have been overlooked and yet the cheery, Karla seems to do nothing wrong.

Karla continues to collaborate with others, seeks their input and tries to learn from every situation. Consider the hunter/gatherer differences that are shared in this situation. Julie is going for the "kill" while Karla is "planting seeds." This is not uncommon with women in business. We have learned from many male role models who are great leaders but because it is not the natural approach for a woman, it does not play out the same. This does not mean that you should be passive, however, learning how to be assertive and when can drive more positive results. Karla stands out because she delivers a refreshing change and gets results. Embracing the differences and doing what is natural, works!

As time passes, Karla tries working more with Julie and each attempt fails. She finally pulls Julie aside and asks what the problem is between them. Julie tells her that she did not deserve the promotion. Julie continues by saying that she may need to work with Karla but she does not need to like her. Karla, surprised by her comments, looks at her and shares the idea that it is not a competition. Each have a dream and there are plenty of opportunities but to get there, you need to first build your ladder. She continues to ask Julie who she can count on. Julie responds by saying she relies on herself and doesn't need anyone else. She has the ability and these people, these men are threatened by her. Karla steps back. She remains silent for a moment and then asks her to walk down the hall where some construction is being done in the building. Reluctantly, Julie follows.

Down the hall, there is a ladder that the workmen are using and the conversation flows as follows:

Karla looks at Julie and says: Go for it.

Julie: Go for what? You are crazier than I thought!

Karla: Look at the top of the ladder. Take your best shot at jumping up there without using the steps.

Julie: I can't get to the top just by jumping. That is ridiculous to even ask me to do.

Karla: That is my point. We cannot reach our dream or achieve our goals if we don't take the time to build our ladder first. We need the support of others and we need to lead by example, allowing others to participate and gain through the process. It's not a competition, Julie. It's a ladder that we must climb. We face many challenges and obstacles of what people think and how businesses have been run for decades. If we try to get to the top without structure, we will ultimately fail. I was promoted because I offer something different than Mr. Smith. He may not even fully understand how I developed a team and may not care but what he does care about is results. Stop trying to mimic the men you see in business and begin building your ladder.

The Quality of Your Ladder

These two young women share the same dream of someday leading an organization but take two very different approaches. Julie expects to walk in and achieve her mid-level dream immediately and quickly move her way to the top. Karla is climbing her ladder. She still maintains sight of her ultimate goal but uses her natural abilities as a woman to succeed. She has learned to harness the power of being a woman in business. It is a balance of logic and emotional intelligence. Karla may have all the details just as Julie does but allowing others to contribute, even if it means the good ideas that were originally hers are credited to someone else or a team leads to greater results. She is willing to share the spotlight. She engages with others and develops relationships. Women are great at communicating and developing relationships. It comes natural! As women, we care about others but when we let go of what makes us unique in the business world, we can become tyrants.

Knowing that 75% of all businesses are run by males (New York Times) and only 4% of Fortune 1000 and Fortune 500 companies have female CEO's (Catalyst) does not mean we need to conduct business as if we are men. There is nothing new or refreshing with that approach. It does mean that there is a ton of opportunity. Male business leaders cannot overlook the change in teamwork, communication and results that can be achieved with a woman leader. Would you rather be on an island surrounded by strangers who you struggle to communicate and identify with or would you prefer to be with friends and family enjoying laughter and love? Be who you are and develop a strong support system early on so you don't become isolated later.

Each person's ladder may be different and that is ok. The important aspects of each ladder include a solid ground, support system and stability. You can and will succeed if you remember who you are, embrace the differences between men and women and allow your heart and head to work in sync. Let's consider some ways of achieving success and moving past the obstacles.

Analyze why you chose the field you are pursuing. What specifically was it that led you down this path? Find your "why." (This is not the monetary gain but the true passion for what you have chosen to do.)

_____

_____

_____

When in business, you not only need to do the tasks and market the products such as the radio station where Julie and Karla work, you need to market yourself. People remember and respect the "why" in our lives. It is this passion or idea that sells you! This is the core of who you are as a person and it has the potential of separating you from the masses. As a female, you may face some challenges especially when you begin to do something different but it is that difference, if you are true to it and willing to pursue it that will make you stand out. Embrace the "why" in what you have chosen to do and do not try to stay on the same path that everyone else does. Dare to be different and take a chance. Follow what you feel is right and be open to ideas and help along the way. When you think of great leaders, is the first image one of a woman or a man? Consider some great female leaders like Mother Theresa, Oprah and those you know locally who have sought to help others and gained credibility and prestige. Change the image in your mind so that your passion can shine by staying true to the natural you.

You need to develop a support system for your ladder. Your support system needs to be able to withstand a lot of weight, not wobble and one that can be relied on over and over. Some examples are women in business networking groups, the women's business association, the Professional Woman Network, and peers who collaborate with you on a daily basis. It also includes a personal or business coach who partners with you to move forward. These are the people who will support your ideas at your company, will lend a hand and want to see you succeed.

Who and what are your support systems? (If you do not have any, take time to research some in your area and list the ones you commit to contact.)

_____

_____

_____

_____

Focus on how you interact with these groups. If you are a member of many groups but not actively involved, they have not yet become a part of your support system. If you attend and use it more as a social event, you may have some support but people don't really understand your goal or know where you struggle. We learn from others and we grow by sharing and accepting feedback. We need to engage and share nuggets of value with others so that we do not expect to just take but we give back to others. Engaging in these support systems should be a picture of collaboration where you share your knowledge, possibly even host one of the events or speak at one, and then in return, you seek guidance. Yes, it is relationship building! How do you plan to engage with your support systems moving forward? (Be very specific and include the action you will take with each one.)

_____

_____

_____

_____

At this point, you have the support for your personal business ladder. Next you need to define each step. As you know when climbing a ladder, you can sometimes skip a step but may find it a little more challenging and may need someone or some type of additional support since it will be a bit more of a struggle. Develop your plan but be willing to step a little over to the left or right on each step. Your goal should include not only moving up but sometimes gaining a breadth of knowledge while on one step before proceeding. Imagine the step has a can of paint on it. When climbing a ladder, you sometimes need to improvise. Stopping to help others along the way when they are struggling will ultimately help you even though it may feel like you are slowing down. Again, imagine being on the step of a ladder and having a team of women right behind you to help push you up. There is strength in numbers and to truly lead and create positive change and results, we need the help of those around us. Rushing to the top won't build the ongoing foundation and structure you will need for longevity.

Let's Build Your Ladder!

Consider your plan of how you will make it to the top. We've already discussed the "why", the "who and what" and now it's time for the real action plan, the "how." To make it to the top or any new level in business, you need to know how you will get there. Some examples of "how" include taking on a new project, enhancing a current product or mentoring someone else. All of these become very visible to those around you without any words. It is the action that is seen, believed and admired. Remember the story above with Karla. She did not go in and ask for special assignments or a promotion. They were offered to her because of her actions. Your actions will speak louder than words and will paint a picture that can be seen and understood by all. Each of the following is a step on your ladder. Take some time to write out specifically what you will do and what each one represents.

What is on your first step? Write it on the step. (example: Developing effective communication)

How will you step up to get there? (Be very detailed, specific and list actions.)

_____

_____

_____

_____

What is on step 2? Write it on the step. (example: Develop a support system)

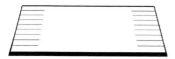

How will you step up to get there? (Be very detailed, specific and list actions.)

_____

_____

_____

_____

What is on step 3? Write it on the step. (example: Position such as Specialist, Manager, VP)

How will you step up to get there? (Be very detailed, specific and list actions.)

_____

_____

_____

_____

You can have as many or as few steps as you need on your ladder. Can you see how developing your own personal ladder naturally leads to achieving your big dream? If you close your eyes and consider the story of Julie and Karla, can you see why Karla was succeeding? Can you imagine yourself on your own ladder? What do you feel, see and hear as you plant your feet solid on each step?

I feel_____

_____

I see _____

_____

I hear _____

_____

When you embrace who you are as a woman in the business world without sacrificing the wonderful differences you possess compared to a man, your journey becomes rewarding with less conflict. The biggest mistake you can make is not being true to you and not allowing your natural abilities and talents to shine. Use your ladder and make sure your foundation is solid and filled with other successful people who can add value and not negativity.

Obstacles Become Opportunities

Finally, we will look at some real obstacles and discuss ways of overcoming them. Becoming a successful woman in business can be a challenge at times but it is your attitude, aptitude, servitude and gratitude that will be your guide. All of these not only help you move from step to step, they are your foundation and purpose.

Some of the obstacles you may face include being treated as having a different focus. Women become wives, mothers, soccer coaches and volunteers. There are some men in the business world that may initially view that as you having a different focus or a conflict with business need and desire to grow. This may even be viewed as a weakness. It is your responsibility to be a professional. Act in a manner that exudes confidence, collaboration and a positive attitude. Offer to help others. Remember, your actions become your image. By not acknowledging what others may say, think or perceive, you are instantly stepping above them and leading. You gain nothing by arguing your points no matter how valid because people focus on action, not mere words.

What are some of your potential obstacles and how will you handle them?

_____

_____

_____

_____

As you progress in your career, you may have times when you feel left out of conversations especially if there are more males in leadership roles than females in your organization. Do not sacrifice yourself by trying to engage in a topic that is male focused. Instead, be creative and interject with an interesting fact or by offering praise for something done well by one of the other leaders. This quickly changes the topic of focus and moves the discussion in a direction that you can participate in and offer value. Men and women have different comfort zones for communication but that does not mean they are not interested in other topics.

Continue learning about your organization. This includes other areas of focus that you may not be responsible for but will increase your ability to understand and engage more in the bigger vision of the organization. Know your aptitude and prepare to spend extra time studying, asking questions and observing areas where you have less strength or knowledge. Do not shy away from the big obstacles on those ladder steps, just proceed slowly and steadily.

What are some areas of growth for you?

_____

_____

_____

_____

In business, you may come across some men that simply refuse to ask you for help. Be the leader. If you see someone needs help, don't make them swallow their own pride by forcing them to ask. You can help break the barriers that exist between men and women by again, remembering that as a woman, we innately want to share and talk. Be a servant leader by identifying others who need help or support without them having to ask. You can simply position is at something you want to share with them to get their feedback. Imagine how that same man will view you in the future after you help him solve a problem or gain new insight. You cannot grow if you are fearful and unwilling to teach others. The more you teach others and allow them to grow, the more opportunity you will have to take on new roles.

Show gratitude in a sincere and specific manner. It is not enough to say "nice job" or "thank you" even though that may be all you hear at times. Your goal is not to follow what others do, it is to be who you are and use your natural abilities to achieve success. In business, especially with men, it is common to hear basic words of gratitude. As a female, we tend to want to elaborate with our words so use this to your advantage. Be specific when saying thank you. What specifically is it that you are thankful for with this employee or peer? Male or female, your words of thanks will hold more meaning and will be remembered if you are specific such as "Hey Joe, thank you so much for working late last night so we could present an award winning presentation. I really liked the animations you chose!" Can you see how this will be more memorable and boost Joe in his support of you too? This is a sincere moment of gratitude that has lasting impact because you will have just added Joe to your support team by elevating him. The other side of gratitude is to remember to be humble. When you achieve a new step on your ladder, take a moment to thank those who supported you. No one wants a boss whose ego is so big they may get stuck in a doorway!

You have all the tools you need to build your ladder and begin climbing it. When you face moments of difficulty, breathe and reach out to your network. Let your support system work. Be engaged, participate and most important, always remember the "why" because without it, you may find years later that you are lost.

You will succeed! Build your ladder then your dream will come true.

Suggested Reading:
Breaking the Barriers, A Woman's Toolkit for Success Edited by Linda Ellis Eastman

Made to Stick by Chip Heath and Dan Heath

The Servant (Leadership) by James C. Hunter

Women as Leaders, Strategies for Empowerment and Communication Edited by Linda Ellis Eastman

ABOUT THE AUTHOR

DR. SHANA Y. PATRICK

Dr. Shana Y. Patrick is the CEO of Infinite Provision Consulting, LLC. She established her consulting business in 2010 in an effort to provide organizations and individuals services related to leadership development, soft skills training, and organizational effectiveness.

Dr. Patrick is also a highly accomplished business analyst with 20 years of combined experience in the public sector (federal), private sector (telecom and logistics), and university setting (Professor). These experiences have enhanced her work performance by allowing her to consider various approaches and solutions to workplace challenges with a clear understanding of how to work decisively, but also with immense consideration for the contribution of others. She is also Six Sigma GreenBelt Certified.

Dr. Patrick earned a Doctor of Management (DM) in Organizational Leadership from the University of Phoenix (UoP), a Master of Arts in Business Administration from Bowie State University (BSU), and a Bachelor of Science in Accounting from North Carolina Agricultural and Technical State University (NC A&T).

Professional & Community Organizations:

Professional Women's Network (PWN)

American Society for Training & Development (ASTD)

International Society for Performance Improvement (ISPI)

Delta Sigma Theta Sorority, Inc.

Rebuilding Together

Make-A-Wish Foundation

Dr. Patrick is available for speaking engagements, collaborative research efforts, and training sessions regarding enhancing soft skills, effective communication, and leadership development.

Contact:

Shana Y. Patrick, D.M.

Infinite Provision Consulting, LLC

P.O. Box 1883

Clinton, MD. 20735

Email: InfiniteProvision@verizon.net

Telephone: 301-351-0162

THIRTEEN

RECOGNIZE THE EMOTION, BUT CONTROL THE BEHAVIOR

Dr. Shana Patrick

How do you address a tense situation that could potentially place you in "hot water?" Are you going to lash out in the same manner as was directed toward you or will you stop to think about the consequences? Many times we act without thinking and in the moment feel that the consequences are worth it, if we even consider the consequences - which we often do not. When we feel disrespected, insulted, or embarrassed we tend to react. One of our first thoughts is "I'm not going to allow anyone to speak to me in such a manner and get away with it." We feel cheated if we do not speak our mind and usually have a strong desire to level the playing field. What's the common denominator here? Feelings! Feelings tend to drive most people into reacting to a situation, me included. However, I learned that reacting to situations in the workplace that are driven by emotions benefit no one, especially you.

I'm sure you already know how to dress the part of a professional, arrive on time, and demonstrate all that you have learned to get you to this point, but do you know how to remain poised in your well-groomed state when you feel disrespected or insulted. In the beginning of my career, I questioned how to hold it all in...the frustration and the perceived disrespect. Everyone kept telling me not to let it get the best of me... but how? I knew that lashing out would get me nowhere, but I also knew that something had to be done. At least I thought that something had to be done. I was still working out the "pick your battles" concept in my mind. My challenge was learning exactly how to do this without giving the receiving party any ammunition against me or giving off the impression of that I wasn't ready for the big leagues. I needed to remain poised, professional, and in control of my emotions.

I learned that some situations just aren't worth dwelling over. To dwell over something you can't change only causes anxiety which is why it's so important to stay in control of our actions in the workplace. Therefore, we can't get bent out of shape every time a colleague says something we don't like or does something we don't agree with during a discussion. I'm not saying to let anyone take advantage of you or speak to you in a disrespectful manner, but I am saying to assess the situation before acting. It's perfectly fine to act in a suitable manner, but reacting without logic or thought gets us into trouble. You've worked too hard to get to where you are just to throw it all away over something like a misunderstanding or someone else's bad behavior.

We must learn to stay in control of our negative emotions in the workplace if we are to be productive and effective contributors. According to William S. Howell (1982), "...emotion generally interferes with task-oriented communication. The emotional person devotes thought and energy to the emotion rather than to the task" (p. 57). While many people view emotions and feelings as one in the same, Howell (1982) denotes the differences and offers a strong foundation for the importance of maintaining self-control in the workplace.

Howell (1982) notes that physiological changes occur when a person reacts to a situation emotionally (i.e., increased heart rate, modified breathing patterns). The author also points out three symptoms that occur when in an emotional state. They are as follows:

1. Shock - In a state of shock, a person's reasoning skills are impaired; thereby, making it more difficult to respond in a calm manner during activities.

2. Diffusion – Reflects an intense and physical response to a situation (i.e., facial expression, shouting, pacing).

3. Transference – Individual tends to blame everyone around him/her for the emotion they are experiencing due to high emotional provocation (Howell, 1982).

Feelings, on the other hand, are not as resolute as emotions in the workplace and do not typically result in a person demonstrating the same extreme physical behavior as denoted when in a negative emotional state (Howell, 1982). Our feelings tend to be a product of personal experiences that we've shared with other people or circumstances that arose from events we've encountered. But unlike negative emotions acted out in the workplace, feelings in the workplace have the ability to manifest in a positive or negative manner. Negative feelings may impact communication while positive feelings have a tendency to bring about increased productivity (Howell, 1982). And although negative feelings have the ability to impair our interaction with others, "…they are easier to live with than emotions" (Howell, p. 58).

Negative Space Can Cause…

• Distractions -

> If you are distracted and unable to focus on the task at hand because of your recurring role as the "angry person in the room," you could jeopardize your position. In the workplace, people are always watching and you need to be cognizant of the impact your behavior has on your position. If you are unfocused due to the fact that you're constantly disconcerted that things are not going your way, you will limit yourself. Opportunities for greater responsibility, promotions, special projects, and even your commitment to the job may come in to question.

- Unproductive time -

  Staying in a negative space breeds unproductive behavior. You may think that as long as you are busy doing something, then your work will not be impacted. However, busy does not necessarily mean productive. Busy can simply mean that activity is occurring. If you allow your feelings to control how you manage your day, you may find yourself constantly moving, seemingly busy working on various projects, but going nowhere.

- Added stress -

  Stress affects everyone, even newcomers to the workplace. However, it does not have to define each workplace discussion or disagreement. You have the power to own it or not. You can accept the situation for what it is, process it, and respond in a mature manner or you can allow your emotions to get the better of you. The latter will only cause increased angst.

- Blocked growth -

  Being at the beginning of your career is a new and exciting time, but uninviting behavior can block you from reaching your full potential. Remember, you have a long road ahead in terms of your career; there's no need to burn out or burn yourself in the first few years of your career all due to the fact that you can't control your emotions or you allow your feelings to guide you when they should not.

• Joy stealer -

Your happiness and satisfaction play a huge role in your behavior at the workplace. It is your responsibility to create your happiness…not anyone else's.

Acknowledging the Emotion…Acknowledging the Feeling

While you do not want to act upon every single emotion or feeling that that you have in the workplace caused by a tense moment or discussion, I would suggest acknowledging how you feel (if only for a brief moment). Many times we are taught to suppress what we are feeling as if it doesn't matter or hold significance. I tend to disagree and believe it's necessary and important to acknowledge how we feel and validate the feeling, even if it's only to oneself. There is no harm in acknowledging that a workplace incident caused you to feel upset, disappointed, embarrassed or angry. I believe getting in touch with how you feel allows you the opportunity to open up and find out who you really are and what really makes you tick. However, blurting out your response when your emotions or feelings are heightened will only exacerbate the situation if it is the wrong time and place. It could also be perceived as unprofessional given the environment you work in. The key is to develop your communication skills and awareness of vocal tones so that you are able to deliver your message in a professional manner at the appropriate time. According to Alessandra and Hunsaker (1993), "Developing the skill to understand vocal tones refines your interpersonal communications ability. It helps in building and improving solid, long-lasting working and personal relationships" (p. 138).

To begin the process of understanding what your behavior patterns resemble, review the following questions:

- How do you express yourself in the workplace during a tense situation?

- Do you openly express your concerns without reservation?

- Do you hide behind the words of others and suppress what you truly think?

- Are your responses controlled or out of control?

- Do you take the time to receive and process before acting or do you simply react without concern for potential consequences?

- What is your typical response when you are pushed into a negative emotional state?

Control the Action…Circle Back to Self

I find it helpful and an overall good practice to periodically conduct a self assessment to see where I stand presently, to reflect on where I've been, and where I would like to go in terms of self-improvement. In an effort to accomplish this task, the following exercises have proven to be useful:

- **Seek continuous emotional maturity** - Emotional maturity focuses on how well an individual responds to a set of circumstances or situations and how well they control their emotions in those situations involving other people.

In an effort to improve one's emotional maturity, it takes obtaining insight into your current state of emotional maturity and then practicing with a new set of tools and resources that aid improvement.

- **Seek balance (stability)** – We all live such busy lives and feel that there is never enough time to do it all, finish it all, or accomplish it all. This behavior can place us out of balance emotionally, physically, and spiritually. Given this upset, we are more apt to respond to tense situations with very little thought about the ramifications.

- **Avert resistance** – Various tools and resources aid us in our efforts to improve our lives, but we must implement a regimen that pushes us to practice what we have learned. While your emotions may be pushing you to shout, stomp or even walk out during a heated discussion in the office, your time spent learning how to deal with confrontation and practicing what you have learned could allow you to avert a disastrous situation.

Every encounter may not be dire, but the principle remains the same. It is critical that you learn how to demonstrate self-control. Practice calming yourself down, taking a step back, and assessing the situation before reacting. Determine the level of gravity. Usually after we calm down, we are able to assess a situation in a clearer manner, allowing us to make better decisions based on facts rather than on emotions. Emotions have the power to get us in a world of trouble. There are situations that will occur and will demand immediate attention, but it's up to you to decide what type of attention to give the situation dependent upon the level of gravity. Every meeting will not be a meeting of the minds, but it does not mean that you should lose control either.

Many people attempt to separate work life from personal life. I believe it's possible to a degree; however, our emotions and feelings about work cannot always be so easily separated from our personal life and vice versa. Thereby, causing the lines to blur and emotions to filter into both aspects of our lives. A bad day at work can cause you to cancel an invitation to dinner, back out of meeting up with friends, or totally engulf your evening with thoughts of despair. While it's commendable for you to show concern and act on work related items that need attention, it is also just as important to be in control of what emotions you allow to enter your personal life. While I believe there is a cyclical connection between our personal life and our work life, we still have the ability and responsibility to create a balance (sense of peace) that allows us to make sound decisions versus always ending up in a world wind of instability causing us to constantly react to situations rather than act upon those situations.

No one is asking that you perfect your ability to control your actions in the workplace, but simply that you make the effort to work towards self-improvement which will require some self-control. And really, that's what we should strive for as we progress in our lives and our careers...to be better that the day before, to do better than the day before, and to give more so that we may inspire others to do the same. I was extremely fortunate to meet mentors at the first two companies I worked for who showed me the ropes. These people not only inspired me, but showed me how to deal with problematic situations without overreacting at every turn.

You will learn that not every organization operates in the same manner and will require that you tweak your approach on how to address certain situations, but your foundation should remain the same which is to remain in control of your emotions. Self-control should be reflected regardless of the situation; regardless of the organization. In reading this chapter, my hope is that you find something of substance to aid you in making more informed decisions when encountering situations that will challenge your ability to stand strong and true to yourself, while simultaneously acting wisely rather than reacting carelessly.

References

Alessandra, T., & Hunsaker, P. (1993). *Communicating at work*. New York: Fireside.

Howell, W. S. (1982). *The Empathic Communicator*. Prospect Heights, Illinois: Waveland Press, Inc.

Notes:

_____

_____

_____

_____

_____

_____

_____

_____

_____

_____

_____

_____

_____

_____

_____

_____

_____

_____

_____

_____

_____

_____

_____

ABOUT THE AUTHOR

JANICE RILEY

Ms. Riley has a B.S. in Marketing from Shippensburg University, Shippensburg, Pennsylvania. Having grown up on a fruit farm in Cumberland County, Pennsylvania, Janice has been in business development since her toddling days of peddling fruit to markets and neighbors. She worked in direct marketing for a variety of companies, dabbled in the government contracting world at Patuxent River Naval Air Station in the '90s and worked as a marketing professional for several firms. Janice even spent a few years working with a small publishing firm as one of their top editors, editing manuscripts from all genres. Janice then spent two years managing her own consulting firm, Janley Consulting, specializing in startups and small businesses.

Most recently, Janice has been conducting business development for Owen Software, an emerging technology company in Maryland. Responsible for managing the NASA Space Grant partnership, she has developed relationships with multiple state space grant consortia and NASA centers. Due to a corporate focus on Science, Technology, Engineering and Mathematics (STEM) Education, she is also involved with several state and national initiatives to engage women and minorities into STEM fields.

In her free time, Janice visits impoverished areas with her husband, helping to educate, encourage and empower individuals in ways that create sustainable improvements to their lives. By helping to create new businesses, coach existing businesses to be more successful and edify people, she and her husband hope to make a lasting difference in the world.

Contact:
Janley Consulting
14411 Pen Mar High Rock Rd
Cascade, MD 21719
www.janleyconsulting.com
janleymd@gmail.com
301-536-2216

FOURTEEN

WHAT I WISH I'D KNOWN AT GRADUATION

Janice Riley

After sitting through hundreds of lectures, taking numerous exams, writing a litany of papers and conducting various research projects, you have finally received that college degree you worked so hard to get. You have learned so much; you are ready to take on the world. Yet, there's so much more for you to learn that, as life would have it, you may end up learning the hard way since there's no former "school" to teach you survival skills. Thankfully, you have chosen to read a book to teach you some professional skills to ensure your future success. Good job!

Let's start with the basics needed for life in the corporate world. These are a few tips that if you surveyed older women and asked for advice, you'd hear at least one of the following bits of advice. Here are your basic survival skills:

1. **Dress for success.** Wear a suit to your interviews. You are making a first impression. Be sure it's the one you want to make. Choose your wardrobe for work based on office guidelines and your professional goals. Examine how your boss dresses and others in management. If you aspire to their positions, dress accordingly.

2. **Never bad-mouth anyone.** Mama always said, "If you don't have anything nice to say, don't say anything at all." Listen to Mama. It is easy to get sucked into gossiping and griping about a former boss or a current colleague. Guard yourself from the negativity. It is bad taste and bad form. Nothing good will come of it.

3. **Be polite. Be sincere.** Be respectful to all, from the janitor to the Chairman of the Board. You never know who knows whom. Your distinctive behavior will be noted.

4. **Don't leave the office before the boss does.** Follow her example and others on working hours. Put in the hours to get the work done. Be reasonable. Don't sacrifice yourself for work. Realize you need your rest and need breaks.

5. **Set realistic expectations**. You're a young professional. You need to pay your dues. Your office may not be the best, your pay may not be what you dreamed of when you were in school, you may not get as many vacation days as your

parents do each year upon hiring. These are things you earn through experience.

6. **Listen attentively!** Listen for what's not being said. Ask questions to understand how your work fits into the big picture. Speak less and listen more. It will make you stand out from the crowd easily.

7. **Ask ONE intelligent question** or make one intelligent suggestion during staff meetings. This establishes you as a bright young lady who is interacting in the meeting, but not trying to steal the show. Get to the point and then be quiet. Wait for a response. Do not feel pressured to fill empty air.

8. **If you don't know the answer to a question, admit it**. Then track down the answer and follow-up with the person to give him the answer. Your honesty and follow-through will be appreciated. Plus, it expands your knowledge so you know the answer for the next time.

9. **Watch your Social Media behavior.** Your Facebook profile, your Twitter account, your online presence is public domain. Be savvy about what you publish publicly for the world to see. Realize potential employers will google you to research who you are. Do it yourself and look at your results with the eye of an HR recruiter. Would you hire yourself? Clean up your online presence if necessary.

10. **Drink sensibly**. Oftentimes, you may find yourself at happy hour, office parties, business conferences, and other events where there is alcohol, especially free alcohol. This is not a

frat party. This is not a night out with the girls. Set a one drink limit per event. You can be social without having to keep pace with others. Do not be the last to leave events and don't be known as the party girl. It won't advance your career.

Upon graduation, most graduates begin the job search process. Even after you land a job, realize that interviews are still in your future: for promotions, new positions and even new companies. There are plenty of websites that detail interview expectations and excellence. Utilize them. Here are a few tidbits to improving your interview skills:

1. *Focus on practical skills.* Apply your coursework and internship experience. (Employers want to know how your education and experience will apply to working for them. Think through how your courses relate to everyday work and be able to explain that.)

2. *Handwrite a thank-you note for interview.* It will make you stand out. (Not a email message, an actual snail mail thank-you note.)

3. *Be humble.* Cocky beginners attract no one. True humility is noteworthy and appreciated by many.

4. *Don't ask* about vacation time, pay scale, benefits in the first interview. Wait for the offer to work out those details, which are negotiable.

5. *Bring notebook to take notes.* Now use it during the interview.

6. *Ask questions*, proving you did your homework. Be sure to research the company and position before the interview to establish a background.

7. *Ask for the job IF you're interested.* Nail down when follow-up will occur. Ask about next steps and when you'll hear more.

Choose Your Attitude Daily

Your attitude is your key to success. Be positive and maintain a can-do attitude. Have fun on your job. Enjoy your work. Life's too short to suffer through boring work or a job you deplore. Your attitude will be recognized and appreciated. Be solution-oriented. Don't focus on problems; focus on how to solve them. Come to every discussion with at least one solution to match each problem on the agenda. Persevere through the tough times. They will come. How you react to them will speak volumes. Accept compliments. Don't make excuses. Don't blow them off. Smile and say thank you. You know how many women will say, "Oh, it was nothing," "this old thing?" "I just did what anyone else would do." Quit demeaning your own beauty, your hard work. Just shush it and say genuinely say thank you. Accept recognition for your work and extend gratitude for anyone who helped you achieve the goal. It builds their confidence and shows you appreciate others.

Get Out of Your Comfort Zone

Work is not about finding your little spot and staying there. Get out there. Be visible. Volunteer for opportunities. Accept assignments that will stretch you. Seek out new learning. If you don't get it, tell the speaker you don't get it. Don't do it incorrectly. Take the blame when it's something you were responsible for. Even if it wasn't your entire fault. Know when to let someone else take credit for something. Help struggling teammates when able, but not at your own demise. Take notes to ensure you remember instructions and comments. Make others, especially your boss, look good. They will return the favor if you persist. Side with your boss in front of others. She will appreciate your loyalty. Be flexible. Be honest and straightforward. Be polite. Push for process improvement. Show how you provide more value. Don't be afraid to voice your opinion. Embrace the discomfort of confrontation. Be a truth teller in the business setting.

A Little Voice Coaching

No, we're not auditioning you for the next Voice series. It is important to realize that your voice impacts your life. How others perceive you and hear you is crucial to you being understood. First, be observant of your tone. It communicates emotion even when you don't realize it. Learn to control the pitch of your voice. Slow down and exercise the bottom range of your voice. Studies show that a slower pace of speech is heard and heeded more than a fast pace. They've also proven what we already knew: higher pitched voices are less likely to be understood. When you take the time to speak calmly and directly, you separate yourself from the competition and others will truly listen to you. Think about it. If you heard a hysterical woman screaming about something, would you respond in a good way? How would you react? If you heard a calm woman explaining her concern about an issue in a reasonable tone, you'd react in a different way. Regardless of feelings, learn to control your voice. It's critical to survival in the corporate world. Additionally, my dad always drilled into me that I needed to "talk like a lady," not a sailor. I've since learned why it's so important. Your vocabulary tells the world who you are and where you've been. Your background and history is communicated through the words, the phrases you use. How do you communicate when at peace, when upset, when frustrated, when depressed? Maintain civility and don't get sucked into inappropriate jokes, lewd comments and other bad behavior. Be direct about your objectives. Be polite and uplifting in your speech. Edify, encourage and empower others. You will notice others around you doing the same as you continue on your course of positivity.

Skills to Learn

First of all, be sure to continually hone your professional skills in your area of expertise. Technology and life is always evolving and changing. You need to ensure your own success by continuing education related to your field. Utilize your company's tuition assistance program to cover the costs of education. Now, there are additional types of skills that are integral to your advancement in the corporate ladder. Learn to manage time wisely. Hand in hand with time management goes organizational skills. If you're a good organizer, you'll be appreciated up and down the corporate ladder of success. Perfect your collaborating skills. You thought you did a lot of team projects in college; that was preparation for life in the real world. It's all about teamwork. People will want you on their team as they see your ability to interact and empower others as well as contribute wisely to the project. Last but not least, work on your technology skills. Learn a variety of programs and applications. The older generations appreciate how you grew up on this technology and understand it intuitively in a way they never will. Be willing to tutor others on your expertise. It may open doors you would have never otherwise had a chance to walk through.

Personality at Work

A highly valued skill by many is the ability to read a room. If you have the ability to assess the situation and those in it, determine the right steps to take, and execute, then you'll go far. Take a variety of personality assessments and learn your own strengths and weaknesses. Study the other types as well so you know how to identify and respond to them.

Keep It Professional

Work colleagues are just that, colleagues. They are not your close friends. Study how others in the company interact. Observe the company's culture and learn how things work. Earn the respect of your colleagues and focus on being professional. Cultivate professional relationships, a strong connection that produces good results and effective deliverables. Keep your personal life at home. Check your issues at the door. Refuse to let the stresses of life impact your work. Learn to focus your mind on the task at hand rather than stewing about personal issues. Men learned to compartmentalize long ago, keeping personal life separate from home life. We women need to incorporate some of that compartmentalization into our behavior. Be able to forget about your dating situation, roommate's drama or sibling rivalry when you're at work and being compensated to do a job. There will be time to deal with the issue later. Focus on your work and let your problems work themselves out. You're probably worrying more about it than is healthy.

Dealing with Conflicts. Remember that the people who drive you crazy are probably not happy people. Do your best to work with them but distance yourself from them whenever possible. When necessary, privately confront them when their actions interfere with your work. Never discuss the issues with other co-workers. Involve your boss and/or the HR department whenever necessary.

Live a Balanced Life

There are multiple facets to your diamond. You are not solely your professional persona. You are also spiritual, mental, physical and social. You need to be developing each aspect of your life simultaneously. Plug into civic organizations, the nonprofit world in order to better our planet. Focus on your physical well-being. Exercise regularly. Your health is important to others. Eat healthy and drink plenty of water to stay hydrated. Your work performance will improve if your health improves. Your mental well-being also is positively impacted by regular workouts. A great way to deal with the stresses of the office is to get in some exercise. Whether you prefer an intense workout, a brisk walk or yoga, making the time to do something several times a week will improve your health physically and mentally. You can withstand more stress if you're making an effort to workout regularly. Take time to develop your spiritual self. Whatever your beliefs are, be sure you take the time to meditate. Joy and peace are your links to withstanding anything. Find your connection to both and develop them. Learn to hold them inside despite your present circumstances. Practice random acts of kindness. Watch it change your life.

Nix the apologies and qualifiers

Ever used any of the following phrases:

- "This might not be a good idea..."

- "I'm sorry but..."

- "I'm not the expert on this ..."

- "I think so and so sort of said this already, but ..."

- "This might be a stupid question..."

These qualifying comments fall under the realm of apologizing too much. Stop doing it. They implicitly weaken you, to yourself and to others. They are unnecessary comments. There is no benefit to them so don't say them. Notice yourself engaging in this behavior and steadily work it out of your repertoire.

Networking

Networking is beneficial in any point of your career. Join trade organizations, nonprofit organizations that match your passions are, local professional women organizations such as American Association of University Women, Women in Technology, or National Association of Professional Women. Get involved in each organization. Get connected to at least one of the committees. Build relationships with other members, learning who they are and what they do. Meet them for coffee or lunch on a regular basis. Plan to meet someone for lunch each week to broaden your network. These women will help you advance in a multitude of ways, professionally and personally. Plug into associations your company belongs to, find meetings that interest you and get involved. The more you expand your area of reach, the more you'll grow.

Be Strategic

Be strategic in every action you take. Delegate tasks when appropriate. Learn that there is no need to do it all yourself. Focus on what you do well and enable others to help you succeed. Draft a 5-year plan. Aim high. Set 3-year goals and 1-year objectives. Then take the available steps before you to put you on the pathway to achieving those goals. Take all the training available to you. Volunteer to do high-visibility projects in non-profit organizations. Participate in informational interviews. Deliver on most promises. Nobody is perfect. Realize you will make mistakes. Select mentors who are at the next step or two beyond where you are. If you want to be a success executive with a family, target a manager who is also a happy wife and loving mother to mentor you.

Know the gaps in your skills, knowledge, experience and network. Ask to be part of the assignments to fill those gaps. Look to change jobs every few years to gain functional experience across different industries and company types.

Be uniquely you.

At your new job, you may find that you are the youngest person in your department, at meetings, etc. In male-dominated industries, you may very well find:

- The majority around you are men whose age is close to your father's

- You are one of the few females on board

- You are the youngest.

Don't let this situation intimidate you. Remember that you are knowledgeable, smart, creative, energetic, and flexible to pick up new things. You are awesome and you have A LOT to offer. Repeat that to yourself. Keep up your professional confidence! Now, go get 'em, tiger.

Notes:

ABOUT THE AUTHOR

DAWN CAMPBELL

You know how people always want more happiness and less discomfort in their lives. Well that's exactly what Dawn Campbell, Master Health Coach and Holistic Practitioner helps clients achieve.

Working together, self-sabotaging behaviour is identified and replaced with positive habits. Following which, clients experience the joys of inner-happiness, blooming confidence and sexier lives filled with vital health.

Freelance for 10 years following a 20 year successful corporate career, Dawn has created a thriving health practice around her home and lifestyle. Thereby offering fellow health seekers an oasis to rebuild, rejuvenate and revitalise their mind, body and spirit.

A lifelong vegetarian, Dawns experience includes being a high raw vegan chef following a natural hygiene lifestyle. By her own admission, her family live the 'good life'. Financially free, they continually strive to be self-sufficient which adds to their contentment. At 50 years old, she's happier, healthier and fitter than ever so must be doing something right!

Dawn's also a 'Heal your life' teacher; Callahan trained Thought Field Therapist and Mentor Coach for Noble Manhattan, Europe's leading coach training provider. She's currently studying Naturopathy and Life Science.

Dawn's ethos is no-one knows our body better than we do. Therefore, her mission is to educate, empower and encourage others to reclaim responsibility for their health and become their own health guru.

Dawn would be honoured to be included in your dream team supporting you achieve your goals, after all, if we don't look after our bodies, where else will we live?

Contact:

E: dawn@holistichealthcoach.eu

W: http://www.dawncampbellholistichealth.eu

T: +33 (0) 2 43 64 37 48

S: dawncampbell1

A: Pays de Loire, France

"BBC radio interviews, writing for national and local press, presentations, in-house company training and workshops with 1 -1 follow up sessions mean that hundreds of clients have benefited from Dawns result orientated supportive style". Erica Connelly, Business Link, UK

FIFTEEN

SELF-CARE IS NOT SELFISH

Dawn Campbell

"So many people spend their health gaining wealth, then have to spend their wealth to regain their health." —A. J. Reb Materi

Assuming you don't want to make this mistake, we'll cut straight to the chase by raising the multimillion dollar question because as we entrepreneurs know, time is money!

Q. What do *you* think is the number one most important resource you'll need to succeed as young women breaking into and making your mark on the business world?

Before reading on

1. brainstorm the question

2. note your ideas in your journal

3. prioritise them in order of importance.

Over many years coaching 'business start-up' clients, I've observed great lists being created detailing numerous anticipated resources. Lists that typically include but are not limited to notable things such as; branding, vision, mission and goals; finances; having an M.B.A.; a database of network contacts; premises, equipment and reliable transport and of course clients.

Undoubtedly, those are some of the great resources we need to help us establish and develop a successful business. However, most entrepreneurs are so busy considering all the external resources they'll need, they usually forgot to consider the internal resources they'll also need.

A resource much closer to home, so close in fact, this one particular resource is right under our noses. Furthermore it's a resource most of us have some control over. It's also a resource that's central to the success of pretty much everything anyone has ever achieved.

I'm talking about health. If we don't value health as our number one best resource I'm not sure what else could possibly be more important? After all, if we don't look after our body, where else will we live? Remember the wise words of Desiderius Erasmus *"Prevention is better than cure"* that's what practicing self-care is about.

The absence of good health means it's difficult for anyone to achieve their maximum potential in any area. You (mind, body, spirit) will suffer; your relationships with certainly suffer; even your home and your business life will not function as efficiently or effectively as they could if you were in good health.

If you doubt the wisdom of Richard Baker who said *"To get rich never risk your health. For it is the truth that health is the wealth of wealth."* then answer the following questions

Q. Which is more important your health or more money?

Q. Which is more important your health or your home?

Q. Which is more important your health or your relationships?

Q. Which is more important your health or success?

Q. Which is more important your health or time?

Q. Which is more important your health or …………

Fill in the blank and repeat this exercise as many times as you need to *until* you believe like Henri Frederic Amiel that "*In health there is freedom. Health is the first of all liberties*".

Extreme Self-Care for Everyday Vitality and Longevity

"A man too busy to take care of his health is like a mechanic too busy to take care of his tools." —Spanish Proverb

Assuming we're now in agreement that health is our wealth, we need to learn how to master extreme self-care by first attaining a good health status, secondly, maintain this valuable asset.

To begin with, let's explore what it is to even practice self-care? Whilst there is no definitive dictionary definition of self-care (except in medical terms), I think it's about practicing empowerment, awareness and assertiveness.

Of course self-care may be misjudged as selfishness. This is never truer than it is for women, especially mothers who are considered to be the 'nurturers' in our society. Regardless of status or sex, someone who practices self-care understands their limitations and needs. They appreciate that unless they are taking responsibility for themselves on as many levels as possible; they are in no fit state to take care of anyone or anything else. So it's about leading by example. A case in point which we've probably all experienced is when we're about to take off in an aircraft and the steward tells us in the event of an emergency to put on our own oxygen mask *before* helping anyone else. There's nothing selfish about that, it's just common sense.

So when we talk about self-care, we are positively, purposely and actively taking time for ourselves in a way that rejuvenates and energizes us. Ultimately self-care makes us a better person to be around at home and a more productive person in the workplace. To deny our need for self-care gradually leads to an air and energy of negativity as we become more repressed and unbalanced.

Plug Into the Power of Self-Care

"No one else can breathe for you, drink for you, sleep for you, exercise for you, eat for you, or get sunshine for you. Health is your responsibility. No one else can do it for you. Health is self-built." —Life Science

The above quote details just a few of the *many* self-care habits we need to practice in order to enjoy a successful personal and business life. After all, these two sides of us don't operate in isolation. To enjoy a successful life rather than just a successful business, we need to invest in self-care. This ensures we successfully merge our personal life, family relationships and home time with running and managing a successful business.

Here's a comprehensive health protocol

1. Breathe clean pure air because pollution is destructive to health and well-being.

2. Maintain a temperate climate, excessive cold or heat drains nerve energy.

3. Maintain internal cleanliness to minimise the risk of disease.

4. Drink plenty of pure water, ideally distilled.

5. Quality sleep allows the body to heal, repair and become rebalanced.

6. Eat a natural diet suited to our physiology; raw fruits, vegetables, nuts & seeds.

7. Regular fasting to improve assimilation, elimination and self-healing.

8. Expose skin and eyes to daily sunshine to top up essential vitamin D3.

9. Daily activity is key to keeping-fit, supple and mobile.

10. Rest and recuperation, essential for the mind body and spirit to develop.

11. Recreational playful activities that rejuvenate our creative self.

12. Peace of mind enhances emotional well-being.

13. Harmonious pleasant environment to live in.

14. Community to participate and interact with.

15. Self-mastery of oneself.

16. Secure outlet and work activities that provides a sense of purpose.

17. Inspiration, motivation and commitment to achieve goals.

18. Instinct to reproduce.

19. Aesthetic pleasures from being in touch with nature.

20. Expression of natural instincts; love, appreciation, gratitude and creativity.

21. Positive self-esteem builds self-confidence, self-reliance, and a sense of self-worth.

These basic self-care practices nurture vital health as well as promote longevity as originally taught by the likes of T.C. Fry, Graham, Jennings, Shelton and Schulz. These and many other early proponents championed the virtues of a natural hygiene diet and lifestyle as some of the keys to good health.

7 Key Strategies for Successful Self-Care

"Love yourself first, and everything else falls in line. You really have to love yourself to get anything done in this world". —Lucille Ball

Most modern day practitioners and followers are still in agreement that these 21 self-care practices are as valid today as they were centuries ago. In fact, some go so far as to say that considering the emotional, physical and environmental stresses we experience today, self-care is more important than ever.

The following 7 practices are the essential keys to successful self-care

1. Sleep and rest

2. Natural diet

3. Sunshine

4. Peace of mind

5. Pure water

6. Fresh air

7. Exercise

Whilst we may not have before fully realised the connection between our personal health and the health of our business, we're now learning to appreciate just how linked these two areas are. Practicing these essential self-care top tips on a daily basis will not only ensure vital health, but a positive work life balance too.

It stands to reason it would be nigh on impossible to feel, sound and look like you mean business when inside, you're feeling unhappy or unhealthy. Likewise, when your work life is making you unhappy and unhealthy, life at home can't help but become stressed and strained as a consequence.

To avoid that vicious spiral, you owe it to yourself and everyone around you to practice self-care first and foremost. Remember, self-care has nothing to do with being selfish despite what you may have been brought up to believe. It has everything to do with being honest about your needs and honouring your boundaries.

When I'm coaching entrepreneurs the work we do together frequently overlaps between personal and business. As a holistic health coach it's my responsibility to check the reality of any given situation with each of my clients. We do this by exploring these 7 self-care strategies. This process enables me to better understand the health of my client and ultimately, the health of their business and vice versa.

7 Step Self-Care Plan

"If you feel "burnout" setting in, if you feel demoralized or exhausted, it is best, for the sake of everyone, around you to withdraw and restore yourself". —Dalai Lama

Why is adequate sleep *and* rest so important?

"One hour of sleep before midnight, is worth 2 after midnight."

This saying may or may not be true, but what is true is that adequate ssleep is essential if we are to function properly during the day.

Sleep has its own natural restorative cycle of repairing itself after an active day; healing cells, tissue, muscles etc. and eliminating toxins so the longer we sleep the better.

If we're in the lucky minority who do *not* suffer with a sleep disorder, a third of our life will be spent healthfully experiencing the 4 stages of sleep (light sleep stage 1 & 2 thetra activity followed by stage 3 & 4 deep or delta sleep which is a cycle that is repeated 4 or 5 times a night).

However, this basic need for sleep as per Maslow's Hierarchy of Needs Pyramid, or the lack of it, is for a growing number of people a vital clue to what lies behind poor health and performance. Adequate sleep is especially difficult to achieve for people who have changed the regulation of their internal biological clock due to shift work, or are living in areas with light and or excess noise pollution. Additionally, sleep deprivation increases our risk of physical injury and mental issues such as depression.

Likewise adequate deep rest is equally important. If we don't get a balance between rest and activity, our nervous system becomes wired, edgy and overly emotional. It's this over sensitivity to constant stimulation that wears us out physically and emotionally. Insufficient sleep and rest creates longer term health issues hence the sayings 'running on autopilot' or 'going through the motions' where we're essentially running on adrenaline.

Business leaders know the value of practicing daily power naps to prevent this happening to them. Just by switching off for 20 minutes a day allows their creative juices to become renewed. As the wise Thich Nhat Hanh says *'doing nothing is doing something'*.

How you will benefit?

Don't worry, you cannot sleep too much. The body will sleep for as long as it needs to repair, heal and eliminate. Healthy sleep essentially equates to a healthy mind and body enabling you to function safely and calmly. It enables us to engage in various physical and mental activities with renewed energy each day. Adequate sleep is especially important while we're growing up or engaged in physical or athletic activities.

People struggling to manage either mental issues such as depression or physical issues such as obesity would benefit from improved sleep which balances their hormones.

Q. When are you going to implement the steps required to improve the amount and quality of your sleep?

A. _____

_____

_____

Why does the best nutrition come from a natural diet?

"The golden rule of eating is; Thou shalt not poison thyself." —TC Fry

The results speak for themselves. Mother Nature provides natural foods already perfectly packaged and balanced with all the enzymes, essential macro and micro nutrients we require.

While commercially produced man-made (thus non real) food items have created an increase in and growing variety of diseases for us to suffer from.

How you will benefit from a natural diet?

By swapping shopping at the supermarket for the green grocer's means you'll make healthier choices. Supermarket trollies are typically filled with denatured, low nutritional, fortified for profit only foods (i.e. items that need an ingredients label to explain i) what it is and ii) what's in it). This type of shopping is bad for your health *and* it's bad for the environment. The only people who benefit from you shopping at the supermarket is the supermarket themselves and their supplier's shareholders.

Shopping at the green grocers or outdoor markets on the other hand means you will be making healthier choices about what to eat. Additionally you are supporting your local suppliers, all the while taking better care of the environment by minimising the need for excess (and expensive) packaging.

Choose to consume a higher quantity and quality of foods that are rainbow coloured. They denote foods that are fresh, ripe, juicy, local (ideally organic), seasonal and above all, are completely natural. That is the only way you will instantly feel your health improve.

Supplementing these steps with an occasional water only fast and the practice of food combining and you'll finally rid yourself of niggling health issues that make you feel sluggish and irritable. Only then will you be truly free to feel alive and revitalised!

Q. When are you going to swap shopping at the supermarket for the greengrocers?

A. _____

_____

_____

_____

Why is sunshine vital to our health and well-being?

"Just living is not enough; one must have sunshine, freedom and a little flower." —Hans Christian Anderson

Nicknamed the 'sunshine vitamin' sunshine is vital to the body as a whole. The body converts sunshine into natural vitamin D3. Vitamin D3 strengthens and conditions our skin; regulates our glands and improves the quality of our haemoglobin in the blood. Natural vitamin D is absolutely essential and the darker our skin pigmentation, the more we need.

How you will benefit?

Low blood levels of vitamin D3 are associated with a whole host of illnesses; especially bone related such as osteoporosis and generally increases the risk of mortality.

By taking the opportunity to expose your skin *and* eyes to direct sunlight, even on a cloudy day, you'll enhance your health and general well-being. It's the sunlight that is synthesized through the eyes that regulates the thyroid. Skin, organs, muscles and blood all improve with sunshine all of which reduces your risk of disease.

To calculate ultraviolet exposure levels for your vitamin D status Google your latitude / geographical location for example see http://nadir.nilu.no/~olaeng/fastrt/VitD-ez_quartMED.html.

Q. When are you going to start exposing your skin and eyes (min. 20 mins daily) *without* sun protection (that blocks your pores) or sunglasses (that blocks UV rays)?

A. _____

_____

_____

_____

Why is peace of mind central to our well-being?

"Do not confuse peace of mind with spaced-out insensitivity. A truly peaceful mind is sensitive and aware." —H.H. The Dalai Lama

Stress is the opposite of peace of mind. Both feelings are internal. Wherever you go, there they are. Hence the saying when people go off in search of peace that it was right there under their noses all the time!

Because the level and type of stress is constantly changing with the times, people are increasingly complaining about their lack of peace. This imbalance between peace and stress impacts on our physical and emotional health and eventually, weakens our immune system thus increasing our chances of become diseased.

How you will benefit?

Practicing mindfulness helps us live in the present moment. Likewise, switching off from negative influences (including negative people who drain our energy) and learning to meditate both limit the constant stimulation that pervades our life 24/7.

Mastering 'monkey mind' helps develop mental poise, maintains healthy blood pressure and protects our adrenal hormones. Unless we take time out to quieten and tame the mind we will always be a slave to it and know no peace.

Q. When are you going to put into practice whatever gives you peace of mind on a daily basis?

A. _____

_____

_____

_____

Why is drinking pure water so critical?

"Water is the only drink for a wise man." —Henry David Thoreau

The majority of people are chronically dehydrated. A lack of understanding about our bodily composition (55- 75% + water), its constant need for water to be replenished *and* the type of fluids needed leads to dehydration.

Therefore, we need on average 7 litres of water a day, especially if consuming a Standard American Diet (SAD) which is in itself dehydrating. The exact amount of water required depends on other variables such as our size, climate and activity.

Water is necessary to help the body flush itself by eliminating toxins through the kidneys, skin, lung etc. Water keeps our blood thin so flowing more freely thus improves the health of your heart and minimises skin issues and so much more.

Additionally, we've gotten so used to eating on the go 24/7 that often as not, our thirst signals are misinterpreted for hunger. This false hunger is habitually dealt with by eating more dehydrating food. The end result is today's obesity problem until the vicious circle is broken through education about what it means to be healthy.

How you will benefit?

By swapping artificial sugary laden snacks and fizzy, caffeinated drinks for fresh ripe juicy fruit (which contains the purest water), also drinking distilled water whenever you imagine you feel hungry.

If after 30 minutes you still feel hungry, and then eat. However, more often than not, you won't be hungry. Instead you'll be learning how to recognise thirst signals over genuine hunger.

As an added bonus to becoming rehydrated, you'll be managing your weight more effectively too.

Drinking sufficient amounts of water means you'll also experience more energy too because often feelings of fatigue are simply early warning signs of dehydration.

Q. When are you going to improve your hydration levels?

A. _____

_____

_____

Why is breathing fresh air imperative?

"Forests are the lungs of our land, purifying the air and giving fresh strength to our people." —Franklin D. Roosevelt

We breathe 21,600 times a day. Our brain and the trillion cells in our bodies all need a fresh constant supply of oxygen which is delivered by our red blood cells to live. Additionally, our white blood cells need oxygen to do their hard work of keeping us disease free.

Without fresh air, we become as stale and polluted as the air around us. A lack of fresh air leads to a lack of energy amongst other symptoms. If you live and work in the city, make time to visit the countryside and enjoy breathing fresher air.

Unless we exercise, we only use a third of our lungs capacity. Combine that with the fact many of us lead sedentary lives, are insulated indoors and it's easier to understand the reason for the growing health related issues we suffer such as asthma and allergies. The air indoors is apparently more polluted than city air due to the vast array of chemicals in our homes and offices.

How you will benefit?

Start each day by opening a window and emptying your lungs by puffing out all the stale toxic air until you cannot puff anymore. Only then breathe in fresh air which is full of negative ions and makes you feel alive. In fact, whenever you're tired, do this for an instant boost to your energy and clarity of thinking.

Also sleep with a window open, if that is not possible, select the appropriate plant for your bedroom to prevent the air becoming too stale.

Minimising the use of chemicals at home will decrease the chances of your health being compromised (as well as the health of your family and pets). That means swapping cleaning chemicals in the bathroom and kitchen for natural animal eco-friendly products. Don't forget your personal beauty chemicals and your fabric cleaners too; there are always natural friendly ways of staying clean and fresh. Finally, avoiding inhaling artificial air fresheners and smoky environments.

Q. When are you going start exercising your lungs?

A. _____

_____

_____

_____

Why the need for exercise?

"Those who think they have not time for bodily exercise will sooner or later have to find time for illness." —Edward Stanley

You know what they say *'use it or lose it'* that's because exercise develops our strength and endurance. It's cumulative and helps our co-ordination, flexibility and agility as we age. Exercise is quite literally 'body building' because our whole being is involved (cells, blood, lungs, heart, muscles, circulatory, cardiovascular and respiratory systems).

So exercise helps us age well, it makes us feel better about ourselves and look good (with or without our clothes), it also improves our self-esteem. Even our mind is improved with exercise because we're producing endorphins that make us feel happy. We're sleeping better because of the additional activity and our weight is managed so it's a win-win situation.

How you will benefit?

Regardless of calling it exercise, keeping fit, working out or training, we must move more vigorously if we are to ensure a comfortable, mobile independent old age. Doing *anything* that increases the heart rate for at least 15 mins daily (be it sex, housework, rambling etc.) will improve the tone of our body as well our emotions.

Q. When are you going to move more and promote your youthfulness?

A. _____

_____

_____

_____

Final Word about Self-Care

"The perfect man of old looked after himself first before looking to help others". —Chuang Tzu

Only *you* can decide to take action and make the right choices for both your personal and business health. You can either have more of what you've already had in your past, or else you can opt for something more empowering and nurturing for your future. One things for certain '*if nothing changes, nothing changes*'. So don't just read this chapter, commit to taking action right now.

Learn to master each of these self-care strategies by focusing on them one at a time, in any order you like until each new habit is formed (circa. 21 days). Consequently, in less than six months you too will be on the road to healthy success both at home and in your business. Additionally, you'll become a great role model for your family and employees alike.

Share your thoughts with me and I will send you a complimentary copy of my Self-Assessment Health Questionnaire worth £47.97 which will help you build on the insight gained from this chapter.

My contact details, photo, and biog etc. here...

ABOUT THE AUTHOR

SHIRLEY A. WILLIAMS

Shirley A. Williams is President and CEO of Leadership in Action, LLC. She has been certified by The Professional Woman Network as a Professional Coach and Diversity Consultant. Through this institute, she conducts workshops and seminars that have been presented throughout the United States and abroad. The workshops and seminars conducted consist of topics such as: Women as Leaders, Leadership Skills and The Superwoman Syndrome.

Ms. Williams' knowledge of business and professionalism is supported by over 20 years of leadership and workplace learning experience in corporations, non-profit, university and faith based organizations. She has over 12 years experience in recruiting and change management.

Among her many accomplishments, Ms. Williams has coauthored numerous published books and is completing her first independently authored book on reinventing yourself. She has been recognized by the Lydia Circle of Christian Business and Professional Women with the Spirit of Deborah Leadership Award. She has also received the Wayne State University Leadership Development Award from Wayne State.

Books (Coauthor) • The Baby Boomers Handbook for Women • Learning to Love Your Self for the African American Woman • Remove the Mask | Living an Authentic Life • Becoming Your Own Best Friend • Raising African American Daughters • Wellness for the African American Woman• Life Skills for the African American Woman • Releasing Strong Holds

Certifications• Certified Professional Coach • Registered Corporate Coach • Volunteer Chaplin • Certified Diversity Consultant • Certified DISC Behavior Model Consultant

Professional Spotlight• The Magnolia Radio Show • Black Enterprise • WLQV-Faith Talk Radio

Professional Organizations • Professional Woman's Speakers Bureau • Professional Woman's Authors Institute • National Association of Female Executives • Coalition 100 Black Women • Campfire USA (Past Board President) • Lydia Circle of Christian Business and Professional Women • Betty R. May Cancer Foundation (Board Member) • ASTD (Association of Training and Development) • Optimist Intl. (Past Lt. Gov.)

Ms. Williams is available for speaking engagements.

Contact:
Website: www.leadershipinaction.info
Email: swilliams@leadershipinaction.info
Phone: (888) 926-9911 | P.O. Box 3238 Southfield, MI

SIXTEEN

WHAT I WISH I HAD KNOWN

(BEFORE STARTING MY FIRST "REAL JOB")

Shirley A. Williams

*"Any woman who has a career and a family automatically develops
something in the way of two personalities, like two sides of a dollar bill,
each different in design. Her problem is to keep one from draining the life
from the other".* —Ivy Baker Priest - Politician

Have you ever accepted an employment or business prospect that turned out to be an experience from hell; because it was totally different from the opportunity presented and what you thought you had signed up for? Did it leave you quietly wondering to yourself; what were you thinking? And did it have you shaking your head as you heard the voice within say; I told you this was too good to be true? After that, you remembered that during your decision making process the thoughts swirling around in your head that made you feel a little uneasy and uncertain about whether this was going to be all *you imagined it would be? (Let me confess; there have been times that I myself have been so captivated by the attractiveness of the packaging; that I didn't and couldn't really think about my own needs at the time. In addition to being taken in by their stuff, I overlooked how relevant knowing and meeting my needs was and how a bad match can impact our personal success.* The point I want to make here is; when we know our needs and understand what motivates us; it becomes a critical factor in establishing a standard for the quality of life that you want. Take a moment and picture a time when you might have had the occasion where you feel you may have made an apprehensive or impulsive decision that sounded or looked good at the time; instead it ended up being everything but what you expected it would be. Was your decision by chance influenced by the conflicting self talk (pro/con) that took place in your head during that time? I sense that you probably know the kind of conversation that I am referring to? It's the conversation where you know in your gut that something was not going to turn out as well as it sounded..... but. Nevertheless you still got trapped by the smooth talk, money, glamour, and compliments of how impressed they were with you and it sounded soooooo good? (Because like me; the packaging got to you.)

And maybe there have also been times when the chatter in your head took you in another direction and had you thinking the presentation/offer was an insult because you believed the offer was beneath you; because of how you see yourself or believed you deserved something better. Then again maybe this offer stoked up some fear that made you feel inadequate and under qualified? Either way there are times when we focus on and listen to the positive and negative self talk without being objective. Sometimes our ego only allows us to hear the biased kind of self not talk; self talk that can cause some anxiety when we consider taking a risk when or it challenges you to search yourself with an honest and objective eye.

When we have these fights with ourselves it our decision making capability that impacts the end result as well. Which only serves a purpose of either generating feelings that cause us to feel greater than we are or less than and in both instances we need to tread carefully. (Projecting an image of our being overly confident or lacking confidence can negatively influence the impressions of those we want to impress or connect with.) Remember, self talk can be a blessing or a curse; it can prevent us from realizing our full potential or compel us to self sabotage ourselves, because we lack the wisdom of self awareness and how to moderate both. I have made it a personal goal to understand myself better than anyone else does, doing so keeps me humble.

THE VALUE OF SELF AWARENESS

*"Do yourself a huge favor and practice positive self talk it will liberate you
from entertaining those negative inner conversations and instead it will
compel you to focus on positive empowering self talk. Remembering always
that our actions are inspired by our thoughts and our thoughts shape who
we become and what we achieve."*
—Shirley A. Williams

Self awareness is the ability to visualize a nonbiased self portrait using a spirit of courage and truthfulness that provides insight into how others see you and how you see yourself when interacting with others. As I Reflect back to the time when I started my professional journey; I wish I could honestly say that I had this knowledge and, how critical being self aware is; but I can't. At the time I was so naïve and inexperienced, that I had no clue in regards to what success for me; or would look like or how to get it. Or to consider the traditional actions to take and behaviors I needed to exhibit to prepare me for standing out and taping into my full potential. I didn't have anyone who could advise me on the proper protocol in advance or what it would take for me to climb that proverbial ladder of success therefore I chose to position myself to become a covert apprentice. Once I got into the swing of things I got noticed and found myself a mentor. Along with that what I learned along the way was, (with the help of a mentor) an open mind can take us on a journey beyond anything you can envision. I also learned that our ego has to be managed at all times. I also reached a conclusion that if I allowed myself to be solely guided by my instincts, inflated ego and delusional perception of self, a closed door will continue to be closed to me. My mentor taught me early on that self awareness improves our judgment and our openness to engaging in ongoing professional and personal growth and development. It helps when we acknowledge our strengths and allows us to accept our weaknesses and focus on a strategy for improvement. (Doing this can be the gift to self that keeps on giving as long as you believe there is and will always be a need for self improvement.)

Knowing what I know today, about self awareness and truth, I can say what a blessing it would have been for me if I would have had a career coach prior to sitting at my first desk. Having a mentor who shared this information with me beforehand might have possibility helped me develop this important capability even earlier in life. The ability to evaluate your, motives, role, beliefs and behaviors can have a profound effect on every area of our life. The fundamental components of self awareness is understanding your thoughts and needs and being able to define your desired end result – what do you want out of life? Being insightful to your strengths, shortcomings, ethics, passions and personality is necessary to the process of making adjustments where required. All right, I will admit that my greatest challenge going through that process was discovering and admitting I wasn't perfect and learning to respect the opinions and feedback of others for the greater good. At the same time I needed to broaden my insight as to why others perceived me as they did and why I viewed others as I did. (The desire to understand those people dynamics was my motivation for connecting myself with the D.I.S.C. Behavioral System.) My investment in D.I.S.C. has turned out to be an invaluable asset and a critical tool for developing and managing the relationships in my life both personally and professionally. Gaining a better understanding ourselves and others can place us in the position to succeed in every area of our lives.

The following list highlights a few significant lessons that I learned along the way:

1. Be careful with your ego because if you are not it can sometimes be an opportunity killer.

2. An open door may not initially have a "BIG" job title on the other side; however it could set the stage for a star to be born and create an opportunity for a superstar audition.

3. Find a mentor (a trusted teacher) and model their behavior

4. When you challenge ideas, processes and a new course of action, quickly follow up by offering a solution. When you fail to do so you will be viewed as someone with a closed mind which is an indicator of inflexibility and a lack of interest.

5. Become an eagle – strive to become a change maker. (Change makers manage to learn not only enough to get by in their position; they also strive to gain understanding of the vision, mission, strategies, goals and values.)

6. Take on extra circular assignments; remember how you benefited from this by doing so when you were in school, you earned extra credit and it helped you boost your GPA. (**G**rowth **P**otential and **A**bility aka **A**cumen in business.)

7. Make it a personal priority to observe the organizations procedure regarding succession planning. (This would be a practice used to identify and fast track individuals who have demonstrated the passion, character, ambition and ability that is seen as the model of those who can add value?)

8. Keeping your skills current is the key to movement and promotion; corporate America refers to this as "up skilling". Make upgrading a priority it will increase your value in the organization.

9. Stay focused on areas of personal and professional development; identify the skills you have that are "transferable/portable". Look for opportunities for skillset-building or enhancement. (That would be those soft skills that will be viewed as an asset in other departments.)

10. Reinstate and practice the old school values of trust, commitment and quality. (With four generations co-existing in the workplace today; your efforts will be recognized.)

11. Speak up – Stand up – Link up and Measure up. (Communicate your ideas with clarity, don't compromise your principles, collaborate when beneficial, do what you say you are going to do when you say you will do it.)

12. Be authentic, resilient and open to varying points of view. (Be real and quick to recover from setbacks.)

13. Periodically seek feedback on areas for potential development and skill enhancement. (Put your "big girl panties on" and accept feedback graciously.)

14. Do not judge or devalue someone based upon where their desk is; doing so can cause you to miss out on opportunities. (Don't underestimate who has whose ear.)

15. Be mindful of your role and the state of affairs when you provide reasons and explanations; I once had a mentor who told me that they were still "just an excuse that I put some lipstick on".

KNOW YOUR PASSION

"The best career advice we can give to the young is: Find out what you like doing best and get someone to pay you for doing it."
—Katherine Whitehorn

Take the time to evaluate your motivation for either accepting a position, client or project; when you act out of desperation or egotistically we tend to regret those decisions. As you think about your choices, honestly take into account the compatibility factor because not doing so can make or break you. Before signing on; ask yourself these questions; is this going to be a good fit or is it just a means to an end? Is this something I am going to enjoy doing or is it something that will I become bored with and will resentment and dissatisfaction grow from it each day that I am doing it? After that look for a cue that will give you confirmation that this experience will be either a launching pad for success or a dark pit you will grow to resent. You can get a feel for the organizational culture by asking a few probing questions about things that concern you e.g. retention, opportunities for growth and philosophy on talent management and performance development. Then you can better determine if this will be a gateway that you will overtime refer to as a liability or a potential path to success; or an environment that you can see yourself thriving and prospering in.

STAND OUT IN A CROWD OF MANY

"It's better to be remembered for standing out in a crowd than to be forgotten for blending in." —Unknown

When I was working at the university we were hosting a conference and there were not enough people responsible for the room set up scheduled to come in early enough to get the set up done. After hearing all the commotion, I came out of my office and started to help with getting things together while others on the leadership team stood around discussing the poor planning skills of conference manager. At our next staff meeting after the event I received praise and recognition from the senior vice president and the president of the University for focusing on getting the job done and not being concerned titles or with who dropped the ball.

I stepped in and helped because I presumed that when the people attending the conference got there they wouldn't care who dropped the ball. I believed the entire University and staff would have received the blame for the lack of planning or the credit for how organized and accommodating we were. The lesson I learned from that experience was; because we were all affiliates of the university, we would all be considered as competent or incompetent. I opted to work for the competent vote.

THINK OF EACH ENCOUNTER AS A FIRST IMPRESSION

"What impression are you leaving behind?"
—Shirley A. Williams

Growing up I remember my mother would remind me over and over again that *"you only get one chance to make a first impression"*. My takeaway from what I considered to be nagging was pretty simple. She was teaching me; to present my best self whenever I met someone new. Of course my inner "sassy little girl" wondered if this meant that after the first meeting; the next time I could show them my not so best self? As time passed I figured out that was not exactly what she was saying. And she did inspire me to make a habit of presenting my best self, no matter how many times I may encounter someone...

A MENTOR IS YOUR ROLE MODEL

"Keep away from people who try to belittle your ambitions. Small people always do that, but the really great people make you feel that you too can become great." —Mark Twain

Selecting a mentor shouldn't be a complicated task. Pretend that you are looking for someone to provide inspiration, insight, strategies and the action steps required to lose 50 pounds. Wouldn't you believe it was an obtainable goal if you found someone who had actually accomplished that goal? Wouldn't it motivate you if they were a walking testimony a symbol of possibility, someone who at one time was a size 18 and is now wearing a size 10 and has maintained their weigh for the past 6 years?

A mentor should be someone who can relate; someone who has achieved the success levels you desire for yourself. They should be someone you respect and is respected throughout the organization or community. You must have confidence in them and consider them to be a trusted guide. They ought to provide encouragement, advice, support direction and constructive feedback on your strengths and shortcomings for the purpose of getting you to the goal post.

In the late seventies, early eighties I applied for a job as a computer salesperson, it was a "job" that was not offered to many people of color or women. It required travel, working long hours, and socializing after work; it was a male dominated field. During my interview I can still remember the woman interviewing me saying that I was not qualified for the job, however they were looking for a secretary/receptionist. I took the job as the secretary and made the best of it. The happy ending to this story is that someone observed my capabilities and interaction with my coworkers and clients and took me under their wing; as a mentor does. (It was a male manager.) The first thing he told me was stop going to lunch with the secretaries and start going to lunch with the sales people. (I know how this sounds, however it was how the men played the game, he advised me "to hang" with the people who had the job I wanted. (It's the soar with the eagles' theory.) He was on point; after I started "hanging" out with the sales people they forgot I wasn't one of them and helped me to become one of them.

PERSONAL AND PROFESSIONAL DEVELOPMENT

"Continuous self improvement increases your intellectual capital and adds value to your professional and personal portfolio."
—Shirley A. Williams

The word ***development*** and a few more words that come to mind are motivational for me. Some of those words are; growth, expansion, progress, improvement, education, enhancement, promotion, upgrading and advancement just to throw out a few. Find the magical words that will inspire you to continue to *strive for personal and professional development daily.*

POSITIONING YOURSELF

The biggest mistake that you can make is to believe that you are working for somebody else. Job security is gone. The driving force of a career must come from the individual. Remember: Jobs are owned by the company; however you own your career.
—Earl Nightingale – Motivational Speaker

When I worked in the staffing industry the corporate mantra was; operate with the mindset of an entrepreneur. The directive was to manage the business as though it was your own. The corporate office instilled a sense of ownership that made us feel empowered. The philosophy was one that encouraged decision making, trusting your instincts and independence; as long as we met our goals and carried out the mission. The freedom to manage in this manner motivated us to work hard and exceed expectations. The knowledge I gained from that experience was the template I used when I started my business.

NEVER UNDERVALUE NETWORKING

"Networking is marketing. Marketing yourself, marketing your uniqueness and marketing what you stand for." —Christine Comaford – Lynch

Networking provides a platform to promote you, your business and showcase your talents and skills. It gives you an opportunity to expedite the relationship building process and discover what others are doing. It can open a door to a more comprehensive group of people, businesses, ideas and trends. The time you invest in networking can be very valuable; it could potentially provide an opening for acquiring new prospects. It can also be a gateway for developing new partnerships and referrals.

A FEW COMMON SENSE THINGS TO REMEMBER

- Keep your personal personal; do your best to keep the professional and personal conversations and issues from colliding.

- Be on time and when it's considered necessary leave late; do not let your success potential be tied to the hands of the clock.

- Your work station is not your home away from home don't decorate it as if it is.

- When you're in a meeting give it your full attention – step outside if you must text, take or make calls. (You are the only one impressed by your importance; it's disrespectful and annoying.)

- Multitasking is not the same as busy being busy; learn to recognize the difference.

- Be quick to share the credit; and slow to point the finger of blame.

- Take responsibility for your own actions.

- Treat people the way you want to be treated.

- Feedback is not criticism; the intent is to use it as tool for development.

- Remember that the words "business casual" suggests "we're doing business".

Dedication

I dedicate this chapter to all those women who have been blessed with the experience of promotion in their personal and professional lives. I commend you for your staying power. I ask you, what are you doing to reassure that your daughters and my two daughters (Trelana and Danielle) will get further up that ladder than we were able to? Can you remember those who helped you along the way and those who were to insecure to do so. I encourage and challenge you to share your wisdom, knowledge, extended hand and open heart of acceptance to help another sister get her foot on that ladder next to yours. Doing so will give power to the one who takes your hand and when you grab hers you will become even more powerful because your legacy will live on.

References:
Quotations cited in this chapter were retrieved from the internet.

Notes:

ABOUT THE AUTHOR

DR. VERONICA EDDY

Dr. Veronica Eddy, President of Dove Consulting and Counseling Group, LLC, is as RN, who earned a BA in Psychology from St Leo University in St Leo, Florida. She earned a Masters in Religious Arts, was ordained into ministry, and continued on to earn her PhD and NCCA licensure as a clinical pastoral counselor from Jacksonville Theological Seminary.

Her nursing career has spanned more than forty-six years with half of that spent working in the Oncology field where she not only administered chemotherapy and counseled patients and their families through very difficult times, but also helped families through the death of their loved ones.

Dr. Eddy has also worked as an administrative assistant in a successful nursing company providing IV services to the nursing home communities around the state of Florida, as well as in MD., VA., Washington D.C., and other regions of the Northeast. Her ability to understand and relate to women in this highly stressful environment keeps her continually in the forefront of providing the necessary tools to work smarter, not harder. About two years ago, she has relocated to Pennsylvania, is working as an Intake Coordinator in a growing home health agency and continues to attend to the needs of the nurses under her care.

Professionally, she is a member of the National Association of Professional Nurses (NAPN), a Certified Trainer with Professional Woman Network specializing in the area of Women's Issues, is a member of The American Association of Christian Counselors (AACC), and The National Christian Counselors Association (NCCA).

Dr. Eddy has had the privilege of being the women's ministry leader in her church in Florida where she applied her expertise in the many areas of the needs of women. She has also designed and implemented a grief recovery program to minister to the countless people needing support after experiencing loss, as well as help to train others to help those in the depths of their grief. After her relocation, she continues to be involved in her church singing on the praise team and ministering to wounded and grieving women. As a licensed clinical pastoral counselor, her understanding of one's emotional needs propel her forward to help minister to and help meet the needs of the physically and spiritually battered women.

Contact:

123 Carriage Dr.
North Huntingdon, Pa. 15642
727-247-7944 or 724-989-9311
Email: nikaron@aol.com

SEVENTEEN

BELIEVING IN YOURSELF

Dr. Veronica Eddy

For we are God's masterpiece. He has created us anew in Christ Jesus, so we can do the good things He planned for us long ago.
—Ephesians 2:10 NLT

Graduation – one goal accomplished! Now, on to the next – that big, wonderful world that has been waiting for you and your first job – the one you have been preparing for all this time. So much excitement with so much to do – job fairs, Monster.com, resumes being sent out with eager anticipation, shopping for that perfect wardrobe and practicing those interview skills.

Or are you that mom who has successfully raised her child or children? They are all in school and now your opportunity has arrived to bring your shelved dream down, dust it off and walk to and through doors of opportunity presenting themselves.

The new graduate is fresh and up on all the latest interview techniques and skills. Her education is up to date and contemporary. However, the mom returning to the work force probably has a good deal of retraining to do. Her education may be dated so a refresher course may be in order, and today the interview process is nothing like it used to be. What once was based on experience and skills is now a process of almost seeming psychological evaluation. Interview questions are behavior based and delve into who you are, what are your assets, as well as your strengths and weaknesses. This line of questioning tries to determine what makes you stand out, yet how will you be a team player? How will you take your weaknesses and turn them into strengths?

Preparation for interviews has always been important, but in today's business/corporate world it is so much more so. Because there are so many people vying for so few jobs it is vital to learn what you need to know. Researching the company and knowing about the position is a necessary task to accomplish. Resumes have changed over the years as well, and what type to use needs to be decided. Again, researching resume types and what each requires may be a necessary process, as well as having a professional help you to prepare it.

In times past, when school budgets weren't cutting out all non-traditional classes, manners and etiquette were taught along with the three R's. Many young people today have never been exposed to etiquette classes, but it is important to know that there is a job interview etiquette that should be known and observed.

According to Lisa Gache, head of Beverly Hills Manners Inc., etiquette is important and "should be thought of as an inner GPS, a navigation system that guides us in the right direction and helps us to do the right thing".

Ms. Gache goes on to list common mistakes those entering the job force need to avoid. They include:

Showing up late: Punctuality is vital as the person doing the interview has set aside time to meet with you, and you have left the impression that you are someone who doesn't plan or may be chronically late for work.

Cell phone being left on: In today's society a cell phone is attached to a person morning to night. It is important to shut it off altogether before entering the office of the interviewer. You do not want the interviewer's concentration broken. Also, it pays deference to the interviewer and shows that this interview is important to you.

A limp handshake: This shows intimidation and that's not an impression you want to leave. But conversely, the grip shouldn't be so hard and tight that you cause pain. Etiquette requires you to wait for the interviewer to extend their hand first.

Being a "Chatty Cathy": Nervousness causes one to fill the silences. It is important to listen and ask thoughtful questions so research and preparation are necessary.

Don't slouch: Impressions are important and body language gives a lot away. Arms and legs should be kept uncrossed as it signals that you are on the defensive and uncomfortable. It sends a message that you would rather be anywhere than here. Hand gestures should be kept to a minimum and feet kept flat on the floor with your hands clasped in your lap.

Not smiling: It's important to smile – be happy! You may be getting the job. The job market is a cutthroat competition and even if feeling discouraged, put on your happy face and "fake it till you make it". A good attitude is important.

E-mail thank you notes: A hand written, snail mail thank you note is vital. A written note demonstrates professionalism. And you would be surprised how many applicants won't bother to send a written thank you note, so you will stand out. Also, this is another opportunity to restate your interest in the position. A written thank you leaves a strong and positive impression.[1]

So much learning and so much to do; so much energy and excitement! Then what – wait! As you know, you weren't the only one being interviewed and most times this process may take months before completed. It's sometimes during this waiting time that we begin to question ourselves. That faint, unrecognized voice of doubt begins to creep in and ask, "Did I look good enough?", "Did I answer the questions correctly?", "Did I project the confidence they were looking for?". And so many more that are a mild, subtle display of our hidden lack of confidence.

Why wouldn't we look at ourselves in the mirror and compliment ourselves on our wardrobe, hair and makeup? Why wouldn't we recall the question and answer time and believe in ourselves enough to wait confidently for that phone call?

Where does all this self-doubt and failure to believe in ourselves come from? It isn't something that just materialized out of thin air. From childhood on, all that we are and all that we believe of ourselves

1 http://www.dailyfinance.com/2010/05/14/job-injterview-etiquette-11-mistakes-to-avoid/

has been shaped from our childhood experiences and memories. These childhood experiences play an extremely large role in developing our self-esteem.

Self–esteem is what people think and feel about themselves. A person with good self – esteem doesn't let the normal ups and downs of life cause them to feel less about themselves. They feel good about themselves and take pride in their accomplishments. People with healthy self-esteem have the ability to look into themselves and accept who they are. They can acknowledge their strengths as well as their weaknesses and still recognize that they are people with worth and value.

However, a person with low self–esteem is drastically affected by the normal ups and downs of life. They do not have the ability to look into themselves, to acknowledge their strengths but only dwell on their weaknesses. Even the good moments are torn apart and shredded and the worst is always picked out. The person with a low self–esteem may feel they do not do anything well, nor do they feel they will be accepted or liked. They rely on how they are doing today to determine their self–worth. They are constantly plagued by negative thoughts and feelings, and need constant positive external reinforcement from friends and family. But these are only temporary fixes and have to be repeated over and over.

I recently read a quote by Marianne Williamson stating, *"Until we have met the monster in ourselves, we keep trying to slay them in the outer world. And we find that we cannot. For all darkness in the world stems from darkness in the heart. And it is there we must do the work."*[2]

2 Williamson, Marianne, Everyday Grace :Having Hope, Finding Forgiveness and Making Miracles, Riverhead Books,NY,NY 2002

Look at your strengths and weaknesses and in a positive way list a plan of action to make your weaknesses strengths. Not knowing our negative characteristics can create roadblocks to developing a positive self-image and increasing our self-confidence. Celebrate each accomplishment instead of devaluing yourself for the shortcomings.

Strengths	Weaknesses:	Action Plan:

Our first encounters that begin to develop our self-esteem are with our parents, siblings and extended family. Our experiences with all these people begin shaping our perceptions of ourselves. How we are treated by our parents begins the process and it extends from there. Being harshly criticized, teased, ridiculed or compared to others whom we are told are better than us, and the implications that we are never good enough causes our self-esteem to plummet even more. When causes us to never measure up to our parents' expectations, or are ridiculed by our teachers, coaches or peers we fall deeper into that pit. Messages of failed experiences are interpreted as a failure of one's whole self.

All these past experiences, even the ones we never seem to think about, impact us continually in our daily lives. That quiet inner voice is berating and degrading and taking over where the other living ones left off. It is a constant, harsh critic punishing mistakes and belittling accomplishments.

A child/person with a healthy self-esteem has experienced being paid attention to, listened to and treated with respect. They have received much affection, their accomplishments have been recognized and applauded, and their failures and mistakes have been accepted. They have the confidence and strength to receive instruction and correction from parents and those in authority. Their inner voice sends accepting and reassuring messages.

All of these messages have taken up residence over the years, and whether good or bad, they will impact each and every day through every experience. So, when you are out there searching for that job and the first or second, and even the third don't pan out, where are you on the self-esteem scale? Are you belittling yourself for being stupid or not good enough, or are you looking at this as a learning and growing experience?

It is important to begin to develop a positive mindset and a confident attitude because what you think, you become. You need to stop listening to that harsh, critical inner voice and begin identifying your worth and value. Forgiving yourself is as important as forgiving others when things don't go as you hoped they would. You must recognize that you are human and <u>ALL</u> humans make mistakes. The compassion you show to others should also be extended to you as a vital part of your restoration as well.

Emotions – both positive and negative – are normal to everyone.

They must be experienced but in a balanced way. It is unhealthy to sway into the depths of despair or to the heights of ecstasy and everything in between. Nurturing yourself, as you would a friend, is important at these times because you should be your very best friend, not your worst critic. We need to lighten up and loosen up. There is a Chinese proverb that states: *"Blessed are they that laugh at themselves, for they shall never cease to be entertained"*.

A great woman, Eleanor Roosevelt said, *"No one can make you feel inferior* without your *consent"*. We all have the power to change; none of us have to remain a captive or victim of our past. Even though we have made poor choices, have no role model or cheerleader, we are not disqualified from being a success. If you have no cheerleader – become your own. If you have no role model – research great and successful women and follow their patterns and values. We all have worth and value, and should never allow anyone to kill our dreams by telling us what we can't do!

It is important to believe in yourself and in what you see yourself doing and becoming.

Brigham Young stated, *"Why should we worry about what others think of us, do we have more confidence in their opinion than we do our own?"* That which you can imagine you can achieve, but the opposite is true as well. If you can't imagine your dream then you will probably not reach or achieve it. You must focus on what you can do, not on what you can't. Obstacles and setbacks are inevitable. Life isn't fair. We can't just wish to be successful; we must push those critical voices down, look at our strengths, take responsibility and move to action. Our motivation must come from within.

Another important fact that influences our life's journey is the relationships we make and keep. It's important to surround yourself with people who encourage, uplift and add value to you. These are people who will help restore and increase your self-esteem. After all, if you are a low self-esteem person you have had enough naysayers speaking over you, pulling you down and draining your energy. It is vital to realize the impact other people have on our lives. The relationships in our lives are positive or negative, they lift us up or drag us down, and they enhance or detract. Identifying these types is vital to our well-being and self-esteem. True friends and family love and encourage unconditionally, they believe in your dreams, give hope and comfort, laugh and cry with you, are truthful with you and always encourage.

These positive energy people are the ones who help you to believe in yourself and develop that self-confidence. Novelist Mark Twain said: *"Keep away from people who try to belittle your ambitions. Small people always do that, but the really great make you feel that you, too, can become great."*

I would like to leave you with a statement made by John Maxwell in his book **Talent Is Never Enough**: *"Life is too long to spend it with people who pull you in the wrong direction. And it's too short not to invest in others. Your relationships will define you. And they will influence your talent — one way or the other. Choose wisely."*[3]

---

3 Maxwell, John, Talent Is Never Enough, Thomas Nelson Publishers, Nashville, TN 2007

ABOUT THE AUTHOR

ALICE J. MAXIN

Alice J. Maxin is President and Founder of **The Write Turn**. Her focus is empowering individuals to express themselves, lead and succeed. She is a published author, an accomplished speaker, a renowned trainer/facilitator and a professional life coach as certified by the Coach Training Alliance (CTA) and the Professional Woman Network (PWN).

With a Master's Degree in Education, Alice enjoyed careers in both teaching and labor relations before forming her own company, **The Write Turn**. She now offers her writing expertise to those looking for the right person to write and express their ideas for them.

Alice's professional abilities include capturing the "write" words, effectiveness in facilitating groups, unique training and seminar development, creative problem solving, and assisting emerging leaders. She is also an experienced, certified trainer and coach with expertise in Emotional Intelligence (EI), leadership, assertiveness, communication, emotional wellness, women's issues, and organizational skills.

Her memberships include the *Professional Woman Network, National Association for Female Executives,* and the *Armstrong County Community Foundation's* philanthropic division, *Infinity.* She is an active member of the *Armstrong-Kiski Chapter of the Women's Business Network, Inc. of SW Pennsylvania* and a volunteer for *HAVIN* (Helping All Victims In Need). Alice also enjoys being a support group leader for the *Pittsburgh North Chapter of the Restless Legs Syndrome Foundation.*

She received recognition for her professional success in Who's Who among American Teachers, Who's Who in American Education, and Who's Who of American Women.

Alice is writing her second introspective book to be published by *Professional Woman Network.*

Books: Co-authored
> **Woman's Journey to Wellness: Mind, Body, and Spirit**
> **Beyond the Body: Developing Inner Beauty**
> **The Baby Boomer's Handbook**
> **The Young Professional Woman: Breaking into the Business World and Succeeding**
> Book: Independently Authored/Privately Published
> **R.S.V.P. ~ An Invitation to Take Control of Your Life**

Contact:
Company: **The Write Turn**
143 Sportsman Road
Leechburg, PA 15656
Telephone: 724-295-4117
Email: ajmaxin@gmail.com
Website: www.alicemaxin.com
Blog: http://ajmaxin@wordpress.com

EIGHTEEN

"HOW CAN I HELP YOU?"

Alice J. Maxin

"No matter how busy you are, you must take time to make the other person feel important."
—Mary Kay Ash, founder Mary Kay Cosmetics, Inc.

You pause in your footsteps and overhear the following "Take turns." "Remember to share." "Be nice to each other." "No tattle-tales." "Cover your cough."

Where do you think you are? _____

Yes, you are outside of a kindergarten classroom!

Kindergarten introduces students to one of the first daily social communities in a child's life beyond her family and after day care or nursery school. The teacher emphasizes acceptable behaviors in parent-teacher conferences and they appear in written reports under "social skills".

"Social skills" is the ability to communicate effectively and to form positive relationships with others in social settings and work group activities.

What do you picture when you hear or read the term "social skills" as it relates to your business or your job? _____

_____

Social Skills, not Social Butterfly

In today's work environment, it is not enough to know your product, to have an MBA, or to be technologically brilliant – you must demonstrate the soft skills (relating to people as opposed to technical skills) necessary to succeed. It matters not whether you work for a huge corporation or start your own company. The key to managing your success lies in how you relate to others.

Robert Fulghum's book <u>All I Really Need to Know I Learned in Kindergarten</u> (© 1986) encourages the reader to share, play fair, apologize when you hurt someone and hold hands when crossing the street. In other words, we are social beings who do not live in a vacuum. To succeed in any business (or in life in general), you must possess the ability to get along with others. For those who worry that they are not proficient in this area, there are training seminars to develop and maintain acceptable social behaviors.

The employee or entrepreneur who makes others her priority; recognizes others' achievements and worth; understands differing points of view; and resolves rather than resents conflicts around her is the one who will succeed. Success, in its most profound, meaningful sense, is a personal matter – measured by the achiever's own standards and societal norms.

On the other hand, a social butterfly flits from one group to another, one conversation to another, or one project to another. She never gives anyone or anything her full attention. Tasks go unfinished while she flutters around ignoring the importance of her role in teamwork and not getting back to her clients in a timely way. Because she is overtly social, she needs to hone the scope and effectiveness of her interactions.

"I am" VS "You are"

What forms a first impression when you are introduced to a businessperson? It may not be the color of her hair, her outfit, or her knowledge. It most likely is the feeling you get when she first greets you.

Describe how you might feel when you are approached in a business setting in each of the following manners. The words you hear may be different, but the message is the same.

1. "Here I am. We can get started now." _____

   _____

   _____

2. "There you are. What can I do for you?"_____

   _____

   _____

The first approach is self-centered; the second is client-centered.

Self-indulgent or Others-oriented?

Take the following quiz to get a better picture of your business relationships. Answer each statement with a true or false response as it relates to you. If you have not experienced the exact circumstance, imagine how you would answer and mark it accordingly.

1. _____ Being punctual, not making trouble, and getting work done on time is enough to get a raise or promotion.

2. _____ I make sure the customer is welcomed and comfortable in my work area.

3. _____I always take incoming calls even if I am on the other line or with a client. It may be something more urgent that the current task.

4. _____ I do <u>not</u> multi-task when I am on the phone with a client. I give the caller my full attention.

5. _____ When I am having a bad day, everyone should take care not to upset me.

6. _____I leave my home problems at home, so I can concentrate on work issues at work.

7. _____ Saying to a client "I don't know" is not acceptable. It is admitting that I am not the perfect representative I want her to perceive me to be.

8. _____ If I do not know the answer to a client's question, it is okay to admit it and assure her that I will find it out and get back to her in a timely manner.

9. _____ Playing fair in business will not get me ahead. It's a cutthroat world out there.

10. _____ I am aware that what the client or the boss thinks of me personally may affect how she thinks of my work/my company.

If you responded <u>true to the even-numbered</u> items, you are others-oriented and put them before your own personal needs – a necessary skill to succeed.

If you answered <u>true to the odd-numbered</u> statements, you need a refresher course in how to get along. You are putting yourself, your needs, and your ego ahead of others. You may be self-centered and missing a vital step needed to climb the success ladder.

If you have <u>mixed responses to the even-numbered</u> items, look them over again and write down what you were thinking when you responded. How strongly do you feel about them? What, if anything, would change your mind? _____

_____

_____

_____

A Look in the Mirror

One personality style is no better than another. It is just different. You may not understand what makes your client or coworker tick. The important thing is to understand your own personality.

Consider the following characteristics. Place a mark in front of the ones that you would identify as part of what makes YOU tick.

_____ Patient   _____ Thrifty   _____ Troubled
_____ Understanding   _____ Caring   _____ Loyal
_____ Hurried   _____ Thoughtful   _____ Pessimistic
_____ Disorganized   _____ Good listener   _____ Great talker
_____ Frightened   _____ Goal-oriented   _____ People-oriented
_____ Punctual   _____ Impatient

Once you understand what makes you the person you are, you will be better able to relate to others. For example - if you are hurried and impatient, you need to make allowances for the slow, methodical worker on your team. For the entrepreneur, being a good listener as opposed to a great talker will benefit you in the long run.

What Would You Do or Say?

Read each of the scenarios below; then answer the questions that follow.

1. A potential new client phones you demanding to know how your product will make her life easier when her spouse does not help, the kids are trying her nerves, and the rent is overdue.

2. You are trying to get your work done so you can get to your next appointment on time when Tina Talker steps into your office, closes the door, and sits down to share the latest gossip.

3. After graduating from the university and armed with your degree, you arrive at your interview with the HR director of

a prestigious corporation. She seems more concerned about the last employee who was let go than about your hiring. She keeps emphasizing "interpersonal skills" and shaking her head.

What do all three of the above scenarios have in common? Or are they all different from each other?

> If you responded that they are all different, you are correct.

> If you said they all have something in common, you are correct also!

The Differences

Each scenario presents a different dilemma complete with its own set of circumstances.

The first one is over the phone involving a product.

The second is in an office with a co-worker.

The third is about a new graduate - not even hired yet.

Commonalities

Think back on the responses if you said they all have something in common. What did you have in mind? If you said any of the following, you are right on target.

• Communication

• Difficult people

- Problem-oriented

- Involving you and another person

- Different focuses

Read the scenarios again – this time read them aloud as though you are relating your situation to someone else. Substitute the words "I, me or my" for "you and your" where appropriate.

How would each of the situations make you feel? What would you do to handle each situation?

_____

_____

_____

The woman who understands her own personality and how she relates to people will usually be able to recognize what the other person wants or needs <u>at that point in time</u>. Below are possible responses to the three situations.

1. The caller needs to vent. You cannot resolve her home issues. Listen attentively. When she is finished speaking, ask her what she would like your product to realistically do for her. Find a common thread, if there is one with your product, and follow it. If none is possible, thank her for contacting you and politely end the call.

2. Understanding that Tina Talker loves to socialize, invite her to join you for a cup of tea or coffee in the employee

lounge before you start your day tomorrow. This will give you the opportunity to get your work done now, leave for your appointment on time, and still meet Tina's need to talk. (Beware of engaging in office gossip. Stick to neutral subjects or excuse yourself from the conversation.)

3. When the HR director finishes, politely ask her to explain to you the nature of "interpersonal skills" as they relate to the job you are seeking. This shows your interest in what she was saying and legitimizes her complaint – which is her need at that moment.

What other responses could you envision based on your own personality and the situations?

———————————————————————————————

———————————————————————————————

Remember that your focus is to satisfy the other person's need at that particular time – if it is in your power to do so.

Satisfying all of the people

Abraham Lincoln, 16th U.S. President, was quoted as saying

"You can fool all the people some of the time, and some of the people all the time, but you cannot fool all the people all the time."

From that saying comes the now-familiar

"You can please all the people some of the time, and some of the people all the time, but you cannot please all the people all the time."

Keeping this in mind will save you a lot of soul-searching when you encounter a difficult client or boss.

How to Lose a Client/Job

Many jobs or clients are lost due to a lack of quality interpersonal skills. It is irrelevant if they are known as soft skills, personal skills, social skills, or people skills – what matters is how you relate to others.

When asked the reasons for their dissatisfaction, unhappy customers/bosses commonly list the following attitudes:

- Negativity

- Self-centeredness

- Laziness

- Not a team player

- Know-it-all

- Self-<u>un</u>awareness

- Judgmental

Perhaps you know of someone who demonstrates one or more of these characteristics. Write about how their attitude affected you/your job.

How to Keep a Client/Job

As important as it is to stay clear of the attitudes listed in the previous section, you also need to emphasize your strong points.

Place a mark beside the interpersonal skills you already have. They are listed in no particular order.

- _____ Communicates well with both spoken and written messages

- _____ Listens attentively, without interrupting

- _____ Considerate of others' feelings

- _____ Positive approach to work and co-workers

- _____ Understands own personality

- _____ Makes allowances for others' shortfalls

- _____ Treats everyone with dignity and respect

- _____ Aware of others' right to disagree/have differing points of view

- _____ Demonstrates humbleness

- _____ Respects another's privacy

Recognizing your own strong points and being aware of negative traits is one of the first steps in landing a job and keeping

it or building a business that clients will be eager to recommend. It is up to you to define your success!

Points to Ponder from the Chapter

A. Lessons about sharing, taking turns, and being kind to others learned in kindergarten will serve you well throughout your career and life in general.

B. Being client-oriented (or others-oriented) indicates that you recognize the client's needs ahead of or in relation to your own.

C. Knowing yourself and what makes you "tick", helps you relate well and appropriately with others.

D. Refined people skills are necessary to succeed in the business world.

Suggested Readings

How to Work with People by Rockhurst University Continuing Education Center, Inc.

The Art of Communicating by Bert Decker

The Communication Coach by Sandie Akerman

The Seven Habits of Highly Effective People by Stephen Covey

Dedication to My Son, Stephen

As I watch you teaching your daughter good manners, kindness, charity, and compassion very early in her life, my heart is warmed. Learning what it takes to be valued and respected and to do the same for others is a life-long skill that will serve her well. Your own brand of charm and interpersonal skills are carrying you now to the pinnacle of success in your chosen field and surrounding you with love from family and friends. May you always recognize the wisdom of knowing the difference you make in our lives just by being you.

ABOUT THE AUTHOR

LYNN ANDERSON

Lynn Anderson is committed to helping busy professional woman align their passions to their life purpose creating their life of abundance. As a Certified Professional Coach, Public Speaker, Radio Show Host, Author, and recognized Executive Leader, she is passionate about helping woman take positive control of their life giving them the power to make conscious choices. As a result, Lynn is creating a powerful momentum of change impacting the lives of millions of working woman warriors worldwide.

Lynn's the author of "Be A Woman Warrior: Twelve Tips & Sips for Unleashing the Power Within You" (Feb 2011) and contributing author to the books, "Madam CEO: How to Think and Act Like a Chief Executive" (Dec 2011) and "Leaders in Pearls: How to Be a Change Architect!" (Apr 2012). She hosts a weekly radio show, The Women Warriors, Wed at noon ET on www.blogtalkradio.com/womenarriors. She provides career and leadership coaching through the following organizations: The Metis Movement (www.metismovement.com), LeadershipGold4Women (www.leadershipgold4women.com), With Gratitude & Grace (www.withgratitudeandgrace.com), and Executive Career Hub (http://www.solutions5consulting.com/).

She has over 25 years in military, government, corporate, consulting and entrepreneur experience including working at Southern Company Services, Ernst & Young, and Capgemini. Lynn owns her own coaching/consulting business, Coaching4Abundance (www.coaching4abundance.com). She lives in Atlanta with her supportive husband, three amazing children, fantastic son-in-law, and energetic granddaughter. You can find Lynn on the tennis courts most weekends and also at her son's baseball games or reading a book.

Connect with Lynn on Facebook (https://www.facebook.com/lynn.anderson84), Linkedin (http://ww.linkedin.com/in/lyanderson), and Twitter (http://twitter.com/#!/lyanders84).

NINETEEN

HOW TO SPEAK UP AND BE HEARD

Lynn Anderson

"The most courageous act is still to think for yourself. Aloud."
—Coco Chanel

The delicate balance between speaking up and being heard or sounding like you are complaining has plagued women professionals for many years. You talk too loud and you are labeled as aggressive or even worse. You talk too softly and you are submissive, shy and not in charge. So, what is the delicate balance that allows you to be heard but also provides you the courage to speak up in the first place?

What you need to learn is to convey your credibility, command greater respect, and become a more influential business professional to develop your empowerment as a woman. This chapter will help you to show that credibility, get the respect you deserve, and be the best leader you can be. With each step, we will examine key insights and exercises you can do to help you learn how to effectively speak up and be heard on your terms. After completing this chapter you will feel confident in your ability to speak up and have the courage to not hold back. You will learn the balance of approaching the discussion with a win-win attitude that will gain you respect and the results you want rather than create confrontation, frustration, labeling, or lack of participation.

Emotional Baggage

Before we look at when and how to speak up, we need to understand the internal feelings we have that are getting in our way to speak up and be heard, our emotional baggage if you will. The heavier the baggage is the more difficult it may be for you to speak up and be heard. You might find it more comforting to just stay silent or run away. That's certainly not what leaders do. Leaders show poise and wisdom that allow them to take risks but reap rewards.

To release your emotional baggage, you first have to identify what that baggage is. Complete the exercise below to help you identify what baggage you are carrying.

Activity

1. What anxieties do you have when speaking up? (e.g. I'm afraid no one will listen. I'm afraid I will look like a fool. I

was told to be seen and not heard as a child. I am afraid they won't understand me, etc.)

_____

_____

_____

2. Where does this fear come from? (e.g. your childhood, what others have told you, a specific incident that occurred in your past, etc.)

_____

_____

_____

As a woman, you face a unique set of communication challenges. Maybe you fear conflict and have trouble confronting others or addressing them with constructive criticism. Perhaps your emotions always seem to get in the way when you're speaking with others on sensitive subjects. Maybe you find yourself feeling self-conscious expressing your thoughts and ideas or have trouble taking the floor and getting the respect you deserve. Whatever your communication challenges ... this chapter will help you and the first step is to be true to yourself and identify your specific baggage and challenges first.

When to Speak Up

Before you speak up, you need to determine if it's the appropriate time, place and issue to speak up about. You want to appear thoughtful, confident and in control of the topic and not just re-iterate what others are saying. Take time to analyze the situation first before just speaking. Ask yourself these questions. Are you prepared to talk about this topic? Is it a good time to discuss the topic? Is this something I should speak up about right now? Am I calm, cool and collected so I can talk intelligently about the topic and not let emotions get the better of me? Once you answer these questions you can move ahead and speak up.

Activity

Ask Yourself These Questions:

1. What is the real issue that I want to discuss (be as concise as possible)? Less is more in this instance. As a confident leader you want to appear in control and confident that an issue needs resolution. You want to capture everyone's attention with a clear, concise statement. Don't be wordy. Women tend to ramble. Don't.

    _____

    _____

2. What is the significance of having this discussion? Look at specific values, numbers, timing, etc. State the facts and values as succinctly as possible.

_____

_____

3. What's my ideal outcome?

    _____

    _____

4. What help do I need if any?

    _____

    _____

5. Invite a response (open door). What can I say to "open the door" to a conversation? Ask someone what they think about the topic. Get others input. Seek out ideas and support.

    _____

    _____

Standing Your Ground

When you are ready to speak up about a particular topic and you answered the questions from the previous section effectively, you want to be able to stand your ground, know your limits, and correct any problem patterns as quickly as possible.

When you set limits, you are creating boundaries of how far you are willing to go with the topic or individuals before taking another approach or tactic. Sometimes, while you may be prepared to discuss a topic and be right on target with your assessment, others may not be so ready. They may be feeling they have been taken off guard and not comfortable with the situation. If you assess that this is the case, you want to be prepared to take the discussion off-line, ask to discuss in more detail at a later date, and look for another approach to deal with the situation. Ideally, you want to be on the same emotional playing field as your opponent. You want to look for a "win-win" situation where you get your ideal outcome but the other person doesn't feel as if they are being taken advantage of or stepped on. You want to be on common ground.

If there are outbursts from others or the discussion appears to be getting out of hand, you want to take these "problem patterns" off-line and approach the discussion from a different perspective. You certainly want to hold your beliefs and point of view but you also want to respect the thoughts, feelings, and actions of others. If someone else is trying to get you off target and out of balance, appealing to your emotional state, again, you want to take a time out and look to discuss the topic in more detail at a future date. That doesn't mean you back down from your position, but rather you look at ways to take emotionally heated situations out of the picture. There are no right or wrong answers, just different perspectives. If this becomes unclear, look at stopping that behavior and addressing the topic at a later date.

Regardless of the outcome, you want to be fair and yet not back down from your statement or discussion. You can certainly look at the situation from multiple perspectives and also see the "other side" of the discussion. However, you don't want to appear "wishy washy" about things either. You want to be respectful, willing to listen, and willing to change your point of view based on discussion but not be pushed into an agreement. The key thing to remember is that everyone deserves their point of view, there are no "right or wrong" answers, and ultimately you want to get the best solution as a whole for the organization. That isn't backing down. Understanding, unfolding, and discussing are all a part of this process. However, running away from the discussion should not be a desired outcome.

Picking and Planning Your Battles

One of the best things you can do to help you to speak up and be heard is to consciously choose to engage in the conversation. When you tell yourself that this topic is worth my input and the topic deserves a discussion you know that it is the right time to speak up. Don't just speak up for speaking up's sake. Know deep down in your heart that the topic being discussed is worth saying something more.

Ask yourself these questions to help you choose the right time and right way to speak up:

- Is a discussion needed for an open, honest conversation?

- What do I need to do to establish a relationship for a "win-win" outcome?

- How can I be direct about this issue, yet respectful of other's opinions?

- Can I be respectful of other's opinions?

Remember, this isn't the time for game playing or aggressiveness. You don't really want to prepare for battle, but be prepared for an honest and open discussion. You want to have total respect for other's opinions, even if you disagree with them. Otherwise, you need to be prepared to walk away and engage in the conversation at another time when you are in control of your emotions. Realize you are on a level playing field (and if you don't feel that way you are not ready to engage). Don't be intimidated by power-plays, wealth, higher socio-economic status or cultural differences. If you are, step back and consider if you really can be objective with the conversation or whether you have to wait for another time to be able to make progress.

Basically what you are doing is learning how to be assertive, yet not too passive or aggressive in the process. You respect others yet hold firm to your convictions with poise and levity. You are able to not put blame on others for having different points of view, express your opinions matter-of-factly and can speak confidently on the subject.

If you are being aggressive, you will have an air of superiority, are critical of others, push your position as the only position, and tend to bully others including ridiculing and talking down to them. If you are too passive, you will skirt around the issue, create win-lose situations, become a victim, not want to rock the boat, and have difficulty defending yourself. Again, you want a happy medium between the two.

Activity

Next time you are having a discussion write down whether you felt you were being aggressive, passive, or assertive.   Maybe you were being all three at various times during the conversation.

I was

_____

_____

If you were not being assertive, list the reasons you felt you were not being assertive:

_____

To allow yourself to learn how to be more assertive and engage in effective communications, you need to create exercises that allow you to clean out the negative thoughts or thoughts that hold you down. This is called "Mental Housekeeping." Recognizing these situations is the first step. Another helpful step is to have a "pep talk" with yourself by using positive affirmations. We find that many women have had their minds "programmed" a certain way since childhood and this negative "self-talk" generally creates your behaviors well into adulthood.

If you hear yourself say inside your mind statements such as the ones shown below, you are allowing your negative self-talk to get the best of you!

"I'm just not good enough."

"I should be seen but not heard."

"I could never talk about that."

"Who am I to dispute these facts."

In order to unlearn these negative old habits, you need to reprogram your mind so that new behaviors or new self-talk become positive and allow you the courage to speak up and be heard.

For instance the statements above become:

"I am good enough to say something about this."

"I am confident I should speak up on this topic."

"I can talk about this and need to."

"I am confident my point of view needs to be heard."

Activity

List out your negative self-talk and then create a positive affirmation to overcome it.   Take your positive affirmations and every night before you go to bed say them over the next 21 days.   Remember if you do something for more than 21 days it becomes a habit. So kick your negative self-talk habit and create a positive one to help you be confident and stand up for what you believe in.

Negative Self- Talk
Positive Affirmation

Now that you have prepared to speak up and be heard realizing it's the proper place, time, and you are mentally prepared, you want to be able to sound confident and assured when you speak up.

How to Project Confidence When You Speak Up

I've learned these three quick tips to developing a stronger, more powerful speaking voice when I was in the military and they work! Practice them, and I'm sure they will work for you too.

1. Posture.   Stand proud with your shoulders back and down. Not only will this command respect, but it will also help you feel stronger and open your passageway (and diaphragm) for better projection.   Speaking is both a physical as well as mental skill. To have a stronger sound, your whole body needs to act as a resonant sound chamber.

Activity

Say "Hmmmmmm" aloud and feel the front of your face vibrate. Keep that vibration going and add a complete sentence after it: "Hmmmmm. I enjoy speaking to such a large group—particularly when they are so complimentary!" Can you feel the sound in the front of your face? This is called mask resonance. To keep this strong sound coming, you'll need to stay aware of what it feels like and practice. Stand up straight and tall, place your weight comfortably on both feet, and create a strong resonance chamber for your voice.   Practice another sentence and keep practicing until it is second nature for you!

2. Passageway.   Shallow breathing results in a weak voice. This is why someone who is hunched over, sitting at a desk, sounds tired, timid, or distracted.   The air flow to their lungs is limited because of their slumped posture. You don't want that! You want the air passageway to be open (hence why the shoulders are back and down to open your chest). I was able to project my speech and announce evening meal down a long and noisy hallway when I was a first year cadet at the Air Force Academy just by practicing this technique. Image being slumped over and talking downward. I would

have been the evening meal if I'd followed that principal. The same is true at a meeting or event. If you aren't allowing your passageway to get air flow, you will cut off your voice circulation. The air behind your voice gives it a rich, full sound. Hence why it's so important to have great posture to enable proper breathing.

3. Passion. Finally, when you have passion, you have energy. That intensity or energy allows you to show excitement about the subject you are talking about. This excitement produces a different cadence in your voice, animation in your face, gestures to emphasize your points, and movement that demonstrates overall excitement about sharing what you know with the people around you. Tap into your passion on the subject at hand to help you project the confidence and excitement you possess. Automatically, that passion will create a full, strong sound in your voice and people will want to listen to you.

Activity

Find a topic you are passionate about. Use the 3 principals just discussed to help you create a powerful speaking voice to discuss the topic.

1. Topic chosen: _____

_____

2. Testing your posture, passageway, and passion, write out what you want to say about the topic: _____

_____

_____

_____

3. Test your discussion out using a friend or co-worker. How does it feel and what is their response? _____

_____

_____

_____

Are You Really Being Heard?

Now, that you are projecting your message with confidence, you must find out if the message is being heard effectively. Verify that what you have said is coming across to your audience. Here are some tips to help you do just that. It's time to "stand up" and take credit for your contributions. This means being more assertive and possibly even unlearning some of the things your mother taught you in good faith. Don't be shy, be in control. Practice these tips to get more comfortable with them.

- **Don't be afraid to kick up your volume** a notch or two in a meeting, especially when people are speaking simultaneously or another starts the second someone has finished.

- **Lower your pitch**. While society equates authority with a lower pitch, most women are born with a higher-pitched voice. You can practice lowering it whenever you are alone. A good tip before answering the phone is to say, "low, low" and then "hello" into the receiver. It avoids that higher-pitched "hi" or "hello" that often happens when it is the first word said. Your first words leave a lasting impression.

- **Vary your tone**. Add interest by emphasizing different words to get your meaning across. One of my favorite exercises when teaching presentation skills involves giving the same sentence different meanings simply by emphasizing different words. This also is an important skill if you spend a lot of time on conference calls, where body language is absent.

- **Similarly, watch your inflection**, which involves varying your pitch to achieve your purpose. It's often common to raise your pitch on the last word when you are asking a question. "Are you going *home*?" Keep your pitch the same or lower it when asking questions. Pitches that are higher than normal indicate nervousness or fear. That's not what you want to convey in a meeting. Someone may take advantage of you and try to push you into a corner if you seem nervous. I had this problem at the start of my career and still struggle today. You want to sound confident, in control, and not questioning what is going on. Ask someone you trust to help you identify your pitch changes if necessary or record the meetings and see how you sound.

- **Keep your rate at an even keel**. Speaking too quickly also can indicate nervousness and make it more difficult for others to follow your logic. Speaking too slowly might suggest a lack of knowledge or concern about being inaccurate, and it is guaranteed to make "type A" personalities want to finish your sentences. So again, be conscious of what you are saying, how quickly and the inflictions you are using.

- **Get used to interrupting and interruptions.** As women, you may have been taught that it is impolite to interrupt and wait until someone is finished speaking. While that's generally true, it is not always the way the business world works. Choose your situations wisely. If two of you start speaking simultaneously, crank up the volume and keep speaking. Men usually think they will get the stage because they speak louder.

Activity

Take a voice recorder into your next meeting. Record the conversation and listen to your responses, discussions, and tone of voice. What do you hear? _____

_____

_____

Now, based on the tips above, what steps can you take to improve your ability to be heard the next time? _____

_____

_____

Practice this technique several times and soon you won't need the recorder to help you see what you need to do.

Lessons Learned on Building Confidence and Rapport

Many times when I was one of the only females in a room filled with men, I did find it hard to speak up and at times when I did speak up, my suggestions fell on deaf ears. Also, how many times did someone tell me to "Speak up. I can't hear you!" Was it me or the way I approached the situation?

The answer was a little bit of both! As women, sometimes we find it difficult to speak up when others in the room have louder voices and seem more confident. We doubt our beliefs or point of view and appear timid in our approach. We also might feel that we aren't being listened to or that on a particular subject we might get caught up emotionally in the topic. What can we do and what were some of the tips I learned to be bolder and to speak up to be heard? I'd like to share these lessons learned with you. Hopefully they might help you to be more confident, speak up, and be heard!

1. **Practice makes perfect.** As the saying goes, the more times you try something no matter how difficult, the easier it becomes. Taking a risk is really challenging the first time (and speaking up in a room filled with out spoken men can be intimidating) but the more you do speak up and work on techniques to be heard, the easier it gets. My confidence did grow as I become more comfortable voicing my opinions. Also, when I brought my passion to the topic, I found I had more energy and more volume to discuss the topic.

The more timid you present a suggestion; the less confident others feel about the proposed solution.

2. **Calm, Cool and Collected.** As the saying goes, "Just the facts Jack." Learn to instill a quiet confidence in your point of view. Have confidence in your convictions but don't get so tied to them that they become you. If you go on & on & on … your message is lost. There is no right or wrong idea. Everyone is entitled to their own point of view. So try not to take things personally. Now, that is much easier said than done, but when you do feel frustrated or your emotions start coming into play, step back, take a deep breath and tell yourself that this is just an idea you are sharing. It's generally not life or death (though when I was in the Air Force there was a few of those situations!). Even in those more critical situations, being calm, cool and collected can really pay off.

3. **Separate.** As I said in #2, your idea is your point of view but is not what you are all about. So remember that the discussion is not all about who you are. Sure the ideas come from your vantage point and from another vantage point there might be some great ideas to share. So, learn to keep the idea separate from you. Be prepared to learn from others and hear about new possibilities that maybe you didn't even think about.

4. **Less is more.** I think sometimes as women we want to explain things to our detriment. At times this is where the emotions come into play. We tend to be more emotional. By stating an idea, linking it to the value it potentially brings,

and closing, you present your position in a strong, confident manner. Also, if you feel you aren't being heard, be direct and say so. Hit the problem head on. Don't grumble about it afterward. Put your idea forward and let the process unfold.

5. **Respect.** At all times you want to show respect for everyone's point of view. Go the higher road whether people are paying attention or not, and listen to what each person is saying. Don't rush right in to defend your position or talk over others to push your idea. By really actively listening, you might also come up with an even better idea than you started with based on a new possibility that someone else spoke about. Therefore, don't get ahead of yourself and just focus on your proposed solution. Show each person the respect you would want for yourself.

6. **Move on.** Sometimes you will be faced with people who just don't listen or want to hear what you have to say. Finc. Go ahead and state your idea, position, or thoughts. Do your part. You can't make everyone else do theirs. Set a good example for others to follow. You might not think you are making an impact but if you keep following these tips, I have found out that in the long run you will be heard and respected. Respect yourself and know you gave it your best shot. Don't run and hide. Do speak up. Control what you can control.

7. **Build Rapport.** I know it's hard to present ideas when you are not comfortable with or have a rapport with those you are in discussions with. I was at a conference this past

weekend and while the women there were wonderful, it was intimidating at the start of the conference to speak up and be heard. But, as the conference went along and I got to know the women, it became easier. So, get to know the individuals around you and establish that rapport. Find out what they care about and what their passions are. You will get more comfortable with being able to present your ideas and others will be more open to them when you take the time and make the effort to establish a connection.

8. **Ask Questions.** Sometimes just by asking the right questions, you get others in the room aligned with your ideas or point of view. So ask yourself, "What questions should I be asking to get others involved in supporting my idea or that I need to know to help resolve the situation?" Thoughtful questions can really establish credibility and a willingness to understand, to be open to new ideas, and to be more engaged. This shows concern for the topic and not just for your solution.

Activity

Take 1 or 2 of the lessons learned above and apply them to your next business meeting.

What specific lessons (list #) are you going to use in your next meeting?_____

How did the use of these lessons change the outcome of the meeting or change the way you approached the meeting (if any)?____

_____

How do you feel about using these tips to get results? _____

_____

What might you try differently in your next meeting? _____

_____

_____

In Closing

Many times as women, our fears and history cause us to recoil and shy from the spotlight. We didn't learn how to project our voice, how to build up our confidence, and were told to be seen not heard. So, when we enter the business world, we are already behind the eight ball in this arena. We struggle with the right balance between being ourselves, being labeled as aggressive, and yet being heard effectively.

This chapter covered some specific steps you can take to identify your fears, build your voice strength, uplift your inner voice, and create an environment where you will be heard. Learning to do so effectively will allow you to be a leader in your life as well as your career.

I'm sure you have some great tips as well on "being heard." Feel free to share them with me and help mentor up. Become a leader and be a confident woman warrior! I know you have it in you, so speak up and be heard. I am listening.

ABOUT THE AUTHOR

JURACY JOHNSON

Juracy Johnson is a Best-Selling Author, an expert in self-growth and a Life and Career Coach.

A National and International Workshop Leader from Mexico with an M Sc in Seismology and a passion for life and self-discovery, Juracy is the author of more than one hundred scientific and self-help articles. She is also a co-author with Deepak Chopra, Marshall Goldsmith and many other self-growth experts.

As a cancer survivor since 1993, Juracy made a choice: She absolutely refused to be a victim. She loves life and is grateful for the support she received from her husband, her family, and her friends during that difficult time. Juracy loves people, and helping them reach their dreams is one of her goals.

Currently, Juracy works as a Life and Career Coach, and is also working as a Math Professor at the Engineering Faculty of the State's University in Ensenada in Baja California. She is also a caregiver to her husband who sustained a traumatic brain injury in 1999. She Coaches and offers Workshops in all Mexico and Latin America. She also participates in conferences regarding Natural Hazards all over the world and she has co-authored many books in that subject. She is the founder of Liderato Femenino (Feminine Leadership).

"I have been offering workshops and coaching services since 2003. I have a passion for helping people overcome their challenges and guiding them into having a joyful life"

Contact:
You can visit my site at: www.juracyjohnson.com
Facebook: https://www.facebook.com/JuracySoaresJohnson
Email: contacto@juracyjohnson.com

TWENTY

FEMININITY: YOUR POWER BEYOND BELIEF!

Juracy Johnson

Many of us are not aware that our femininity is more than a tool, it is an inner power by nature, that enables us to achieve our success. We seem to have accepted the idea that if a woman is feminine, she is weak or less intelligent than a man, but that is far from the truth. We do not need to act like a man to succeed in our profession. Know that it is no longer a man's world, instead it is a world of opportunities for all. Feminine power is in all of you! It is softness, compassion, intuition and openness which is not opposed to capacity, intellect and ability. Perhaps you haven't thought about this, or haven't allowed yourself to believe it or integrate it into your professional life.

So, in order to make the most of your feminine power and enjoy it while you do,   as a young professional woman entering the career world, the first step toward your realization is to have PERSONAL AWARENESS, that is, to understand who you are and the image you project, having no difficulties at all in modifying whatever is necessary to achieve your wants and needs.

After you understand who you are and what your emotional patterns are, you will be able to lead yourself and make profound leadership connections with others, influencing your team and the organization where you work in a positive way. Are you ready to take this Journey? Then let's begin!

To start this process, define and describe what you want:

I WANT:
DESCRIBE IT IN DETAIL:

HOW DO I SEE MYSELF? Build a list of every attribute you see in yourself, good and not so good in every aspect of your life that you can think of. Write everything that comes to mind, no matter what order it is in (character, clothing, relationships, etc.), just write! Stop and take 10 to 15 minutes to do this. This is very important before you continue with this chapter.

HOW DO I SEE MYSELF?

After you finish, notice the first 5 statements you wrote. How many good and how many not-so-good traits do you see in those 5? This could show if you tend to see yourself more often in a positive or in a negative way. Be aware of this. If you see yourself more in a negative way, you must learn to love yourself more (hire a Coach, participate in a Loving Yourself Workshop, etc.). Loving yourself is the first step for Success! Remember that Real Power is about your presence... it is the energy of knowing that you are who you are. So please, appreciate and love yourself RIGHT NOW, just the way you are. You will find that you don't need to change your essence, you just need to change the patterns that are stopping you to live and love yourself fully!

HOW OTHER PEOPLE SEE ME: Ask people who have known you as a classmate or as co-workers -if you worked while you studied-, what are your best attributes and what are the areas where you could develop. Accept objectively what they say as an opportunity to see yourself through the eyes of others without justifying or criticizing yourself, or loving yourself less because of what they say. Just say thank you and make a list as follows:

POSITIVE ATTRIBUTES	AREAS OF OPPORTUNITY FOR GROWTH

Check if some of them appear more than once. Keep in mind this exercise is just to notice what potential clients could see in you. Don't be too harsh on yourself; maybe you were not showing all of your potential at the time, maybe you thought it wasn't necessary, or maybe they haven't seen you in a while and don't know that you have changed. Analyze and answer the following questions: a) What aspects of my personality do I need to modify? b) What qualities can I make the most of? c) What attributes do I want to bring out so I can be successful at my job? When you do this exercise remember YOU are your Best Friend. YOU are doing this because you want to succeed. Just a few people have the courage to do this in an objective way, so please avoid negative thoughts like "I am not good enough" or "I am not smart enough". You want to redirect your energy to the path of achievement, prosperity and victory.

FEMENINE TRAITS THAT CAN HELP YOU IN YOUR JOB: In addition to softness, compassion, intuition and openness, other feminine characteristics are gentleness, sensitivity, empathy, listening and caring. These qualities give you a distinctive power for inspiring the organization where you work, for <u>*constructively*</u> but not aggressively confronting others when necessary, and for understanding their needs, as women leaders do not avoid emotions, they recognize them in others as well, see them as important sources of information and use them to empower their leadership. Also, remember that acting childish has nothing to do with femininity, instead it has to do with immaturity, so avoid tantrums, giggling or using a childish voice to ask for something. When someone at the office is having a tantrum, your best response is no response at all. Stay quiet or politely excuse yourself and leave if this angry outburst is taking too long.

It is also important to take a look at your VALUES and BELIFES. Values are the ideals about how things ought to be. They serve as the basis for conducting one's life. Mostly they were learned and influenced in our early years by observing and listening to what others with authority (parents, siblings, teachers, etc.) told us or showed us. As you get older your values can be aligned with your friends and role models you associate with. Beliefs are generalizations or assumptions we make about ourselves and the world around us. It is the way we "see things". Are those values and beliefs serving you or are they limiting your progress? Do you think being feminine will stop you from achieving success? The good thing about values and beliefs is that you can always change them!

What are your most powerful values and beliefs you have about being and behaving feminine in the workplace? Take your time and write down 5 of each of your most cherished values and beliefs on this matter.

VALUES	BELIEFS

How did you acquire them? Do they serve you or control you? In what way have they changed your nature? Maybe those values and beliefs served you at a different time in your life, but they are no longer true for the person you currently are or the person you would like to become. Remember we live in a dynamic system where everything is constantly moving, so it is constantly changing and shaping a new world. If you want to change some of the values and/or beliefs that no longer serve you now, start doubting those values/beliefs. Look for evidence to question them so your brain will associate doubt with the values/beliefs that you want to change. At the same time, build evidence that supports both systems you are creating to empower you and start acting congruently with your new set of systems. Don't force anything. Your new values and beliefs must be aligned with your true identity: a feminine identity. As Andre Gide so eloquently said: *"The belief that becomes truth for me is that which allows me the best use of my strength, the best means of putting my virtues into action."*

Notice how your Attitude and Behavior are the result of your Values and Beliefs. So choose them wisely.

In order to perform to your highest level at the office, think of yourself as your own ultimate role model. What will it take for you to be your own role model? Write the things that will demand the best of you:

Your EXTERNAL APPEARANCE: To dress in a feminine way, you don't need lots of money to buy beautiful clothes that suit your personality. Don't overspend buying brand clothes if you cannot afford them and avoid buying imitation brands as connoisseurs can detect them in an instant. You don't want to give a false image. Buy clothes that are comfortable to you in colors that agree with your personality. Even if you work inside an office, you don't need to wear black, blue and gray all the time. Your clothes must reflect YOUR beauty. Do not use daring, bold, tight clothes or a big cleavage. It is ok to look a bit sexy if you are in good shape, but always do it with class; avoid crossing the limit and ending up in the vulgar zone. You will send the wrong message if you do. Your shoes must be clean, even if you are not a shoe person. People notice and they don't want to have a Leader with dirty shoes. If it is raining, wear something comfortable and take an extra pair of shoes with you, so when you arrive at the office you can change them in the restroom. Also, nowadays, there is no need to match your shows with your purse. If you take a briefcase of a business bag to the office, make sure you don't take a handbag also. Not only it is difficult to manage both but you end up taking unnecessary stuff to work.

You accessories should be delicate and feminine. When you are a Woman Leader, you want people to focus on YOU, on what you are saying, not on your necklace, rings or bracelets.

What about your makeup? Avoid shinny and glossy eye shadow at the office, even if you are planning to have fun afterwards. In such case, you will need to touch-up your makeup at a friend's home or at yours, but not in the office restroom. Try to separate your office life from your private life as much as you can. If the party is at the office, make sure you follow office rules and etiquette rules at all times, regarding the way you will dress and wear your makeup.

YOUR PERSONALITY: Do you have a strong imposing personality? Does it reflect the best side of you? You can be soft and determined at the same time. If you have a loud or a fast voice, try to speak slowly and with the right volume. Practice at home, practice with your best friends. If they ask what is going on, just tell them you feel relaxed that day, don't tell them you are practicing, as nobody needs to know your plans to succeed. Your friends just want to have a good time with you, so enjoy! On the other hand if you have a quieter voice, make your best effort to speak out loud. Go to your kids' baseball or soccer games and yell your heart out! Practice, practice, practice. Also, be aware of your body language. What is it saying? Are you seen like an Open Feminine Leader? When you are standing up, your heels should be apart a distance of half your distance between your shoulders and please don't shake your legs. As they say "your car describes your personality", I say "It is not the only thing that describes it". Personality is made focusing on the person as a whole.

If you can't afford a new car at this time, that is fine, just make sure your car is sparkling clean outside and inside. Don't leave coffee cups, food, facial tissues or kids toys in it.

CHOOSING YOUR WORDS: Your thoughts come before your words. Choose to think the best about yourself, your coworkers, your profession and the events surrounding your world. When you direct your thoughts in this way, you will be happier and you enable yourself to create the best. If you need to acquire more vocabulary, join a Toastmaster's Club, read out loud, or find your own 'word-of-the-day' at the dictionary and use it at the office, supermarket, with your family and at every chance you get. Don't overuse it, just use it once at each different place you go.

OFFICE ETIQUETTE. One of the things that is always in discussion is "Should I touch my coworkers? What if it is a man?" First of all, treat all people equally: males and females. If you are the "touching kind" then do it wisely and touch people on the elbow. If you are not sure how to do it, then don't! Inappropriate touching is a sure way of finding yourself accused of harassment. If you have a great smile and are polite, you do not need to touch people. Remember you are working with others who come from different cultures and you don't want to offend anyone. YOU are the Female Leader. Lead by example.

When having lunch with your coworkers make sure to cut your food into small pieces and take small bites so your cheeks don't expand while chewing. If you eat smaller portions at a time, you won't make any noise while gulping. Practice at home! There is no other way. If you want to succeed, you need to grow! Now I am not saying that there is something wrong with you, I am just emphasizing the need to learn to behave well socially as a Female Leader. After lunch, don't go into the public restroom and brush your teeth in front of everyone. If there is a private restroom for one person at a time, then you can get away with brushing your teeth there, but I truly don't recommend it. If you really feel the need to do it, then do it in a place where you are alone and make sure nobody outside the restroom can listen.

I always carry mints and a portable facial tissue box in my bag. When someone has a cold or a sore throat I offer some tissue and a couple of mints.

YOUR PRIVATE LIFE: Don't give too much information about your private life. Notice how people's working spaces are decorated. You can get a glimpse of their private lives if you watch closely. So, take note on this and be careful and wise about how much information you want to display. If you are having troubles at home –and we all have, sometime or another- keep those troubles private. It works both ways: If you are having problems at your job, keep the problems there and don't bring them home.

Remember at all times why you are there. Women have the gift of socializing in a natural way, so take this to your advantage and build good relationships and avoid gossip. Focus on your job and do your best. If you see the need to take some course via Continuing Education at the University or at your local College that will help you develop at your job, don't hesitate and do it!

Don't open your personal Facebook page at work. Act professionally at all times and don't make personal phone calls using the office phone nor make personal copies on the copying machine at the office.

If you feel overwhelmed by all of this, maybe it is time to rethink your goals. Don't become someone who you are not. Be true to yourself while enjoying the process. A Feminine Leader is a Woman who lives her life on her own terms, who doesn't settle for less than all that she can be, who is happy while growing, who feels alive when she expands into her true self feeling rich and fulfilled, happy to be Her. It is all about who She becomes.

Is this You?

ABOUT THE AUTHOR

E. JOYCE ROLAND, RN. PHD, MSN,CNE

Dr. E. Joyce Roland is a doctorally prepared registered nurse with expertise in women's health from a wholistic perspective (mental, physical and spiritual). She is currently an clinical associate professor of nursing at North Carolina Central University, Durham, North Carolina. She is also president and founder of Roland Essential Services, a personal service entity that focuses on Wellness and Health Maintenance, Career Coaching, Leadership Development, Stress and Conflict Management, as well as the mental, physical and spiritual health of women. She is a teacher, writer, and researcher in mental and physical wellness for women, and especially for African American women. She has co-authored several books in the PWN series, the most recent of which were *The Young Woman's Guide to Personal Success(2007), Survival Skills for African American Women(2007), The BabyBoomers' Handbook (2008),and Wellness for the African American Woman:Mind, Body &Spirit(2009)*.

Dr. Roland has a BS in Nursing from Winston-Salem State University, a masters degree in Nursing from Seton Hall University, South Orange, NJ, and a doctorate in Community Psychology from North Carolina State University, Raleigh, NC. Since 1978 she has worked as a nurse educator and research psychologist. In 1999 she completed post-doctoral studies in Alcohol and Substance Abuse Epidemiology (as it relates to women) at the Alcohol Research Group, University of California, Berkeley (1997-99), and most recently completed research on posttraumatic stress disorder among women veterans (2004-06). She enjoys working with women, adolescents (male and female), teaching them self-care and self-improvement strategies and providing mid-career advice to women. She also teaches courses on health and aging.

Her most recent community work has been with a Durham based Rites of Passage program for African American girls and with the Urban Ministries of Durham – a community agency for the homeless - teaching life skills development for women and preparation for re-entry into society. She also serves as a support group leader for women in the maintenance of breast health. She enjoys travel and has visited Mexico, Haiti, Barbados, and other Caribbean Islands. In 2004, she traveled to England with a U.S. contingency, visiting Coventry Cathedral to discuss and learn more about strategies for promoting peace and reconciliation in the world.

Dr. Roland is a member of the Professional Women's Network, a life member of Delta Sigma Theta Sorority, and a member of N.C. League for Nurses, the American Nurses Association, as well as the Central Carolina Black Nurses Association. She is an active member of St. Paul AME Church in Chapel Hill, NC, serving on the Christian Education Board and the Health committee. She also sings in the choir. She enjoys reading, writing, crocheting and quilting.

She is married to her husband, Lewis, and has three fabulous adult daughters: Leslie, Kaifa, and Lisa, a son-in-law (Richard), and two beautiful granddaughters, Cameren and Asha, and one grandson, Richard III.

Contact:
E. Joyce Roland, PhD, MSN, CNE
125 Hidden Springs Drive
Durham, North Carolina 27703
Phone: (919) 598-1917
E-Mail: jroland67@gmail.com
www.protrain.net

TWENTY-ONE

SUCCESS BECOMES YOU

Dr. E. Joyce Roland, PhD, MSN

"Let your light so shine before others that they may see your good works
and glorify your Father who is in heaven".
—Matthew 5:16 (King James Bible, Cambridge version)

In the 1980's, two popular buzz words were Buppy and Yuppy. These words constituted a new language used to describe Black Urban Professionals and Young Urban Professionals (who presumably were not Black). These terms were used to describe young people usually in their late 20s and early 30s, who were successful college graduates who had found high paying jobs, and who exhibited a lifestyle that reflected their new status.

These young people, both male and females, were able to attain certain standards of living seemingly by taking advantage of educational and job opportunities available to them at the time. This privilege enabled them to enter the workforce at a salary level that improved their standard of living precipitously. They became a much sought after resource and profited much from the experience.

How is today's new professional unlike the new professional of the 80s? What, if anything has changed our perception of the professional, and what message can we give to today's young women entering the workforce about what it means to be a professional. What else do they need to know to succeed in their chosen endeavors.

Defining Professionalism

The key word in both "Buppy" and "Yuppy" is "professional". What is meant by "professional"? How will we know it when we see it? According to Merriam-Webster's on-line dictionary (2013), the 'professional' is defined as an "individual who participates for gain or livelihood in an activity or field of endeavor that requires a certain style or level of behavior". The persona of the professional may be described as courteous, conscientious, and generally business-like especially in their work with others. What traits does the professional woman need to become successful in her chosen career? Being professional may not automatically guarantee success.

Gender Differences

Over the years the role of the professional may or may not have changed as much for males in society; however, over the last 2 decades the field has really blossomed for females; today, the female student now makes up the majority of college students and college graduates. Given that the player on this field has changed from male to female, how is today's young woman impacted by these changes?

First Step- Be Prepared

If this is your year to enter this world of work you might benefit from a few "pearls of wisdom" about 'success' in the modern work arena. Remember, you <u>are</u> the professional graduate who has prepared and groomed herself over a number of years to meet this challenge. You chose the right undergraduate degree, and remained in school just a bit longer to get the right degree: be it Law, the MBA or the MPA, or MA, or the PHD for that matter. You are ready to present your best to the world. A new world and era opens for you. I think this is a good time to discuss some particulars of being a "new urban professional" (NUPPY) in the 21st century. What do you think you need to know to succeed in your chosen work?

I'd like to offer the word SUCCESS as a basis for describing some of the characteristics of a successful professional. What does Success look like?

-S = Self-Confidence

-U = Unique and Understanding personality

-C = Collaborative work ethic; (learn to work with others)

-C = Collegial and cooperative attitude

-E = Experienced, and having expertise (being good at some one thing)

-S = Self-knowledge and a success-oriented work ethic

-S = Spiritually guided

As we go through this chapter focusing on some of these success strategies that will allow you to "s**ucceed against the odd**s", the writer will occasionally integrate some of the terms above into the discussion to illustrate what your success path entails.

Let us reflect on the work environment today. Today is a different world than it was two or three decades ago when the economy seemed at a very high and productive level. Opportunities may be not be out of the ordinary for those with talent, but certain personal and professional attributes will make you stand out among a pool of many. You should have *Self-Confidence* about your abilities. Know what you know, and acknowledge what you don't know, but don't be afraid to strike out and learn something new. Don't be afraid to be a 'risk-taker'. <u>Do</u> know your strengths and weaknesses?

Corporations, small and large, are looking for the best worker to help them achieve their financial goals. Your goals should align with the companies for the best outcomes for you and them. Before joining a company, be sure you know as much as you can about the firm or company. Can you work in this environment? Do your values and work ethic align with the employers? If not, perhaps this is not the company for you, regardless of the attractive starting salary.

Be prepared! Having additional work experience in addition to credentials may make **YOU** the better choice as a new employee. Youthfulness is often helpful also, because as a new employee, your salary demands may not be as great as someone with 10 or more years of experience Opportunities for you to grow and achieve your goals may be best at this point in your career. Look at opportunity as well as financial benefits, including starting salary. If you take the position, use the time to grow into the position by learning as much as you can and by being focused, well-rounded and productive. Develop good work habits, and for heaven's sake don't forget to *pay yourself first and tithe!*

In today's work world, technology reigns, yet everyone is expected to have some degree of ***Understanding and Uniqueness*** *as well as* ***expertise*** in a particular field . What is yours? You should know your field as well as, and if not better, than anyone you come up against. You may be wondering what is expected of me? How great is the challenge of being my own person, and yet finding success in my chosen work? Having some work experience helps you in meeting this challenge. This is one reason internships are encouraged in undergraduate school. By the time you enter the real arena of work, you have some idea of what the tasks of the work world are. Some are concrete and some are 'ethereal'. Based on the knowledge you gain in a work environment, you choose the appointment (job) that offers the most of what you are looking for.

Take a moment and jot down past work experiences you have had that helped you qualify for your new position. What needs do you still have?

1. _____

2. _____

3. _____

4. _____

Mentorship

Perhaps you feel you could benefit from some assistance as you move up the ladder? After a few months (six months to a year, perhaps) consider finding yourself a *mentor*. As you begin your ascent up the career ladder, you want to look for someone you admire or someone who has the position to which you aspire. Ask that person to be your mentor, and use that relationship to gain new skills and attitudes that will enable you to move up in the firm or corporation. A mentor can help you avoid pitfalls and assist you in decision-making about moving forward in your new career. A mentor can assist you for a life time -or a short while.

You can also have more than one mentor at one time, depending upon your need. One mentor might help you in building relationships in the work arena, while another may be your guide for overcoming issues related to obstacles related to diversity in the workplace. Diversity differences can be related to gender, age, ethnicity and/or political differences. Your work environment has become a microcosm of the society we live in.

Some women leaders suggest accepting ***challenging*** assignments in order to augment your present skills and to show your willingness to learn new skills, which will help you and the company reach stated goals. You can't afford to become complacent or stagnant and just do what has been defined as your job. Find and ask for assignments that help show off your skill set. Become a part of the solution as a problem solver and a go-getter. Volunteer for difficult assignments if they meet your skill set. Show you know how to 'work smart' as well as 'work hard'!

Often gender difference is a difference you encounter, especially if the leadership in the organization tends to top heavy with males. Have you prepared yourself to confront and move past these challenges that can deter you and get you off course? Again, this is where a mentor may be helpful. You might even choose a male mentor. This will help you learn how men think and problem solve which can be much different than women in some instances. Your generation may be better prepared to deal with this than previous ones.

As you start on this new journey, you must prepare yourself by having specific questions answered before you walk into the door where competition in very high. You must know the jargon and language of the department and the field. Stay open-minded and make it a goal to learn something new as often as you can. Be seen by the leadership. Meet often with your supervisor to share where you are in the company. Ask for new assignments if you feel ready for them.

What will be your responsibility for growth as you enter the work world? How will you manage your personal success? Who will be responsible for your success? YOU, or will you leave this in the hand of some the new bosses or the guidelines of some corporate entity. It can be a very challenging task, indeed. Prepare yourself!

There are so many aspects of this venture. Take a few minutes and write down questions you might have. What do you envision as the major obstacles that you will have to overcome?

_____

_____

_____

Let's move on to discuss some other areas that might help you as you begin your new venture.

Secondly - Know Yourself

You should thoroughly know yourself by the time you enter the work world. As mentioned above, be aware of your strengths and weaknesses. What are you good at? Why did you accept this job and what did you expect to be able to do in your first year? What goals did you or have you set for yourself for the next five years? Have you given this much thought as you anticipate collecting that first pay check? In the next few spaces write down your strengths and weaknesses: Write down what you like about yourself. Describe your values related to work and your personal life. All of these are important as you strike out on this new professional path.

1. _____ (Strengths)

2. _____(Weaknesses)

3. _____ (Goals Set)

4. _____ (Values)

What did you find out? Are you a loner or do work well with others?. Are you an extravert or an introvert? You may find this knowledge and insight related to personal competences make the difference in your success in the workplace. What values undergird your behavior approach to work? Will you be a leader in your work environment or will you follow the crowd? These are questions to ask yourself as you seek to know your 'professional' self. In the long run, self- knowledge will be very important to career growth.

Whatever you do, don't lose sight of your values. And better still, be able to articulate your them. Coming out of college and entering a work environment means you are likely to be working in an environment that is diverse in more ways than one. There may be older and younger people working together. The level of technical know-how may be different among groups of people of different ages, races, educational level? We refer to this as an intergenerational gap in the work setting. All of these present challenges to you - the new professional? How will you prepare yourself to deal with all of this? College classes don't always address these topics. There is much to think about as you begin the next phase of your life. But don't despair. Cheer up! Dig in! You are more ready for this challenge than you know.

I asked one young lady who is now in upper management what she thinks the new professional woman should be about as she begins a new role. What she shared with me was quite interesting. She gave the following advice:

1. Get to know people in your work in your work environment

2. Know and continue to learn your CRAFT

3. Build relationships with others in the workplace

4. Share your expertise with Leadership and others (not at others' expense)

5. Don't get involved in office politics

6. Develop working relationships with co-workers and supervisors

7. Realize what you do better than others and do it consistently

8. Be a problem-solver

9. Don't forget your spiritual roots

10. Don't forget who you are and whose you are

One last reminder about being successful in your new career: Remember, there is no such thing as "being lucky". My brother taught me that "Luck is where preparation and opportunity meet". That always stood out for me, because what he was saying was, "your make your own luck." If you are prepared, recognize the opportunity when it comes and "go for it". You never know what might happen. That is the **"LUCK." – RIGHT PLACE AT RIGHT TIME!**

Are you prepared and very well versed for the next level in your field? Are you the best you can be AND better still, have you positioned yourself to be in the pathway of new and greater opportunities? If you are not where opportunities for success abound, you may never reach the pinnacle you are reaching for. Maybe you need to choose that job that is out of your hometown. You might want to go where the opportunities are, and not be bound by your own self-imposed restrictions. In other words, you have to have guts, bring something to the table, and you have to recognize opportunities and be ready to reach for the 'brass ring' as it passes by' This is often involves being assertive and taking risks.

Stop again and recall times when you have taken risks and taken advantage of opportunities that may have been new for you. Do you reach out boldly when something new is offered to you, or do you shy away and then say you never get the chance to try something new? Be aware of your own behavior. Are you assertive, aggressive or nonchalant, caring about nothing specific in particular? Only you can address these questions. What you learn can hinder you or take you far above your expectations.

Summary:

In this chapter the author has tried to cover essential components of being successful in a new business/work endeavor. You are encouraged to: ***Be bold and Be brave; Be passionate and compassionate***. Much of what happens will be up to you and how you've prepared yourself, and your trust in yourself, God and your abilities. Sometimes, you have to strike out without all the confidence you need, but asking for help as needed along the way. That is probably the last best advice: Know when to ask for help.

Someone once said: The world is your oyster. Open it, taste it and savor it!

_____

_____

_____

_____

_____

_____

_____

_____

_____

_____

ABOUT THE AUTHOR

ALLISON TIBBS

Allison Tibbs is an entrepreneur, author, speaker and certified marketing and business coach, who is the CEO of Marquise, LLC where she specializes in providing comprehensive marketing strategies for small business owners, entrepreneurs and solopreneurs in the form of laser focused coaching and consulting. Her goal is to create an environment of entrepreneurs who are competent, confident and empowered to successfully run their businesses.

With a Bachelors of Science in Marketing from The Pennsylvania State University, Allison has had the opportunity to coach, train, and provide and consulting services to numerous clients all over the United States and Europe, including CEO's, professional athletes, recording artists, and public speakers. Her greatest asset is her ability to quickly assess how to enhance the marketing potential of her clients by thinking outside of the box and providing resources to help take the mystery out of marketing for her clients.

Allison also conducts workshops and provides resources that educate and empower youth, women and entrepreneurs to shift their mindset on how to successfully market themselves and their businesses. Her platform focuses on teaching "The 6 P's of Marketing for Small Businesses" and "The 6 Steps to Personal Branding Success".

Contact:
Email: atibbs@marquisemarketing.com
Website: www.marquisemarketing.com
Blog: www.marquisemarketing.com/blog
LinkedIn: www.linkedin.com/allisontibbs
Facebook: www.facebook.com/marquiseLLC
Twitter: @MarquiseLLC

TWENTY-TWO

POSITION YOURSELF FOR SUCCESS

Allison Tibbs

Being a Young Professional Woman is one of the most empowering things that you will ever experience. I remember when I was stepping into my role as a Young Professional Woman there were things that I had to learn and put in place to truly have the success that I wanted. Now, as a full time entrepreneur of four businesses and a non-profit, I still hold a few things near and dear as I position myself for success.

Over the next few pages, I'm going to share with you 5 pieces of advice that I learned along the way and I hope that will be beneficial for you as you continue along your journey of being a Young Professional Woman. It is important that you understand how to properly Position Yourself For Success, so that you can have a fruitful, fulfilling, and abundant future in your personal and professional life.

1. Define What Success Means To You

I remember, a few years ago being interviewed by a radio show that was geared towards Young Entrepreneurs and the host asked me a question that stumped me. He asked, "What is your definition of success, Ms. Tibbs?" As I sat there, completely speechless, I slowly repeated his question, to buy more time, and then gave him the first thing that popped into my head. To be honest, I don't even remember what I said, but I guess it was good enough because he responded with "Wow! That's great, I'm sure our listeners can relate to that!" After the radio show was over, I realized that I had never taken the time to really think about what my definition of success truly was.

Yes, I had achieved certain accolades in my life like writing nearly a dozen books and starting a couple of businesses, but there was so much more that I wanted to achieve out of life. But, as I sat there reflecting over the past few years of my life, it almost seemed like my success was haphazard and just "happened". I also began to think about all of the things that I truly wanted deep down in my heart and realized that I was pretty far off from reaching those things, if I stayed on course to let things "just happen".

That's when everything changed in my life. I sat down and wrote out exactly what success looked like to me. I had to examine my personal life, my professional life, my relationships, my finances, my faith, my health, and other areas in my life. In each of those areas, I wrote down what

Success would mean in those areas of my life. I encourage you to think of all of the areas in your life and jot down a few sentences for each area, in terms of what would deem you having success.

What I realized from this exercise was that the most important things to me, were being put on the back burner. For example, I wanted to be able to deepen the relationships with my family members and friends, because over the past few years, I had to sacrifice spending quality time with them in order to build my business. I missed baby showers, birthday parties, annual family vacations and even weddings! I knew that, it didn't matter how successful my business, if I didn't have my family and friends in my life, it wouldn't mean a thing. I also felt the same way about making a lot of money, what's the point if you have no one to enjoy it with.

I encourage you to take time to think about where you are in your life right now and figure out what Success truly means and looks like to you.

This is important because it is YOUR definition, and many times we let other people's definition of success define who we are and what we do and go after. When this happens, we are usually left feeling unfulfilled since we have been chasing someone else's dream.

I had a friend who was the first to graduate college in her family. She had a degree in Finance and went on to pursue a finance position in a very big company. Yes, she was good at finance and excelled quite well in her position. Her parents and peers were grooming her to one day be a CFO of a large company, which touted a large salary to afford a big house, nice clothes and cars, and a very plush lifestyle. However, as she continued in her career, she found that really didn't enjoy what she was doing. Moreover, the thought of being a CFO was not only undesirable but also repulsive. She had spent roughly 5 years of her professional career charting her success based on what others wanted for her.

However, when she took the time to think about what she wanted out of life, she realized that she was living someone else's dream. Eventually, we went back to school to get a Master's Degree in a completely different field and now she is enjoying a much more successful and fruitful life. She is doing what she loves and if you asked her, she is on her way towards her success breakthrough.

When you have clarity in what success looks like to you (based on what YOU want), the easier it will be for you to have success. When I think about success, I don't limit it to just one area of my life. I know that most people equate success in terms of financial and social status; but I like to include a bit more in my vision and definition of my success.

I encourage you to take some time to write down your definition of success. There is something magical that happens when you write things down, it's like your heart and soul solidify it into existence. After you write it all out, mine was an entire page, read it a few times aloud. Doing this help you to visualize your success and make seem even more real. I read my definition often just to make sure that I am on the right track.

2. Self-Assessment is Key

Self-awareness is a critical component to achieving your success breakthrough. If you are not sure what you bring to the table and what you need to improve about yourself, chances are you will never reach your full potential. One of the best ways to get a holistic view of your potential is to conduct a Personal SWOT Analysis.

A SWOT Analysis is used in business to gain insight on the chances for success, because it examines internal factors – the Strengths and Weaknesses that the company possesses – as well as, the external factors – the Opportunities and Threats that are present. In the same way that companies conduct a situational analysis, you should do the same thing.

Your Strengths will help you to move closer to your success, while your Weaknesses may hinder your success. When thinking about your strengths, they can include your talents, skills, abilities, education received, certifications achieved, or anything else that could help you achieve success. Your Weaknesses can include the skills or things that come difficult to you or that you don't necessarily enjoy.

You also want to consider the Opportunities and Threats that are present that could assist or sabotage your success. Your Opportunities are external things that could help in achieving your success breakthrough. For example, if you want to get promoted, having a key relationship with an executive in your company could be an opportunity. While, your Threats are external and could prevent you from achieving success. For example, if getting that promotion is very important to you, but there may be others who have been at the company longer or have a larger skill set than you, this could be a threat to your success. Identify certain things, people, and situations that could help and prevent your success.

Once you have completed your SWOT Analysis, you can identify some key takeaways to give you insight in how to proceed. Below are a few questions to help you engage in a deeper analysis.

- How can I capitalize on my Strengths and opportunities?

- How can I turn my Weaknesses and Threats into Strengths and opportunities?

- What will I need to do get closer to my definition of success?

I know that this part can be a bit rough because it requires you to take an honest look at yourself, but this clarity will give you the momentum and direction you need.

3. Set Effective Goals

As you work towards your success breakthrough, setting goals will be critical for keeping you focused and on track to succeed. When creating goals there are a few things that you should consider.

First, your goals should be very clear and include specific metrics of success, like a deadline. Let's use the promotion example again. If you want to be promoted, you will need to be specific about what position you want to be promoted to and when you would like to be promoted. Saying, "I want to be promoted to Assistant Director, by June 30th" is much more clear than saying "I want to be promoted." The goal is to know exactly what you want to accomplish and by when.

When you put a date or a time limit on a goal it automatically puts a sense of urgency with the goal, which will prompt you to take the necessary actions needed to make it happen and avoid procrastinating.

Think about your definition of success and write down at 3 long-term goals that you would like to achieve over the next 5 years. For each long-term goal, write down 5 short-term goals that you will need to do to make this happen. Remember to be very specific and put a due date for each goal.

There is power in writing down your goals and this is setting you up to have your success breakthroughs in your life. My suggestion for you is to type out your goals and post them in a place where you can see them on a daily basis. This will help you keep your goals top of mind and to propel forward to reach your success.

4. Develop an Action Plan

Action is one of the key differentiators between people who say they want success and those who actually achieve it. When I think of successful people, one thing I know that they all have in common is that they didn't wait for things to happen. No, they went out and made it happen by taking action. If you want success in life, I mean really want success; you have to commit to taking action and putting in the work that is required. This may require you to do things that are uncomfortable and it will require you to make sacrifices. However, the good news is that your success lies right outside of your comfort zone!

Below are a few areas where you will need to take action:

- **<u>Vision Oriented Tasks</u>**: On a daily basis, you should be doing things that will move you closer to your goals. Think about your goal and think about some things that you could begin to do everyday. Can you think of 3 Vision Oriented Tasks you should do on a daily basis?

- **<u>New Habits</u>:** There will also be some habits that you will need to form to help achieve your goals. They say it takes 21 days to form a habit, so think about the habits that you would need to adopt. What are 3 new habits can you pick up over the next 21 days?

- **<u>Distractions</u>:** If you want success you will have to make sure that you are able to identify potential distractions and then do your best to eliminate them. What are 3 distractions that you can work to eliminate?

- **<u>Success Partners</u>:** Accountability is key and by finding people who support your goals can be very helpful. Identify people who will join you and be positive sources of energy and make an effort to speak to them on a weekly basis. Name 3 people that you could partner with for accountability?

- **<u>Negative People</u>:** You should also understand that there will be certain people in your life who won't be the best source of energy for you. It would be in your best interest to limit your communication and interactions with these people, as they could wear on your confidence and motivation to achieve your goals. Name 3 people that you should eliminate or reduce contact with?

Putting these action items in place can help you to be better positioned for your success. Remember, your journey to your success isn't necessarily an easy one, but it is one that is definitely worth it!

5. Staying Motivated

The journey towards your success is one that can be a bit challenging as it will require you to make sacrifices, step out of your comfort zone, and make big changes in your life. There have been times in my life when I wanted to throw In the towel and give up. However, it was in those moments that I had to tap into something deep to keep pushing on.

In order to stay motivated, I encourage you to truly identify your "WHY?" or your reason for doing what you are doing. For me, it's simple. I want to be able to create a life of freedom where I can travel, not worry about money or debt, spend time with my loved ones, and create a legacy that will impact the world in a big way. When I think about my legacy I think about how my companies, Marquise LLC and Allison Tibbs International, will allow me to help millions of people have success in their businesses and their lives. I also think about how my non-profit foundation, Empower A Girl Foundation, will empower 1 MILLION girls across the globe.

When I put it all in perspective, it becomes a mission, a life purpose, and a responsibility to be successful, because every moment that I'm not living in my full potential businesses are failing, people are struggling, and young girls are suffering.

I keep my "WHY?" in the forefront of my mind and it serves as a reminder for me daily. I have even created a vision board where I cut out photos and words and glued them to poster board that I hang in my office. When I am having a moment, I look at that board the motivation to push through kicks into high gear.

Let's take a moment to stop and think about your "WHY?" This must be something that is very personal to you, like your definition for success, and there is no right or wrong answer. The only requirement is that you make it meaningful to you, because if you don't care it won't matter if you succeed or fail.

These questions will help you to determine and understand your "WHY?" and help to keep you motivated.

- What are your reasons for wanting more success in your life?

- How will your life change as a result of your success?

- How will you feel when you have achieved your success?

- How will your success impact the important people in your life?

- How will your success impact the lives of your community?

Your success doesn't just affect you, so keep that in mind when you want to throw in the towel. Having a mindset of a champion, where failure is not an option, is necessary when you are positioning yourself for success.

You Deserve Your Success

One of my favorite quotes is "Don't be afraid to give yourself everything you've ever wanted in life." I share this with you because whatever it is that you wrote down as your definition of success, I want you to know that you can have it. However, I also want you to understand that there are certain things that must be in place if you are to ever achieve the success that you aspire to have. As I mentioned earlier, my goal for writing this chapter was to share with you some things that I learned in my journey of achieving my success. I'm excited for you and your success and I hope that after reading this chapter, you are too!

ABOUT THE AUTHOR

DARLENE HUNTER

Darlene is a powerful motivational speaker, author, radio talk show host and life coach. She is an experienced manager and leader with excellent listening and team building skills. She takes great pride and satisfaction in motivating individuals and teams to exceed their goals and expectations.

Darlene stands with her clients and helps them turn their challenges into victories and holds them accountable to reach their desired goals. Darlene is a charismatic, natural leader with a passion for people. She is enthusiastic and highly driven. She has been viewed as a top performer throughout her career as well as having exceptional interpersonal, business and leadership skills.

Darlene is the author of the book "Overcoming the Obstacles, Releasing the Winner in You", a motivational, inspirational book with the message of never giving up! Darlene is the host of "The Darlene Hunter Show". It airs every Saturday from 12:00 pm to 2:00 pm EST on the Fishbowl Radio Network, the largest Internet radio network of its kind. The theme of the show is "Motivating Real People through Real Issues". The purpose of the show is to make life changing differences in the lives of people by motivating, inspiring and encouraging them through life's issues and challenges.

TWENTY-THREE

PERSEVERANCE AND PERSISTENCE

Darlene Hunter

In business and in life each of us have experienced difficulties, we have faced obstacles, challenges and failures and have been faced with opposition. It is at that time when we had to make a decision rather to give in and give up or keep moving forward and stay in the race of what we call life. It is always easier to just throw in the towel and quit, but quitting is the easy way out.

I once had a conversation with a young man who did very well running track. He won all kinds of awards for coming in first place in meets throughout the states.   He shared with me that when he ran in track meets involving hurdles and happened to hit one while running in the race, he would not be disqualified from the race. If he fell he was allow to get up and continue running. I then asked him if anyone had ever won a race after they have hit a hurdle, he replied with a resounding yes.   Life is just like the meet with hurdles. There are times where you will go through life without hitting any hurdles, obstacles, challenges or failures, but there are also times when as soon as you start out you hit some type of obstacle. The important thing that we all have to remember is that we cannot give up just because things do not work out the way we wanted them. We are not disqualified from life or the things that life has to offer. We must be persistent and press our way through until the end.

What does it mean to be persistence? The definition according to the Merriam – Webster dictionary says that to persist means to go on resolutely (a firm determination) or stubbornly in spite of opposition. To be insistent in the repetition or pressing of, to continue to exist especially past a usual, expected or normal time. It simply means to keep pressing towards the mark, the goal, the dream without ceasing, or without stopping until you get to the desired, expected and completed end. It really is all about pushing and working hard with a drive and determination to win.

Below are five elements involved with persistence and perseverance in the professional arena that should be followed. You should grasp and embrace them as you move forward in your professional career.

You should always...

1. Be Plan-ful

2. Be Goal Oriented

3. Be Driven for Results

4. Have A Winning Attitude

5. Be Focused

BE PLAN-FUL

As a professional, you must know what you want and have a plan of action to get you there. Planning to a major component to success. Winston Churchill said *"He who fails to plan is planning to fail"*. Planning your day, week and month are critical ingredients to becoming a successful professional. The how and why elements are important factors in planning, as they guide you in the direction in which you are to go in achieving your goals, plans and intentions. Many in business use the SMART Action Planning model when setting goals and planning. This model was developed by psychologist as a tool to help people set and reach their goals. The components are listed below.

SMART Action Planning

Specific

Measurable

Attainable

Relevant

Time-bound

Specific

To achieve a goal, you need to be specific about what it is. Is your goal defined? Avoid setting unclear or vague objectives; instead be as precise as possible.

Measurable

Be clear, how will you know when you have achieved your goal. Using numbers, dates and times is one way to represent clear objectives. Making a goal measurable makes it possible to monitor your progress. It also forces you to become clear on where you're starting from which is always important. If your goal is too undefined, you'll find it's impossible to tell when you have even achieved it.

Attainable

Make you goals challenging, but realistic. Research has shown that one of the most important elements of success is having a goal that's achievable. Setting impossible goals will only end in disappointment.

Relevant

A goal is relevant if it ladders up to your larger goals and even your purpose statement.

A goal is also only relevant if it's personally motivating for you. If you are setting out to achieve something to please someone else, it's unlikely you'll last the distance.

Time-bound

Deadlines are critical. They keep you in action and they keep you motivated. Without a time limit there's no urgency to start taking action now. Make sure you are realistic with your time frame. There's nothing less motivating than missing your goal all because you didn't allow yourself the right amount of time. Set a time scale for completion of each goal. Even if you have to review this as you progress, it will help to keep you motivated.

Once you have plans in place, you may have to go back and make adjustments when necessary. As you move forward with your plans it is important that you do so with perseverance. Perseverance goes hand in hand with persistence. It involves the continued effort to do what is needed to be done despite any difficulties you may face.

BE GOAL ORIENTED

The purpose of setting goals is to help you get to where you want to go. Goals are action steps needed to get you to your plans or end results. Goals help you to continue on your path to achieving what you are striving to gain. Once you set goals the next step is to work on completing them, that's why it is so important to ensure that the goals in which you setting are ones that you can accomplish. Once again you need to be persistent and press your way through to achieve them. Each time you reach a goal that you have set for yourself you get closer to reaching what ever you have set out to achieve. The sense of accomplishment that comes from reaching even the smallest goals will help keep you moving and striving to get to your desired end. Goals are critical factors when setting out a course of action and are like steps taken when climbing up a mountain or setting out on a marathon race or walk. They are the forward motion that gets you to where you want to go. Think about a steep mountain that one climbs to get to the top. Many may reach the top, but not everyone will follow the same steps. In many occasions, the steps that you take may be unique to you. No one takes the same steps, however, any steps that you know have been successful in helping someone get where you are working to get to should be used, this is what I call using a **Best Practice**. A **Best Practice** is something that has been used and proven to be effective.

DRIVEN FOR RESULTS

Being driven for results is a key factor in success of professionals. When you are driven you have a compulsive and urgent desire to accomplish what you are seeking. You do not let obstacles or challenges that may get in your way stop you from getting to the desired end. You keep pushing and striving to get to where you want to go. The results that you may be seeking could be anything from a bonus, a promotion, more knowledge in a particular area or reaching a goal that you have set. Knowing that you are working towards an end result will motivate you to keep pushing and increase your drive to get you there. The important factor is to always know what you are seeking. What are the results or conclusion you are trying to achieve or reach. What outcome would you like to see. A results driven individual focuses on meeting objectives, and delivering the goals set either by yourself, your boss/supervisor or the organization in which you work. This would involve not only meeting the goals or outcome, but meeting all of the components involved, such as cost, and the time frame which has been set. Many companies include ***Driven for Results*** as a performance measurement and core competency for their employees.

HAVE A WINNING ATTITUDE

To be successful as a professional in any field you must have a steadfast winning attitude. You must be determined, dedicated and devoted to succeed. This requires a firmly fixed mindset to learn all you can around the profession and then be devoted to the cause and purpose.

Many who are entering into the professional arena for the first time may have predetermined ideas about what they perceive the job or career should look like. Once they enter the profession their predetermined ideas may change. The important thing to remember is that the profession in which you decided to enter was selected by you for a reason. Something about it sparked something in you and steered you in that direction. You should never give up on it because something went wrong or because you are not getting to where you hoped you would be fast enough. I believe that there is a time, season and reason for everything.

There are multiple stories that can be told about people who failed in the beginning, but made it to the top of their profession because

they did not give up after being told that they were not good enough to go forward in the profession that they selected. We all know the story about how Michael Jordan was cut from his high school basketball team and then went on to become one of the best basketball players ever. Michael Jordan dominated the sport from the mid-1980s to the late 1990s. He wanted to play basketball and was persistence in his drive to make it happen even after being told that he was not good enough for the team. JK Rowling, the author of Harry Potter was rejected by publishing companies time and time again, but she did not give up because someone thought her work was not good enough. She pressed her way through in spite of her current situation, which was not good at the time, only to become the author of the books that has gained worldwide attention with multiple awards and sold more than 400 million copies. They have become the best selling book series in history. We all know Oprah Winfrey, she was fired from her television reporting job because they told her she was not fit to be on screen. Oprah rebounded and became the undisputed queen of television talk shows and is now a billionaire. Her drive and determination to be successful paid off. She did not give up, because someone else did not believe in her ability.

The capability or ability to keep trying and keep pushing no matter how many failures or obstacles you hit is the the power of perseverance. Achieving your goals may be slow and require patience and stamina, but it's endurance that will make it happen. Endurance enables you to withstand any hardship, adversity or obstacle and allows you the ability to sustain a prolonged stressful effort or activity. You cannot give up, you must stay the course and keep pushing to achieve your goals. Every ounce of progress and all the time you put into reaching your goals and dreams are going to get you to the expected end. You must go into your profession with a winning attitude and a mindset that quitting is not an option.

BE FOCUSED

As a professional you must be focused and determined to move forward. There may be challenges and obstacles that might get in your way, but you must stay focused with a drive and determination to win at what every you choose to do. Think about the long distance runner who will run a 26 mile marathon. They find their pace and then they stay with it. All of their elements, mind, arms and legs are working together in unison. They may get weary and tied but they find their zone and stay focused and concentrate on what is needed to get to the end. Focus means that you must have a point and a direction of concentration. A place where you attention is directed to achieve what you have set out to do or accomplish. When you are focused you have a clear perception and understanding as to what you must accomplish and where you need to go to get there. Once you are focused you will place a center of activity, attraction and attention on the project, plan, problem, program or system that is presented to you. Like the lens of a camera, focusing facilitates and influences perception and will enable you to grasp what is needed with intellect and understanding.

Every professional must perseverc and be persistent when breaking into the business world. This will enable you to reach any goal and accomplish what ever you seek to do. Take some time to write down the goals that you are seeking as a professional. Below you will be able to write not only your goals, but also the purpose for which you are developing them. Remember, goals help you to continue on your path to achieving what you are striving to gain.

Listed below are questions that you can start asking yourself as you start setting your goals. They are simply sample questions, you may have different questions as you challenge yourself.

Goal Setting Questions:

1. What do you want to achieve?

2. What do you want to be known for?

3. What improvements do you want to see in yourself?

4. What do you want to master?

5. What do you want to be?

6. Where do you want to go?

7. What are the three biggest changes you want to make in your life over the next five years?

8. What do you want your salary to be?

9. Where do you want to be in one year?

10. How much do you want to save?

11. What do you want to accomplish over the next three months?

12. What additional classes do you want to take?

13. What training to you want to acquire?

14. What books do want to write?

15. What car do you want to drive?

16. What debt do you want to pay off?

Be Persistent and Persevere

My Purpose	My Goals

SMART ACTION PLAN WORKSHEET

S	**Specific** What am I going to do? Why is it important to do at this time? What do I want to accomplish? How am I going to do it?
M	**Measurable** How will I know that I have reached my goal?

A	**Attainable** Can I see myself achieving this goal? Can I break it down into manageable pieces?
R	**Realistic** Is the goal too easy or to difficult?
T	**Timely** What is my target date for reaching my goal?

ABOUT THE AUTHOR

SAMI KAY MARTIN

Sami Kay Martin is currently a reporter living in New York City. When not writing, Sami works at the Valley Stream Presbyterian Church in Valley Stream, Long Island. She is also on the ordination track for the Presbyterian Church and has worked extensively in youth ministry.

Sami recently became a Certified Life Coach and has led various workshops on teen suicide, dating violence and sexual assault. She is the author of "Becoming the Butterfly: New Life, New Hope, New Joy," which is available on her website www.samikmartin.com.

TWENTY-FOUR

HOLDING OUT HOPE

Sami K. Martin

As many of us know by now, it's not the easiest time to apply for a job, which is why I believe in holding out hope during those times of frustration or lack of work. Right now there are jobs advertised nearly everywhere, but with thousands of people fighting for the same job, what are the odds that you will be hired? Believe me, I understand the frustration, the disappointment that can come with not hearing back for a position for days, weeks, or months. Actually, I held out hope for two full years before I finally found a position... it took me another year before I received benefits, and now I have stability. For now, though, let me encourage you: hold out hope.

The Bible teaches us that hope and faith is all about what is *not* seen, not what is already seen. **BIBLE VERSE**: Hebrews 11:1-3 reads "Now faith is the assurance of things hoped for, the conviction of things not seen. Indeed, by faith our ancestors received approval. By faith we understand that the worlds were prepared by the word of

God, so that what is seen was made from things that are not visible."
Applying for jobs is just like that, right? You find a job that you think
you'd be perfect for; it almost seems a little too good but you take
the chance and apply anyway. You're already exercising your belief in
hope – you're sending information about yourself to someone who has
no idea who you are or what you are all about. One to two pages of
information can determine whether or not you get the job you want
or need.

You place your hope in the person who will read your cover sheet
and resume. But what if that person doesn't call you back? What if
that person never responds to your submission? It may sting a little,
but you soon realize that you need to try again and you either begin a
fresh job search or you tweak your resume/cover letter and email it to a
fresh set of eyes. You again exercise your hope.

Who (or what) else do you put your hope in while you search
for a job? I believe that you put your faith in a Higher Power, in
God, who has promised to provide and meet all your needs. **BIBLE
VERSE:** Philippians 4:19 states: "And my God will meet all your
needs according to the riches of his glory in Christ Jesus." After all,
just because you're unemployed doesn't mean you don't have financial
obligations to meet: rent, food, the basic needs of living. God has said
that if we have faith, S/He will provide and meet all of those needs…
not all of our *wants* but all of our needs.

We also put faith in ourselves, right? We have to believe that we
are qualified for a certain position, are deserving of the job and the
benefits that come along with it, that *we* are the right person for the
job. If we lack that faith, what hope do we have of getting that call
or interview? What hope do we have of a complete stranger taking a
chance on us and saying those two words, "You're hired"? The simple

answer is none. You have to have faith in yourself... and have the confidence necessary to obtaining the job.

Hope is what sustains us through those times of doubt, through those times when the phone doesn't ring or the checking account balance gets too low. Hope is having belief when there should be none. Hope says, "I have faith." And if you are willing to put faith where it belongs, in God first and yourself second, you can achieve anything!

I found that oftentimes when my own bank account was running low, I would receive an offer to babysit or organize an office, both of which I love doing. God would provide the opportunity for me to make a little money to tide me over until the next assignment would present itself. But I also had to work and take advantage of the opportunity given to me. That's the way things play out sometimes — God presents the opportunity and gives you the freewill to decide whether you'll take it or not. It's often said that God helps those who help themselves, and in this case, I found it to be true.

Where does hope go once you finally get that call or interview and hear those magic words? It lies within each day that you show up to work— –you hope and have faith that you will do the best job you can. You hope to show yourself as a worker approved by God and always strive for greatness. **BIBLE VERSE:** 2 Timothy 2:15 reminds us, "Do your best to present yourself to God as one approved, a worker who has no need to be ashamed, rightly handling the word of truth." Yes, there will be times when greatness or Godliness is the furthest thing from your mind, but it should never leave your heart. After all, God is the one who brought you this far, gave you this job/opportunity and provided for you along the way.

ABOUT THE AUTHOR

LORI RUFF

Lori Ruff, The LinkedIn Diva™, is among the Top 3 most-connected women on LinkedIn. A Microsoft Certified Master Instructor and internationally recognized Social Media Privacy authority, Lori writes, speaks and trains on Relationship-Driven Business Development via LinkedIn and Social Media.

Lori is a published author on the topics of LinkedIn, Social Media and Privacy: including *Rock the World™ with your Online Presence, #PrivacyTweet Book01*. She speaks on LinkedIn, Social Media, and Privacy at conferences and gatherings and is in high demand by executives working to establish best practices.

Inspire your audiences; hire Lori to tell her story. She is a survivor and passionate influencer. Even before a near fatal motorcycle wreck in 2005, Lori won Small Business of the Year and numerous awards because of her generous spirit and willingness to help, whether professional, community, or personal goals were at stake.

Today Lori has twice been named to Forbes list of the Top 50 Global Social Media Power Influencers and their Top 10 Women. She works tirelessly to bring quality education about the new world of Social to everyone. She and her partner created RockLinkedIn.com, a free high quality on demand training portal to serve everyone seeking to use LinkedIn to improve their lives, their career, or their results, whether they can afford the help or not.

Connect with Lori at http://LoriIsOnline.com or at a conference near you.

Contact:
Lori Ruff
The LinkedIn Diva™
Training@IntegratedAlliances.com
www.RockstarNetworking.com

TWENTY-FIVE

SEEDS OF GREATNESS

Lori Ruff

Celebrate Your Genius; Do Something Magical Today!

Graduating from high school or college, starting your adult career with that first professional job, finding your first mentor… these are defining experiences of youth that inspire hope and set expectations for an incredible and "successful" adult life.

But it's not long before seeds of doubt are tossed upon you, either by people (even loved ones) who utter careless words or by your own self-doubt. I'm here to tell you that it's ok. Those doubts plague us all. People who achieve success, experience joy, and make a difference in the world are those who hear but do not give into the doubt or the naysayers.

So let's get this over with… what doubts do you secretly hold. Come on: I know you have them. It's impossible to get through your teenage years without them. So let's put them down and air them out so we can address them and then move on. List them here:

_____

_____

_____

Whew! That was great! Now look back at what you wrote. Claim it. Understand that you are better than that. Once you look over the list, run a web search on those phrases. You will find that you are not alone. I'll confess… I've had many of those same thoughts; in fact, we all have. And it's ok. What matters is that you pick up and move on.

Journey

Remember that life is a journey; so is success. You can have one success and call yourself a success when in reality you only *experienced* one success. A successful life is a full one: full of all kinds of experiences, full of good and bad choices, full of incredible friendships, full of other mutually beneficial relationships.

Think of it this way: when you get up in the morning, in order to have a successful day at work, you have to actually go to work! Think of your successful life in terms of getting up and going to claim it. Success is not delivered, you have to chase it. You have to get up and work for it.

But going on a journey requires a bit of packing. So let's think about the things that you want to bring on this journey to help you achieve a life full of success. What do you have that you can pack for the journey?

How about a talent for talk? Are you creative, musical, athletic, well-connected, or funny? Even if you are shy, an average student, or emotional, those things could be turned on their head to help fuel your success. So list your talents here. What do you want to continue to bring along on your personal journey?

_____

_____

_____

Aside from the items you just packed for your success journey, let's discuss a few you might not have thought about but should probably include.

Tenacity

Tenacity is one of the traits successful people all have in common: they are *tenacious*. Successful people are resolute in following their passions no matter what life might throw at them. Successful people are persistent. They don't give up easily but practice a dogged determination to "make it work". Just because one person says: "you can't do that!" or "that's not possible!" it's up to you to investigate and figure out how to make it work.

How can you practice tenacity?

Take a deep breath and face the challenge, no matter if the challenge is in your own head, or if it is real. Perhaps something you wrote above—one of your doubts—is true. So what? Did you know that some people who are widely recognized as incredibly successful had good reason to doubt themselves?

Einstein was just an average student and 20% of today's billionaires did not finish college; among them Bill Gates, Michael Dell, Larry Ellison, Steve Jobs and of course, Mark Zuckerburg. Many also suffer major setbacks, failures, and poor choices. But they keep getting back up, sometimes completely starting over, and tenaciously move forward to claim their prize.

I'm sure you've already practiced tenacity; perhaps you didn't realize what it was. But now, looking back on your life's experiences so far, can you remember a time when you wanted something so bad, you couldn't let go of the thought? That is what tenacity feels like. Why not record the experience here so you will have a vivid reminder for days ahead in which you might begin to lose hope in your goal.

_____

_____

_____

Heart

The greatest people I know are people who have the tenacity to live their Heart: whether it's Larry Page, Ted Turner or the Olympic Athlete whose Heart is in the Competition or Mother Theresa, Mahatma Gandhi or the volunteer whose Heart is in Service. No matter what people do, when they do it from their Heart they do it best and shine brightest.

I've been blessed to be surrounded by great people in my life: My Daddy whose Heart was in his faith and family; my sister Terri, a nurse practitioner whose Heart is in caring for others; my partner Mike, whose Heart is in the joy of authentic relationships; I have been touched by many Hearts modeling Greatness for me.

Who inspires you with their Heart?

_____

_____

_____

Honestly, you want to fill your life with more people like this. If you must work, if you must engage in relationships of any kind, why not search to work with and build relationships with people who inspire you?!

Networking

In today's connected world, it is easier than ever for average people to experience more success because it is possible to not only know more people—to be better connected—but to also know more about the people you do know. That is what will give you and your circle of influence the power to tap into each other's greatness, knowledge, experience and network.

Remember the words John Kennedy made famous: "A rising tide lifts all boats." Help others lift their tide while you work to lift your own and you will experience better than average success. A fabulous way to build your network with people who are interested in you is to start providing value.

Provide value to everyone, whether you know them or not, whether they know you or not. By consistently providing value, your network will grow. People will want to be near you because you feed them.

What do you feed them? What value can you offer? How about:

- Knowledge—don't make assumptions about what people know, instead offer your advice or your take on the topic. *You can't be thought of as a though-leader if you don't share your thoughts!* So get started now. And don't think you're too young. Smart people want the opinion of a diverse group of people to help them make better decisions.

- Understanding—people want to know they are not alone. By talking about shared experiences, you let other people know you've experienced some of the same things they have. You literally make the connection to the "human you" possible. People want to know someone in the world understands them; someone else has been where they are.

- Empathy—perhaps you didn't experience what they are experiencing but by offering a non-judgmental ear, you can offer tremendous value to others and perhaps learn something yourself!

- Sharing—share thoughts, articles, good deeds and #GreatContent of others. By sharing their work, you will build a circle of influencers who will be willing to reciprocate.

  o Sharing Rules: only share what is relevant to your audience and don't expect anyone to share your content or work product with their audience if they don't feel it is appropriate. Sharing willy-nilly is good for no one.

  o Another good rule of thumb is to focus on your own and related topics as far as choosing other content to share.

○ Keep it real: if you are sharing from a personal account, it's ok to share struggles. It makes you human. For example, I suffer with Rheumatoid Autoimmune Disease (typically referred to as "Rheumatoid Arthritis"). Talking about it out loud and in public not only gives me a voice to be heard, but gives others permission to talk to me about the struggles they are facing too.

• Praise—people want to feel appreciated and recognized for a job well done. How do I know? Don't you feel this way too? It feels good when you are praised…recognized for a job well done. Well, pass it on! You'll be amazed at what a difference it will make in your life to recognize the genius in others as you ask them to recognize the genius they see in you.

Think about it: what value can you offer and how? List at least three value propositions you have to offer here.

_____

_____

_____

You're well on your way now to consistently being alert for how you can provide value to others. Don't worry: the law of reciprocity will bring it back to you.

Success

Well, we've talked all about success, but let's define it. If you don't know what success is; how will you know when you've achieved it?

Think about it… did you know a successful student. What was it about them that makes you believe they were a success? Did they study hard or did it just seem to come easy? Were they the valedictorian? If so, does that mean that the rest of the school was not a success because they weren't at the top?

How about a successful co-worker… do you have a co-worker you would define as being successful in their job? What are the traits they practice or display that make you believe that? What were the outcomes of their work that you believe prove their experience of success in that role?

Have you ever thought of interviewing people who you feel are successful and asking them how they reached that pinnacle in their life or career? Here's your chance. Choose three people you know and three people you'd like to know and arrange to interview them as if you were writing an article or doing a talk show. Complete the table below before we move to the next step: asking for the interview. I'll get you started:

Successful person	Know them personally?	Best method to contact
Lori Ruff	Not yet	www.LinkedIn.com/in/LoriRuff

Notice that under the column "Know them personally" I entered "Not yet" ... because once you reach them for the interview, you will! Remember: be tenacious; be bold; and start your Journey. If you ask and they say no; what have you lost? Nothing!

In fact, I'd argue that with a rejection you increase your stamina for this very real and all too often experienced feeling. But tenacious people...successful people...overcome it and just move on to ask someone else.

Happiness

One way to tell that you have reached a level of success is to look at it from the outside in. Do others believe you are happy? I almost don't like using this particular word because happiness can be based on circumstances. But if you can live your life, finding joy in every day, in every experience, you'll quickly grow to understand that nothing is ever perfect; however, we can be "happy" and share that happiness with other people too. Focus on the joy.

In my 40s, I learned that while I was a student, working hard to finish high school and to finally achieve the dream of adulthood, my sister was jealous of me because of her perception that school came so easy to me. I never felt that way, I thought it was tough, but that was the way Terri perceived the situation. Neither of us was wrong, but I was finally old enough to understand that we can certainly appear successful even when we don't necessarily feel it.

Watch the duck swim smoothly through the water, all the while his little duck feet are paddling madly under the surface. Often people will see the cool, collected exterior without understanding how hard you are working. No one really needs to know so don't brag about your effort; let the result speak for you. Keeping quiet will help you avoid being perceived as haughty.

Be sure to listen to how your friends describe you and perceive your work. Perhaps you're happier than you think! So here's your last assignment: list three reasons you have to be happy and beside that, list a friend or two who knows about it. When you're done reading, reach out to those people and ask them how they see you. It's a good idea to check your alignment every so often. It makes for a smoother ride!

Great job! Now it's time to put it all into action. "Celebrate your genius; do something magical today!" Who do you want to be and how do you think you'll get there? Start logging your journey now with the understanding that there will be detours along the way. Something might cause you to sideline your existing goals to take advantage of an unexpected opportunity.

Things will not turn out exactly like you thought; but if you write it all down and try to work within a plan, you'll be amazed at how close you come.

Finally, remember that you'll experience the most success when you can incorporate your passion into your work or into your life. For example, look at my friend, an airline steward who works a flexible schedule two months on and three months off to have the time and flight opportunities to snowboard around the world.

What are your passions? Your goals? The success you want to achieve? No matter what you want to achieve, I believe you can.

I wish you all success!

ABOUT THE AUTHOR

Dr. Claire Maguire

Dr. Claire Maguire is the creative program director at The Retreat at Split Farthing Hall, a place where women come to be inspired to take the next step towards living a fantastic life. As a well-being and food coach, Claire combines transformative life coaching techniques with the power of alkalising and energising food to bring about clarity, focus and momentum. Claire draws on her diverse background and experience to create truly comprehensive programs that address all aspects of our well-being - health, energy, fitness, passion and emotional strength. With a PhD in medical biochemistry followed by working in top universities as a researcher Claire uses her analytical mind to laser in and get results whilst her background as an independent music company director utilises her creative mind to evoke fun, laughter and out of the box thinking to create lasting change. Her own health challenges with breast cancer and overcoming the devastating results of treatment have reinforced in her the upmost importance of our own self-worth, health and positive body image. This is what drives her to inspire other women feel fantastic about themselves.

Claire was nominated as Start-up Business Woman 2012 by Forward Ladies in Business and APCTC Health Coach of the Year 2011 for her work with women; is involved in creating a community of entrepreneurial women to thrive and is a supercoach graduate.

Her passions include dancing; watching her children grow and having fun; travel and yoga.

Dr. Claire Maguire is available for seminars, workshops, keynote addresses and corporate and/or personal coaching.

Contact
Dr Claire Maguire
The Retreat
Split Farthing Hall
Bagby, Thirsk
North Yorkshire YO7 2AF
United Kingdom
Tel: +44 (0) 1845 597 041
Email: info@splitfarthinghall.co.uk
Web: www.splitfarthinghall.co.ul

TWENTY-SIX

THREE WAYS TO INCREASE YOUR VITALITY AND THRIVE IN YOUR PROFESSIONAL LIFE

Dr. Claire Maguire

Being a busy young professional is time consuming. Your focus, your energy, your thoughts are on work and succeeding. You want to do your best and achieve. Yet as great as all this is, there can be moments when you're wondering if you're doing the right thing, anxious about your workload and worrying if you are good enough. This all gets too much leaving you exhausted and stressed. With your energy levels depleted and your mental strength dwindling you are looking at burn out. It's time to start focusing on increasing your vitality and caring for you, so you can thrive in your professional field.

How can you increase your vitality?

1. Be Present

We often live in the past or in the future (or both) yet rarely in the present moment. Do you wonder "what if I had done this differently, I should have said that, what will that person say about me, I know this is going to go badly" and so on? Wishing to change the past or predict the future? We cannot change anything about the past, as much as we would love to, and we cannot predict the future, as much as we try to. For sure, we can make a good guess based on past experience. We think we know, but the reality is we don't really. Yet we make preordained, often emotional responses to what we can do little about. Responses such as judging situations without seeing a full picture; making up our mind about things yet to occur, sliding into 'pity me' victim mode for past events and expecting people to act according to your emotions.

This may well sound harsh, but by clinging to the past you are not fully living and forgiving. And projecting into the future allows the beauty of everyday to pass you by and stops you engaging in life.

Both of these scenarios deplete your vitality as your emotions drain your energy.

It is, therefore, imperative to your wellbeing to be in the moment, to be present. Yet what exactly does that mean? It means living from moment to moment. Let go of the past and not worry about the future. Understand that you cannot change the past and that you cannot predict the future.

Does this mean that you drift through life never achieving? As a busy young professional woman this seems at odds with your desire to achieve and succeed.

In short, no! It does not mean that at all. For you need to have your goals and know the results you wish to attain to keep you happy. We all like to think we are heading somewhere. There is the old saying: *life is not the destination but the journey*. If we keep our focus so much on the destination we don't enjoy the moments that take us there.

I will never forget an episode as a 21 year old exploring the rainforests of Indonesia with our leader rushing us through to the final destination. I was very interested in botany and stopped to examine an exotic insect-eating plant. I called over others to look at it. But no, we had to move on, to get to the destination. It was as though getting there quicker was somehow better. Why? When was I going to be in the rainforest again? Was I ever going to see that plant again? What difference would it have made to arrive slightly later? My point being if we are so keen to rush forward then we forget to see what is around us.

But if we don't have an eye on the destination then how do we know if we're heading in the right direction and we could end up lost! So you need to have both – the result you wish to achieve and the enjoyment of the moments along the way.

How can you be present and enjoy the moment?

You need to stop! Stop everything that you may be doing and look around. What can you see? Really look hard at all that is around you. Notice the colours, the objects, the view, the furnishings, the people, anything within your vicinity. Then start to engage the other senses. What can you smell? What can you hear? What can you touch? And if you are eating, what can you taste? By using all the senses you take yourself out of your head and move more fully into the body. In doing so, you can stop the on-going internal chatter and focus on what is really happening around you. Right now - not in the past and not in the future.

You can then ask yourself the question – at this very moment is my world okay? Is anything really bad happening to me? Again think at this very moment. For sure, you may have a pressing deadline and it's stressing you out finishing it and you wonder if you will ever finish it on time, which leads onto thinking of all the consequences of what will happen if you never finish and then you remember a time when something awful did happen when you didn't complete on a deadline and so on and so on. The pressure and stress builds up and it's all you can think about. But again I am asking you to stop! Really ask yourself what is happening right now. Is anything awful, right this very second, occurring? Most of the time, the answer is no. We build the tension up in our head. The stress is made by us. When we let stress take over, the adrenalin kicks in and cortisol floods the body. That stress then becomes physically very real and as a consequence your health can suffer. This is why it becomes so important to recognise the stress you put upon yourself by not being present.

Keep practising the technique of stopping, engaging the senses and observing what is really happening around you at any given moment.

Try it when you are waiting in line at the grocery store, stuck in traffic or on the commute to work. Find other times when you can practise. What would be a good time for you stop and engage the senses, for you to be present? For the more you practise this technique when you are under less stress, the easier it becomes to employ when a major stressful event occurs.

Ultimately by the practise of being present you can get things done quicker, have more time, enjoy life more and as such your vitality increases.

2. Breathe

It seems an obvious statement to remind you to breathe. It is an unconscious act that if it didn't happen you would die. And quickly! Breathing is essential as the oxygen it delivers plays a crucial role to the functioning of your body. However, over the years your breathing often becomes shallower resulting in you taking in less oxygen. This becomes even more pronounced when you get stressed, anxious or worried and this in turn depletes your energy.

Take a moment and focus on your natural breathing. As you breathe in, notice if the breath is stopping at the chest or does your belly expand outwards? If it stops within the chest, as it does for so many women, this indicates that your breathing is shallow and your body is not getting the full amount of oxygen it needs to function optimally.

Now take a bigger breath in and focus as you inhale deeply. Allow the breath to expand your belly and as you exhale let the belly deflate fully. Continue this cycle. As you do this you are filling your lungs with air and flooding your body with oxygen.

This simple act of breathing deeply increases your vitality in a wonderfully simple way. Plus focusing on your breathing gives you the added benefit of switching off from your internal chatter thus allowing you to become present and in the moment. This is why the act of meditation is so highly regarded as a way to rejuvenate the mind and body.

If you can also step outside or at least be near an open window or door, you can combine deep breathing with the benefit of fresh air. The fresh air will help to increase your energy and vitality even more plus give you a sense of connection to nature, which is often sadly missing in our everyday professional work environment.

3. Food

In busy times, food is often just a grab and go affair. And with the availability of fast food, pre-packaged food, processed food, the food we grab is not always of the best quality. Combining this with feeling pressured, anxious or stressed means we are even more likely to reach for food that is unhealthy yet feels as if it brings comfort and satisfaction.

This may make you feel good for a moment but ultimately it drags you down and depletes your energy and vitality even further as sugary, salty or nutrient deficient foods leave your body searching for the minerals, vitamins and nutrients that are missing. Think of burgers, fries, chips, chocolate, cookies, cakes etc.

We could talk about the physiology of why highly processed foods are bad for you, particularly white flour and highly processed sugars and how they produce a roller coaster effect on your mood and energy levels or why it makes us feel bloated and/or lethargic, but this is not a diet article!

Instead I would like you to think about your food, over a typical day, from waking till you go to bed. Take a note of all the things you eat. There is no judgement here, just a way for you to see exactly what you consume within a day. Ask yourself, what time was it when you reached for a certain food? Were you really busy? Did you eat at your desk? Or did you give yourself a break and go off and eat elsewhere?

This exercise gives you an awareness of the types of food you eat and your patterns of how you eat.

Do the same again on another day, changing nothing about how you normally eat, and this time note down how you feel after eating a certain food. How do you feel immediately after eating? Be truthful… you may have felt euphoric and in heaven after eating your favourite cookie! Then note how you feel an hour after you have eaten. What often happens is you start to feel not so good. You may feel guilty that you ate the cookie or you might feel uncomfortable in your body or you may feel tired and lethargic.

You are now tracking your emotional and physical response to the way you are eating.

This may all seem too much to do, as you are busy. It may appear pointless, as you have deadlines to meet. Yet the reality is if you make the decision, these two exercises around food will not take long. The important bit is you have to want to. You have to desire to find out how food affects your vitality. Once you have that desire in place, it becomes fun to examine the effects food can have not only on your vitality but also on your mood.

It is from this place of fun and investigation that you will gain valuable insights and the knowledge of how and why you can effect changes to the food you consume.

When you have identified the various foods and how they affect you, you can start to ask the question, do I want to remove this food from my diet and if so what will I replace it with?

It is easy to think you will just remove something from your diet if it doesn't serve you. Yet if that food provides comfort, or a distraction, or some emotional response of some kind, then it becomes harder to just take this food away. You will crave it on a deeper level than just satisfying hunger, as you really want the emotional satisfaction. It, therefore, becomes crucial to ask what other healthier food option can give you the emotional lift you seek. Alternatively once you have identified the emotion, what can you do to satisfy that feeling without involving food at all?

For example, you have found that you constantly eat cookies around 3pm at your desk and then you feel disgusted with yourself, guilty that you ate too many, you feel fat with low energy. You dig a bit deeper and find that around 3pm you are fed up and want to go home from work, you are feeling tired and a build-up of anxiety is forming in your body as you don't think you will get all your work done for the day. By reaching for a cookie (or 2 or 4 or more!), you firstly might think it will give your energy levels a boost with the sugar, then secondly you are giving yourself a bit of love and encouragement to keep going and thirdly the 'hand to mouth' action of eating creates a mini break from what you are doing and quells the anxiety building as it acts as stress relief.

If you remove the cookies altogether and do nothing, you are not boosting your energy, you are not giving yourself love and encouragement and you are not getting any stress relief. And this is what keeps you trapped craving the cookies.

As we are trying to increase vitality and you know the end result of eating this snack is not more energy and a big dose of love but actually feeling lethargic and guilty, then this cookie is seriously going to have to go.

But, knowing you have to satisfy the emotional aspect, you need to find a different snack which will boost your sugar levels sensibly, increase your energy and be healthy too. Options include a piece of fruit and a handful of nuts, a piece of raw chocolate or a green smoothie (if you have access to a blender) made up of fruit and greens such as spinach and cucumber. This allows you the sweetness that you crave together with a longer lasting energy boost. You also get your mini stress relief break by eating and consequently lower your anxiety, all with the added benefit of removing those feelings of guilt as you know you are consuming food which is healthy and full of nutrients.

Alternatively, you could say no to food totally and satisfy these emotional needs with some deep breathing, a couple of minutes of meditation and/or spending five minutes becoming present by noticing what is around you and increasing your awareness.

Enjoy using these three different yet complementary techniques to boost your vitality and thrive in your professional life.

ABOUT THE AUTHOR

MALA SHAH

Mala is an Author, Speaker, Trainer, NLP coach and a business woman. She is of Indian Origin, born in Kenya, and grew up in United Kingdom. Mala has grown up surrounded by the very positive, entrepreneurial spirit of the family. She joined her father's business where she expanded her organizational and communication skills and learnt about international business etiquette.

She believes **"Nothing is impossible if you put your mind to it"**.
In her mid 30's she returned to education at Birkbeck College where she achieved BSc in Psychology. During this time she had joined European Bank for Reconstruction and development where she travelled to Ukraine, Bulgaria, Latvia, Georgia, Azerbaijan and Russia. At the bank and from her personal travels she mentored and coached bankers and organised workshops at business libraries.

She left the bank in 2007 to start her own coaching and mentoring business. Mala's unique style of coaching, leadership and management skills led her to create her own model called "C.I.P", which was launched in her recent book. Mala's vision is to inspire women by doing and showing that one can achieve whatever one decides to do.

Her leadership style has attracted new business offering managerial expertise at seminars and events where attendance has been 500 to over 8,000 participants. Her team has assisted at seminars and events with keynote speakers such as ex-President Bill Clinton, Sir Richard Branson, Lord Alan Sugar, T. Harv Eker, Robert Kiyosaki, and many others!

She has defied odds, co-authored three books in less than 10 months and climbed Mt Kilimanjaro, the highest mountain in Africa. Mala is available as a personal coach and speaker.

Books co-authored
Breaking Free: Overcoming Self Sabotage: Chapter Title: "Mission to Success" (2013)
The Young Professional Woman: Chapter Title: "5 Elements to Success" (2013)
Breaking the Barriers: A woman's success tool kit   Chapter Title: "Be a Core Genius" (2013)

Expertise:
Formulae for Self Confidence and Self Esteem building
Creator of "C.I.P" model

Seminar and Training offered:
Mission to Success   5 Elements to Success
Power your Success   Be a Core Genius

Association:
The Professional Woman Network (PWN)   http://www.prowoman.net
The Professional Woman International Speakers Bureau http://www.protrain.net
The Society of Neuro-linguistic Programming   http://www.society-of-nlp.net

Contact;
Email: mala@malashah.com
Website: www.malashah.com www.mds-events.com

TWENTY-SEVEN

5 ELEMENTS TO SUCCESS

Mala Shah

"I have come to believe that each of us has a personal calling that's as unique as a fingerprint – and that the best way to succeed is to discover what you love and then find a way to offer it to others in the form of service, working hard, and also allowing the energy of the universe to lead you". —Oprah Winfrey

Oprah Winfrey respected as "America's most powerful and influential woman". According to Forbes' international rich list, Oprah Winfrey is listed as the worlds only black billionaire from 2004 to 2006 and named her the world's most powerful celebrity in 2005, 2007, 2009 and 2010. CNN and Time.com called Winfrey "arguably the world's most powerful woman. Life magazine named Winfrey one of the 100 people who changed the world. Winfrey is the only living person to make the list, alongside such luminaries as Elvis Presley and Lady Mary.

I converse about Oprah Winfrey as **one** of the most dynamic individuals who influenced my life. I remember back in late 1980's I would rush to watch her show on TV where she interviewed experts and ordinary individuals about their work, life and challenges they overcame. Some of the episodes had significant impact on me and challenged me to open the door to my destiny. Some of the things I learnt by following her story and others such Richard Branson, founder of the Virgin Group, Anthony Robbins, Wayne Dyer and many others who have shown great business skills and wisdom worthy of emulation.

Over the years I made notes of what happened when I made a decision whether a right or wrong one, analysed the patterns which moved me forward and the ones which became obstacles in achieving my goals. Five things came up again and again, which, had I not nurtured these, then I was almost sure to delay the time-frame of achieving my goals. We must understand that in order to appreciate an exotic flower such as an "Orchid" we have to plant the seeds, water it regularly, look after (and yes some of us do talk to our plants!) and watch it grow. But these days we can buy these ready flowering plants from the super-market without having to plant the seeds. However, we would still have to nurture the plant otherwise it will die. Similarly the 5 Elements to Success are Personal, Values, Health, Professional and Spiritual will need nurturing during our life-time.

5 Elements to Success

In my opinion each of these five elements has an **attitude.** It is how we approach each one of these that will define the path to our success. What intentions do we carry? Do we even know ourselves fully? With what purpose and sense of satisfaction are we carrying on with our daily routine? All these questions are inter-connected and the answers lie within our-selves!

Below I have added a couple of questions against each of the 5 elements:

1. Personal: How do you approach things in life? Positive vs. Negative thinking

2. Values: What are your opinions? How do you define your values?

3. Health: What are your thoughts on healthy living?

4. Professional: How do /will you manage your time or change?

5. Spiritual: Meditation, Music, inner conscience

Ask yourself: Look at each of the 5 Elements and write down your own thoughts or questions against each one of them.

Personal Element: For me the Personal Element consists of Positive Thoughts, Communication, Relationship, Reflect and Self-Development.

Personal Element

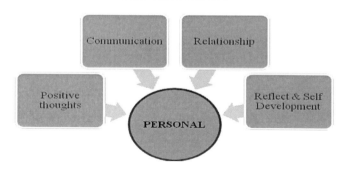

"Positive thinking will let you do everything better than negative thinking will". —Zig Ziglar

Positive Thoughts: Our mind works in two parts: conscious and sub-conscious. Whatever we do consciously and repeatedly, will get registered into our sub-conscious mind. The sub-conscious mind does not reason, it does not distinguish between right and wrong, it does not know whether it is silly or practical, it does not judge, what it does do is it routinely stores all the information. The sub-conscious will then retrieve these thoughts and produce a result, so if you have more negative thoughts stored the result will be negative and vice versa.

<u>For example:</u> You are invited to a party, that you had been waiting for so long, but between the time you received the invitation and the date of the party, you had an argument with your best friend and stopped talking since, the party is on the other side of the city from where you reside and you did not want to go there alone and on top of this the weather forecast is for heavy rain. So already even before stepping into your party dress you have created all the negative thoughts in your mind before anything really has happened. You have created your own bad mood. You are now tense and grumpy which means when you do arrive at the party if someone irritated you or spoke out of context you may leash out (get angry) at the wrong person.

Learn the art of the Power of positive thinking, change (turnaround) a negative thought pattern in to a positive thought.

Negative: "It is not okay to think about my needs".

Positive: "My needs are equally important are as anyone else's".

Negative: "I cannot do anything right. I am a failure".

Positive: "I can do many things right, I succeed and get better each time".

Ask Yourself: What are your current thoughts? Write down those that do not work for you and begin replacing them. Once you have reviewed these repeat the positive ones.

Communication: We can communicate in three ways, Oral, written and non-verbal.

To communicate effectively we must learn to listen to others too. For example, if your boss gives you simple, but straight-forward verbal instructions but you failed to listen with a clear mind as you were thinking of something else or were tired at that time, you may miss vital points which would assist you in completing your task on time. Now if your boss had followed it up with clear written instructions, you may have been able to finish your task on time. Another thing to remember while communicating is not only how **Clear** you are but talk with concise, **straight to the point**, do not go round and round in 3 different sentences when you can communicate it in one sentence. Know your topic, make sure that you have the **correct** information in full. Is your information **consistent** and in line with reality? Does it exist? Finally ensure that you convey your message with **politeness** taking into consideration the diverse audience, their culture background and ensuring that you use **right non-verbal cues**, body language, facial expression and tone of voice during oral communication. Correct communication builds good personal or business relationships. While it is important to present ourselves with **clarity**, **consistently** and **politely** it is equally important for us to learn to listen. Listening requires **patience.** By tentative listening you are showing empathy and expressing interest not only in what has been said but the person too. Listening **builds** **trust** and bonding in both professional and personal relationships.

Ask Yourself: How do you know when someone stops listening to you? How often do you listen tentatively or pretend to listen is there a pattern with a particular person, place or topic?

Relationship: Invest time in relationships, to add to **your** success and happiness.

In the work-place or your own business, **focus** on introducing (networking) yourself to others whenever the opportunity presents itself: at meetings, during seminars, celebrating a co-workers' birthday or promotion, establish contacts with other departments within the organisation. Assist in house pilot schemes, become a committee member, or offer your Volunteer services through work schemes. Every time you introduce yourself you are raising your profile and making others aware of who you are, so when you do communicate with them with a proposal or suggestions they will have some background information about you. Remember, people will not know of you, unless they have met you or you made an excellent impression on them on your first meeting. People cannot read our minds so it is important to establish and be part of a good network of people. For example: when I was working for a bank I took the opportunity to know of any new systems to be introduced in the team and offered my time during the trials, to learn and give my feedback. By doing this I gained a first-hand insight into the programme /system. Later I realised the impact it had both on my personal growth, it boosted my confidence but most importantly I continued to build a trusting, working relationship with my colleagues. Trusting relationships, whether professional or personal, are based on **truthfulness**, **clarity** and about your **promise to commitments**.

Keep It Simple and Straight forward. (KISS)

Reflection and Self Development: Self Analyses your weaknesses and strengths. At the end of each day or at least weekly reflect in your mind, or better still write down what went well and what you could do to improve analyzing the opportunities and threats that flow from them. SWOT Analysis is a useful technique that helps you do this.

SWOT Analysis

	Positive factors	Negative Factors
Internal Factors	Strength	Weakness
External Factors	Opportunity	Threat

Once you have analysed your thought pattern, relationships, communication and reflected on strength and weaknesses, it is time to step up to the next level. Keeping yourself informed by reading books, checking/researching on the internet, attending events, seminars on personal development, it is important to take on interesting yet challenging training courses. These courses do not have to be work-related you could learn to paint or learn a new language or even take on dancing classes. Keep on improving yourself in different areas.

If you wish to achieve worthwhile things in your personal and career life, you must become a worthwhile person in your own self-development".
—Brian Tracy

Values

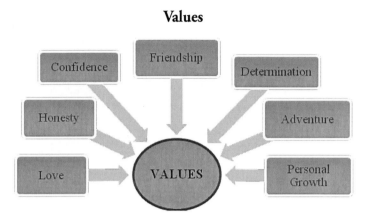

Values: Everyone has core values. By discovering your values you can begin to determine the hidden conflicts in your life. Some people are more aware of their core values then others, for example they may believe that love, and determination, honesty, confidence, friendship, resourcefulness, adventure and personal growth makes them happy and fulfils their purpose of life. These core values align in making decisions in your life.

"Here are the values that I stand for: honesty, equality, kindness, compassion, treating people the way you want to be treated and helping those in need. To me, those are traditional values".
—By Ellen DeGeneres

Ask yourself: What are your core values? Do you believe in these values? Do you actually follow these values? How do they enhance your life?

Health is Wealth

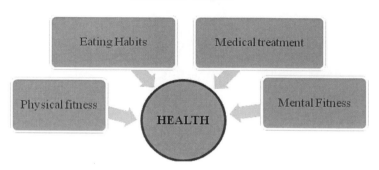

Health is very important. Although I have sub listed: Physical fitness, Eating habits, Medical treatment and Mental Fitness in the above chart, I am not going to bore you by going into details as there are many books and research information online in the market which you can access to read according to your needs. However the point I am trying to make is that one must not forget about taking care of **physical fitness.** This can be in the form of a 10 minute brisk walking from your train station to your work and the same on the return journey home. For example: Leave work with an aim to reach your station minutes before the train is going to depart, this way you may save gym membership and yet get exercise in the fresh air.

Eating Habits: Many of us will have that extra helping when we know there is no need for it. If your body could talk, what would it state about your eating habits? We must treat our body as a temple and respect what we serve/ put inside it. Eat wisely to live well.

Medical treatment: Have regular health check-ups at your local clinic. Keep track of your medical needs. If you are not happy, Always ask for a second opinion from another medical expert.

Mental Fitness: Train your Brain. Spend at least 10-15 minutes every day. For Example challenge your brain by doing Crosswords,

Sudoku and or play electronic games. These games rely on logic and math and words and can improve your brain's speed and memory.

Ask yourself: Do I get breathless after climbing a flight of stairs? Do I have regular meal times or do I eat too late at night? Is my brain alert at remembering things? How fast can I memorize or calculate simple math?

Professional Element

Time Management: Is all about prioritising things. Make a To Do list, prioritise what needs doing first. Set your Goal/s for the day or week. Do not take on more work than you can handle, learn to say NO or if you are in a superior position schedule a meeting with your team and delegate the work. Do not get distracted by others or tedious tasks. Take regular breaks away from your desk or office. Get Focused on what you are doing rather than multitasking e.g. writing emails while trying to converse on the phone will actually increase time spent on these tasks.

Change Management: We all go through change in our personal and professional lives. Every organisation goes through change so be prepared. How? Recognize the positive side to any change and have clarity on what you want to achieve, what is your mission? It is out of fear of the unknown that we resist change. Change is inevitable, and heavily influenced by technology, world financial economy, globalization and consumer demands.

Negotiation Skills: Some say negotiation is an art. I would agree (to a point) if we follow some of the points: Know your client, find out what you can do your due diligence and you know where you stand. Listen to the full "deal", do not be the first one to make an offer, this will put you in a poor position. By keeping quiet you are making the opposite person nervous and to react and make an offer. Be reasonable about accepting the offer. Do not always squeeze for more. On the other hand if you were offering the deal, then accentuate on your strong points and point out the weakness of your opponent. Negotiate with clarity and etiquette.

"Good Manners will open doors that/the best education cannot"
—by Clarence Thomas

Etiquette: Good manners/ behaviour in the workplace. Treat your boss and colleagues, with respect. Support them when you think they are overwhelmed with work. Avoid gossip about other colleagues. Keep your personal life private but do find common ground to share. When doing business with other countries, learn the business culture, like timing keeping of meetings, methods of greeting, exchanging business cards and do they mix personal and business life?

Spirituality: should not be limited to religion but extend it to our **self-awareness.** How often do we take time out to listen to our breathing? May be 45 seconds to a minute. Breathing, meditation, music and even smiling is related to our spiritual welfare. When you meditate you focus on one thing, become aware of your breathing, or you listen to music to relax your mind and body. People notice when you smile and wonder what are you up to? You use more facial muscles when you frown then when you SMILE. Enhance your spirit by understanding forgiveness and finding out how to give generously not necessarily monetarily but with love and passion.

Be true to yourself, discover your purpose, be bold, work hard, rise to the challenge and you will find success. Oprah worked hard for 25 years to attain the status and continues to work on her OWNetwork. She faced many challenges but never gave up on her dreams in fact she commits 100% to everything she does.

Ask yourself: How ready are you to manage your time and change? Are you flexible and adaptable to situations? How well do you know the opposite person? Are you 100% committed to your goal to success? Do you need a coach/ mentor to help you along the journey?

I have shared with you my 5 elements to success which have been useful during my journey. I leave you with the thought:

"Winners do not do different things, they do things differently.
They put in the extra mile" —by Shiv Khera

Tips:

- Choose someone who has the skills to Mentor /Coach you to your next level of your career or your business.

- Surround yourself with like minded positive individuals.

ABOUT THE AUTHOR

Pauline Duncan-Thrasher

Pauline Duncan-Thrasher helps women of all ages and some men to enhance their communication skills on and off the platform.

As a certified consultant /trainer she specializes in helping leaders use Language Behavior Profile to take their teams to new heights of awareness.

She has practised skills she teaches during thirty years as an active Toastmaster, leader, mentor and award winning speaker.

Her Speak and Lead manual provides practical tips for professional speaking by leaders in every walk of life. Pauline wrote her first book "Swimmin' Women" after retiring from a rewarding career as an educator. "Out of Frenzy into Focus" is a workbook that she developed to help those suffering from the kind of anxiety that she had experienced as a young woman.

Pauline has recently added inspiring presentations for spiritual groups and churches to her Amazingly You company.

In addition to her love of camping holidays in a tent with her husband Dan. she is a trained Prayer Chaplain who enjoys volunteering with a Breakfast program for children. a contributing author to Expert Women Who Speak... Speak Out,

The Power of a Woman... Embracing the Woman Within and the soon to be released Celebrate Life and The Young Professional Woman.

Contact:
519-681-9238
beamazinglyyou@gmail.com

TWENTY-EIGHT

BE TRUE TO YOURSELF: LESSONS FOR YOUNG WOMEN

Pauline Duncan-Thrasher

This is a chapter about Happy Life skills.

Without joy all of the so called "hard" skills are pretty meaningless.

"Be true to yourself" sounds awesome to me. How does it sound to you?

To me "Being True to Yourself" could be a motto on the shield of a warrior charging into battle.

Can you hear stirring music and see yourself astride a beautiful white horse ready to gallop into battle?

Joan of Arc was one of my childhood heroes even though she was burned at the stake.

Thankfully being martyred is not an inevitable result of self honesty.

Being honest with yourself, knowing what truly matters and being congruent with values and behavior is the secret to genuine, lasting happiness.

Money can't buy self truth. Being candid with who you are and what you value will open you to receiving rewards immediately.

One of the many uplifting message that's been on our fridge door for more than ten years is a tiny picture of our then one and half year old granddaughter. Her tiny face smiles out from inside a frame that proclaims: "Life is good… eat it up!" "C'est bon la vie…savourez-la!" The dark brown smiling eyes of an innocent, jubilant Mackenzie proclaim a delight in life we all want to have.

Perhaps you have such photos of you as a very young child, looking gleefully into the camera, rejoicing in life. We can recapture that joy by knowing who we are and living according to our own values. Discover the many joys of daily life and absorb them with as much gusto as you do nutritious tasty food. Discovering your values, your dreams, your connections with others can be an exciting life long adventure.

Or you can take the easy way out and just accept your current status. Choosing not to explore might feel safer and easier but it is certainly not as interesting .Following your own ideals rather than the ethics of someone else builds inner strength. Like everything worthwhile this journey requires courage and perseverance.

We'll talk about those traits later on.

First we need to address two pivotal questions.

How can you be true to yourself until you know yourself?

Answer: You can't. Until you recognize what you value, accept and act on it you will sway in every wind that attracts you, listen to every voice but your own, never building roots of confidence.

What is the process in learning more about yourself?

Four Stages

1. Recognize the filters that may cloud your reality.

Filters cloud the real picture of the amazing person who lives under all of the directions, interactions and experiences that flood us while we are growing up. Assumptions about us by other people can dry up our creative juices because when we accept labeling filters as permanent we often cease to grow.

Filters are a lot like those super sticky labels that require massive elbow grease to remove. They come from our teachers, classmates, parents, siblings, friends and sometimes even ourselves.

Have you heard any of the following applied to you?

"She is so polite, so quiet, so noisy, so argumentative, so kind, so nice, a bit rough, a tomboy if you ever saw one, so shy…" The list is endless.

Filters may label a relationship we are perceived to have with others:

"She's a mother's girl, a daddy's girl, the life of the party, a real loner, a book worm." Sometimes adjectives come from bullies who describe us in nasty terms that serve only their purposes. "Apple polisher, baby, sore loser." If not dealt with those filters can leave lasting scars. Sometimes the filters are an honest reflection of what people see at the time.

As we mature hopefully we begin to realize that what people say about us does not define us. It's merely their perception.

2. Remove the filters.

During the process of removing the filters or at least looking at other aspects of ourselves we discover the amazing opportunities that await those who are ready to expand their horizons. If people have called you "so quiet" as they did me, perhaps you can turn this to your advantage by realizing that in your quietness you are listening to others, reflecting and responding thoughtfully. Moving from "shy" may involve learning to communicate more effectively by sharing with children or seniors in nursing homes.

3. Describe yourself today.

Because I was lucky enough to teach young children for more than thirty years I meet many former students to the delight of both them and me. Eight year olds who had to gaze up at me are now twenty eight year olds (or older) often with their own eight year old children. Some students appear only to have grown taller physically. In other ways they seem still quite similar to the children I once taught. Others look more confident, smile more readily, speak more clearly. Some have surpassed their goals set in grade school. Others have settled for less than was expected.

How would your former teacher describe you now?

More important than that, how would you describe yourself now?

Being true to ourselves is about learning to understand our own values, being congruent with actions and those values.

4. Create your own Kudos.

We need to create our own kudos for the times when others are too busy or too distracted to build us up. "Kudos" can be a mantra that lets you know if you're on track to discovering the real you. Kudos can also let you know if you are being true to your real you as opposed to the person others may have misjudged or underestimated.

> **Know** what is important to you.

> **Understand** that others may not agree with your values and that's okay.

> **Do** what matches your values. Be congruent.

> **Open** your mind and heart to positive possibilities.

> **Sing** a song of joy in life each day.

When you make these five activities a daily habit you can create a life that is Amazingly You! You can glide joyfully into your own "amazingly you" identity.

Keep a journal outlining your Kudos for the month, the week, each day.

Your journal doesn't need to be complicated. It can be for your eyes only.

Evaluate your actions based on your priorities.

1. **KNOW** that what is important today may be quite different than what was important in high school.

Perhaps you are at a stage where a well paying job is more important than being popular with your friends. For you being fit may take precedence over going out partying every Friday night. Someone else may enjoy getting together with friends. They may see this as essential for mental health and well being after a challenging week of work. If you are a parent or a newly wed, your time with family may rank number one after your work. Enjoying a balanced life with time to relax as well as to learn may be most important to you. Engaging in an ongoing program of spiritual growth may engage another individual eager to venture into new territory.

Not one of these choices is necessarily right or wrong. So many alternatives can seem daunting but they are also freeing. Because you are an adult you get to choose.

You have the right to decide where, how and with whom you will spend your time.

You have the right to determine where you will direct your energy.

You have the right to change direction if you feel you are not being true to yourself.

2. **UNDERSTAND** that although everyone seems to have free advice the bottom line is that you are the one who needs to wade through all of the ideas until you arrive at what suits you Your choices may mirror what your parents want for you or they may be vastly different. You may need to put your foot down to let family and friends know that your right to decide is your right. Each of us has the right to choose what we believe to be important. You may be the first in your family to graduate from university or you may be the first to choose to **not** enter university, instead embarking

on a year or so of traveling, volunteering or combining work experiences with part time study.

Filters are descriptors that are attached to us often by well meaning people who love us.

When they include "always" or "you can count on "you may feel as I used to, a little trapped. You may need to consciously fight the urge to always be as others expect you to be. Rebel if you are not meeting your sense of what is right.

3. **DO** focus on creating a life that is wonderfully fulfilling every day. Starting fresh each day gives us permission to forgive ourselves for past mistakes, to forgive others and to concentrate on enjoying the moment before us.

How often do we find ourselves complaining about what is going wrong: the weather, our looks, our relationships, and our work?

Taking charge of our thoughts is a necessary discipline for anyone who wants to be happy. Positive or negative thinking influences all of our actions because our mind is always with us, waking or sleeping.

4. **Open** your mind to a life that is creative, joy filled and rewarding: a life filled with possibility thinking followed with action.

All of us need messages that help to keep us on track .Some positive reminders are small enough to be enclosed inside a hand.

When I was teaching grade school, looking for an uplifting message for my students I bought a little stamper that still sits on my office desk. Although the edges are a little frayed it still encourages me to continue encouraging others as well as myself. It's a picture of a small train chugging up a hill. The little train has a smile on its face. The words beneath the mini tracks say "You Can Do It!" You may recognize it from the inspiring children's book by Watty Piper called *The Little Engine That Could.* When much bigger engines were too tired, frightened or busy to accept the challenge of hauling a long train of freight the smallest engine accepted the challenge. After much huffing and puffing, with repeating over and over "I can do it! I can do it!" the little engine was successful.

Going down the hill on the other side the words changed to "I thought I could. I thought I could." There may be times when you are the only one who thinks you can.

Being belittled by others who may have louder voices or greater stature in the company or business world can happen unless we take steps to insure that we know where we stand

Persevering in our journey of self discovery may be difficult at times. I can recall many times in my life filled with self doubt, wondering what others were seeing that seemed missing to me. Could I actually do the task before me? Occasionally a little doubt still sneaks in, especially when facing new challenges. Affirming what is important, restating personal strengths, reflecting on past victories all help to make life doable and even fun. Realizing that the words of others do not impact us unless we allow them in has helped me. A major advantage of being an adult is accepting the power of choosing for ourselves. We no longer need to obey blindly the whims of our friends or the will of the crowd.

5. **Sing.** *"A bird does not sing because it has an answer. It sings because it has a song."*

Chinese proverb

Your song begins as an independent spirit. You may still remember your rebellious nature as a teenager. Maybe you argued just for the sake of arguing. Maybe you kept your responses churning inside. Maybe you couldn't wait til you were old enough to make up your own mind. As an adult you discover that there is a price for independent thinking but also a joy.

As I wrote in my first book Swimmin' Women "*Life without independence is like a shell without the egg.*" Enjoy freeing your creative spirit by independent thinking. What joy when you can look your self in the eye, stand up straight and declare with conviction. "You are amazing" to your reflection in the mirror. My own little fridge mirror was purchased a long time ago in a ten cent store! It was my response to living alone. What a breakthrough to finally realize that waiting for the compliments of others kept me feeling too needy. The message on my mirror always gets a laugh from my audiences because women relate to the need for self acceptance. It says "Looks Good to Me!" Because looking and feeling are so interconnected you may have already learned that determining what you are passionate about gives you a head start.

What excites you? What makes you want to dance for joy? What traits are parts of your life style? The best way to celebrate you is to be true to yourself.

Rate the following twenty two traits as (**E**) Essential, (**I**) Important or (**N**) Non essential.

Consider an activity that you currently engage in or a possible new activity for each trait that you deem as necessary for your happiness and success. How do you interact?

How might you interact if you used these traits effectively?

Be mindful of your mini and major victories. Reflect on a time when you did achieve at least a partial success by accomplishing or rejoicing. Small pleasures abound : seeing your neighbor wave from her front porch, witnessing a teenager help someone to cross the street, learning a new phrase in another language complete with a friendly hug from a newcomer to Canada, getting all hot and sweaty from your favorite Zumba class, laughing with participants of all ages, meditating quietly in your favorite park, enjoying music with a good friend, savoring a delicious treat, smelling freshly mown grass at the start of spring, rereading an enjoyable book, eating popcorn while watching a good movie, encouraging a needy friend who is feeling sad. What does your list look like?

For much of my pre-adult life the only place I felt confident was when speaking to a group of fellow students. Because of my teachers' brilliant insight it was possible to become passionate about public speaking from an early age.

Be true to what totally engages you. Challenges will still come but following your passion will energize you. You will rejoice every day. Throughout your life you will need sometimes to be tough with others or even yourself in order to protect your own values. Saying "yes" when you really mean "NO" may seem easy but the pain has lasting repercussions.

Remember your own spirit is amazingly resilient as long as you believe in your dreams.

BE bold. BE positive. BE true to yourself.

Original Poem by Author Pauline Duncan-Thrasher

Perseverance

Pluck armors us to wage daily battle

Obstinately deny defeatist thoughts

Soar with exhilarated optimism

Intent focus on the task at hand

Tough enough to stay the course

Intelligent or so we'd like to think

Versatile

Exciting

Lasting beyond all expectations

Young at heart

Passion pushes us to create priorities

Able to persevere through blocks that stop smooth journeys

Uncork hidden energy to sustain momentum

Learn to laugh and love despite disappointment

Inner fortitude beneath an outer calm

Notching new cuts in our experience belts

Energizing our spirits with visions of what we most desire.

Recommended Reading:

Finding Joy by Mac Anderson

Esteem by Kathy Glover Scott MSW

Swimmin' Women by Pauline Duncan-Thrasher

Notes:

_____

_____

_____

_____

_____

_____

_____

_____

_____

_____

_____

_____

_____

_____

_____

_____

_____

_____

_____

_____

_____

ABOUT THE AUTHOR

Jaelyn Davis

Jaelyn Caprice Davis has volunteered for her town clean-up day and was the Barnes &Noble Winner of How My Teacher Helped Me Learn Essay Contest, Best Athletes in AAU book, Student of the month, Honor Roll, Chorus, Library Helper, and participated in several plays in school including Guys & Dolls, Seussical, Canterbury Tales & Story of 3 Bullfrogs. She attends modeling and acting class with hobbies that include writing, track, soccer and shopping.

Her dream is to one day be a successful author and Lawyer. Her parents always told her that she could be whatever she wanted in life and she loves them very much for believing in her. They said Jaelyn she would have to study hard and believe in herself that would lead to confidence. God has blessed her with many talents which she wants to share with others, which is why she chose to write about the Importance of Having Confidence for young women. By having Confidence it gives you many opportunities in life. She feels blessed that to have had this opportunity to write her story.

Remember Dream Big and have Confidence in yourself!

THE IMPORTANCE OF CONFIDENCE FOR YOUNG WOMEN

Jaelyn Davis

For young women and teens who seek confidence
What is the importance of confidence for young women? Well, personally confidence means feeling sure about the right thing to do. For example, I always wanted to be a young author, but at first I did not have confidence in myself until I realized that I could do

it! Don't be afraid to express yourself. Also don't be afraid of doing something that you want to do (even if it means stepping out of your comfort zone)

To start with, everyone needs to have confidence. For young women, you need to have confidence so you do not get bullied or picked on in school. I never got bullied because I always believed in myself and I had confidence. Bullies tend to seek out the meekest and weakest- they prey on young women who can't defend themselves. So, stand tall, shoulders back, look others in the eye, use a firm voice, and *appear* confident! You might be trembling on the inside but on the outside you *look* confident and generally the bully will pass you by. (The more you step into this 'confidence role', the more it will feel comfortable in time).

Having inner confidence is huge as well. I talked about 'looking the part' but deep within yourself, consider all the things you do right! Are you confident in your friendships? Sports? Music? Owning a pet? Succeeding in school? Standing up for those less fortunate? Never give up believing in yourself! Do you want to have a life with no accomplishments, achievements, or a time when you stood up for yourself and what you believe? Or do you want to show your talent with great confidence. Don't be afraid to show what you have as a talent. Why? We were all blessed with a special talent and gift. Put your shoulders back and stand strong by believing in what you stand for! What are your values? What will you stand strong for and voice your opinion?

Below are eight examples of how important it is to have Confidence in your life.

Follow Your Dreams

First, you should always follow your dreams. Never be a follower, always be a leader. If you slowly get pulled into peer pressure, then that's when you have to know how to speak up for yourself and have something called confidence. Has anyone ever told you "here try this"? Or "come on do it, stop being a baby?" If so, they are trying to influence you to do something whether it is drugs, alcohol, or sex. It still doesn't matter, either way you're still getting pulled into peer pressure. Have the confidence to say "no"!

Stand Up for What You Believe In

Second, stand up for what you believe in. For example, if you see a kid getting bullied or picked on, stand up for them. Do what you what you think is right. Stride to go in the right direction. Here is a little tip: just imagine that you were the person being picked on. They are hurt and probably torn inside. Many people just walk right on by and ignore the situation and the bullying and taunting may escalate. Step in or find someone in authority! Do what is right!

Be Friendly and Accepting of Others

Third, you should always be a relaxed and friendly person in order to have confidence. Reach out to others who are different than you in race, appearance and personality. Judge not. Learn to *accept* others rather than *tolerating them.* Don't worry about what others may say about you. Be confident in standing up for others and befriending those who are different.

Try to Practice and Build Up Your Self-Confidence

Forth, try to build up your self-confidence. That means don't be afraid to do what you know is right. Do what your heart tells you. For example, if you are an extremely shy person and you get nervous when people or someone talks to you that may mean you don't have self confidence. Think about this when you are in school and you are extremely shy to talk in front of the whole class while reading an essay. Everyone else in your class has to read an essay, don't they? Do you think that some might be as shy and nervous as you? Probably! They might feel the same exact way that you feel. But, there will be those who will muster up the confidence to read the essay believing in themselves and that they CAN do it! That should be YOU! You can do it!

Talk to yourself positively.

Remember Times When Your Were Successful and Overcame Fear

Fifth, my story relates to having self confidence. One time I walked past a board that said "**School Talent Show: Auditions will be held next week.**" I really wanted to try out for this so my friend and I made up a dance and were pumped up and ready. The day of the talent show, I looked around and I saw a bunch of other students waiting to audition, too. I was getting really nervous and felt like running out of the room and screaming in complete fear. I then realized in my mind that all of the kids were also auditioning and probably as nervous as I was! We weren't the only ones. At that very moment, I realized that I needed to have confidence in order to do well. So we auditioned and because of our confidence, we made it into the talent show.

Stand Up for Others

If you see an animal being abused, stand up for it! If you think something is unfair in life, write to the company. Take action! It takes a confident voice to make a difference in the world!

Make a Difference

Be a confident, trustworthy friend. Be known as a person who holds confidentialities, doesn't gossip, and is honest and fair. Listen to others; empathize with their sorrows and celebrate their joys. Don't compare yourself to others. You are unique just the way you are. Be the role model for others so you can make a difference in their lives.

Practice Random Acts of Kindness

Eighth, practice random act of kindness for someone else each day. What I mean is that confidence is sticking up for someone who needs it. And a random act of kindness is helping someone without an applause or trophy. You help them just to help them. If you put the random act of kindness and mix it with confidence, you feel so good on the inside and know you don't need recognition from others to fee the satisfaction of kindness toward another human. Let's say you wanted to help an elderly woman cross the street, then you can't be afraid to help her, or she may not cross the street safely. Have the confidence to do what's right.

Next, if you're thinking confidence is not important, then you are 100% wrong. Let's think about the President for a quick second. We all know that all of the Presidents need to have confidence. Why? Well, they had to have confidence or they wouldn't be where they are today, especially our recent President Barack Obama. He had to go through so many obstacles to reach the level where he is today. But he focused on his education, became an attorney and then an eloquent speaker. If he is nervous, you'd never know it! He has stepped into his confidence and so can you!

As you can see, you can be anything you want to be if you set your mind to it and have confidence. If you want to be an actress or a lawyer or anyone you want to be, don't let anyone or anything hold you back. Do what you want to do. For the hundredth time, have confidence! Believe in yourself! Confidence goes a long way in life. If you want to have a leading role in a play or musical, then do it. Later in life you'll reflect back to the time when you were shaking in your boots and thought you couldn't muster the strength to try out for that musical, but you did, and you also got the part! When you're an adult and trying for a new job or position, you'll remember the times you mustered up the confidence with shoulders back, standing tall with firm voice and saying to yourself " **I can do it!**"

Conclusion

In conclusion, I hope my short little story helped you understand the true meaning of the importance of confidence. The importance of confidence will help now and you get older in life. Having confidence is important and it gives you the courage to stand up to a bully. Whether you are the one being bullied or you are the one helping someone else being bullied. And if you are a bully, just think of the victim that you are making feel really small. They might not know what confidence really is. Try putting yourself into their shoes and see how you feel. If you are the victim, have confidence in yourself and show the bully that you are important no matter what they say. Everyone in the world is important in their own special way. Also, when you do a random act of kindness, do it because you want to, not because you have to or you were forced to.

I always dreamed of being a young author and sharing my words with others. Now I am. It took confidence to overcome my feelings of "Can I do it?" "Maybe I shouldn't!" So for you, the young reader searching for confidence, take a chance on yourself! Believe in yourself and don't ever let anyone make you believe that you are inferior to anyone. Remember, shoulders back, my friend. Confidence comes from within.

THE PROFESSIONAL WOMAN NETWORK
Training and Certification on Women's Issues

Linda Ellis Eastman, President & CEO of The Professional Woman Network, has trained and certified over two thousand individuals to start their own consulting/seminar business. Women from such countries as Brazil, Argentina, the Bahamas, Costa Rica, Bermuda, Nigeria, South Africa, Malaysia, and Mexico have attended trainings.

Topics for certification include:
• Diversity & Multiculturalism
• Women's Issues
• Women: A Journey to Wellness
• Save Our Youth
• Teen Image & Social Etiquette
• Leadership & Empowerment Skills for Youth
• Customer Service & Professionalism
• Marketing a Consulting Practice
• Professional Coaching
• Professional Presentation Skills

If you are interested in learning more about becoming certified or about starting your own consulting/seminar business contact:

The Professional Woman Network
P.O. Box 333
Prospect, KY 40059
(502) 566-9900
lindaeastman@prodigy.net
www.prowoman.net

Women's Empowerment Series

The Young Professional Woman: Breaking Into the Business World & Succeeding

A View from the Top: Exceptional Leadership Strategies

Getting Well: Mind, Body & Spirit

How to Break the Glass Ceiling Without a Hammer

Breaking Free: Overcoming Self-Sabotage

Creating a Blueprint for Inner Change: Tools for personal growth

How to Survive When Your Ship is Sinking: Weathering Life's Storms

Leaders in Pearls: How to Be a Change Architect

Celebration of Life: Inspiration for Women

Releasing Strongholds: Letting Go of What's Holding You Back

The Power of a Woman: Embracing the Woman Within

The Power of Change: Reinvent Yourself at Any Age

Life is an Attitude. The Power of Positive Thinking

Transformation: Reinventing the Woman Within

The Self-Architect: Redesigning Your Life

Becoming Your Own Best Friend

The Woman's Handbook for Self-Empowerment

Remove the Mask! Living an Authentic Life

The Woman's Handbook for Self-Confidence

A Journey Within: Self-Discovery for Women

Learning to Love Yourself: Self-Esteem for Women

The African American Library

Sister to Sister A Guide for African American Girls

Bruised But Not Broken

Learning to Love Yourself: A Handbook for the African American Woman

Wellness for the African American Woman: Mind, Body & Spirit

The African American Library
Sister to Sister A Guide for African Americans

These books are available from the individual contributors, the publisher (www.pwnbooks.com), www.amazon.com, and your local bookstore by request.